Applied Econometrics Association Series
General Editors: **Jean H.P. Paelinck**, Emeritus Professor, Erasmus University, Rotterdam; and **Henri Serbat**, University of Paris 2

The vital importance of econometrics for understanding economic phenomena is increasingly recognized in every field of economics.

The discipline is based on 'scientific processes which aim to identify, explain and forecast economic phenomena using formalised tools to produce, measure, structure and model the information' (Gérard Duru and Henri Serbat, 1991).

The Applied Econometrics Association, established 1974, seeks to develop the use of econometric tools by regular updates on the state of the art and the progress made in each specific field, and so to further the transformation of unconnected facts into pertinent information for use in analysis and decision-making.

The series was conceived to form a set of working references for advanced students and researchers in each specific field, as well as a guide to development across the discipline more broadly.

This exchange of knowledge will be continued permanently by the opening of a debate site on the Internet (http://www.aea.fed-eco.org).

Titles include:
Patrick-Yves Badillo and Jean-Baptiste Lesourd *(editors)*
THE MEDIA INDUSTRIES AND THEIR MARKETS
Quantitative Analyses

Françoise Bourdon and Jean Bourdon *(editors)*
WAGE ECONOMETRICS AND MODELLING

Fabrizio Carlevaro and Jean-Baptiste Lesourd *(editors)*
MEASURING AND ACCOUNTING ENVIRONMENTAL NUISANCES AND SERVICES

Arthur Getis, Jeśus Mur and Henry G. Zoller *(editors)*
SPATIAL ECONOMETRICS AND SPATIAL STATISTICS

Siv S. Gustafsson and Danièle E. Meulders *(editors)*
GENDER AND THE LABOUR MARKET
Econometric Evidence of Obstacles to Achieving Gender Equality

Hans Heijke and Joan Muysken *(editors)*
EDUCATION AND TRAINING IN A KNOWLEDGE-BASED ECONOMY

Pavlos Karadeloglou *(editors)*
EXCHANGE-RATE POLICY IN EUROPE

Pavlos Karadeloglou and Virginie Terraza *(editors)*
EXCHANGE RATES AND MACROECONOMIC DYNAMICS

Sandrine Lardic and Valérie Mignon *(editors)*
RECENT DEVELOPMENTS ON EXCHANGE RATES

Benoît Mahy, Robert Plasman and François Rycx *(editors)*
GENDER PAY DIFFERENTIALS
Cross-National Evidence from Micro-Data

David Marsden and François Rycx *(editors)*
WAGE STRUCTURES, EMPLOYMENT ADJUSTMENTS AND GLOBALIZATION
Evidence from Linked and Firm-level Panel Data

Danièle Meulders, Robert Plasman and François Rycx *(editors)*
MINIMUM WAGES, LOW PAY AND UNEMPLOYMENT

Carine Peeters and Bruno van Pottelsberghe de la Potterie *(editors)*
ECONOMIC AND MANAGEMENT PERSPECTIVES ON INTELLECTUAL PROPERTY RIGHTS

Emile Quinet and Roger Vickerman *(editors)*
THE ECONOMETRICS OF MAJOR TRANSPORT INFRASTRUCTURES

Philippe Thalmann and Milad Zarin-Nejadan *(editors)*
CONSTRUCTION AND REAL ESTATE DYNAMICS

Applied Econometrics Association
Series Standing Order ISBN 978-0-333-91990-3 (cased)
and 978-0-333-71460-7 (paperback)
(outside North America only)

You can receive future titles in this series as they are published by placing a standing order. Please contact your bookseller or, in case of difficulty, write to us at the address below with your name and address, the title of the series and the ISBN quoted above.

Customer Services Department, Macmillan Distribution Ltd, Houndmills, Basingstoke, Hampshire RG21 6XS, England

The Media Industries and their Markets

Quantitative Analyses

Edited by

Patrick-Yves Badillo

and

Jean-Baptiste Lesourd

palgrave
macmillan

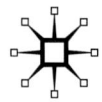

Selection and editorial matter © Patrick-Yves Badillo and
Jean-Baptiste Lesourd 2010
Individual Chapters © Contributors 2010
Foreword © Dominique Roux 2010

All rights reserved. No reproduction, copy or transmission of this publication may be made without written permission.

No portion of this publication may be reproduced, copied or transmitted save with written permission or in accordance with the provisions of the Copyright, Designs and Patents Act 1988, or under the terms of any licence permitting limited copying issued by the Copyright Licensing Agency, Saffron House, 6–10 Kirby Street, London EC1N 8TS.

Any person who does any unauthorized act in relation to this publication may be liable to criminal prosecution and civil claims for damages.

The authors have asserted their rights to be identified as the authors of this work in accordance with the Copyright, Designs and Patents Act 1988.

First published 2010 by
PALGRAVE MACMILLAN

Palgrave Macmillan in the UK is an imprint of Macmillan Publishers Limited, registered in England, company number 785998, of Houndmills, Basingstoke, Hampshire RG21 6XS.

Palgrave Macmillan in the US is a division of St Martin's Press LLC, 175 Fifth Avenue, New York, NY 10010.

Palgrave Macmillan is the global academic imprint of the above companies and has companies and representatives throughout the world.

Palgrave® and Macmillan® are registered trademarks in the United States, the United Kingdom, Europe and other countries.

ISBN 978–0–230–27770–0   hardback

This book is printed on paper suitable for recycling and made from fully managed and sustained forest sources. Logging, pulping and manufacturing processes are expected to conform to the environmental regulations of the country of origin.

A catalogue record for this book is available from the British Library.

A catalog record for this book is available from the Library of Congress.

10 9 8 7 6 5 4 3 2 1
19 18 17 16 15 14 13 12 11 10

Printed and bound in Great Britain by
CPI Antony Rowe, Chippenham and Eastbourne

Contents

List of Figures	vii
List of Tables	ix
Acknowledgements	xi
Notes on the Contributors	xii
Foreword by Dominique Roux	xiv

1	Introduction Patrick-Yves Badillo and Jean-Baptiste Lesourd	1
2	Impediments to a Global Information Society Robert G. Picard	14
3	Transformation of Internet-based Companies' Business Models: Ten Years after the Dot.com Burst Christophe Garonne and Félix Weygand	26
4	The Management of a Hybrid Broadcasting Model: Reconciling Public and Commercial Interests Suzana Zilic Fiser	49
5	The Dynamics of Media Business Models: Innovation, Versioning and Blended Media Patrick-Yves Badillo and Dominique Bourgeois	64
6	The Dynamics of Media Concentration: The American Experience Eli M. Noam	87
7	Measuring Media Concentration for the Purposes of Ensuring Pluralism and Diversity Petros Iosifidis	108
8	Concentration in the French Press Industry: Quantitative Analysis Patrick-Yves Badillo and Jean-Baptiste Lesourd	125
9	The Effects of Competition on the Profitability of European Television Channels Juan P. Artero, Cristina Etayo, Mónica Herrero, Mercedes Medina and Alfonso Sánchez-Tabernero	141

vi Contents

10 Preference for Flat-Rate Media Access Fees: A Behavioural
   Economics Interpretation 155
   Hitoshi Mitomo and Tokio Otsuka

11 Explaining Prices Paid for Television Ad Time:
   the Purchasing Profile Model 171
   W. Wayne Fu, Hairong Li and Steven S. Wildman

12 Advertising Media Strategies in the Film Industry 195
   Caroline Elliott and Rob Simmons

13 Demand for Movies in Europe and the Effects
   of Multiplex Diffusion 207
   Orietta Dessy and Marco Gambaro

14 Quantitative Analyses of the Media Industries and
   of Their Markets: Concluding Comments 220
   Orhan Güvenen

Index 226

List of Figures

2.1	Average monthly broadband subscription prices, October 2008 ($US PPP)	23
5.1	Newspaper advertising revenue in the United States, 2004–2008	65
5.2	A representation of the dynamics of old media and new media	70
5.3	Surveys about the sources of news in the United States	71
5.4	French press resources (in constant euro) (GI = General Information Press)	72
5.5	French press, total paid circulation (volume)	73
5.6	Advertising resources in France 2008	73
5.7	Turnover of free information newspapers in France	74
5.8	Diagram A: The traditional model of the press	76
5.9	Diagram B: Coexistence of free press and paid-for press	78
5.10	Diagram C: Complexity of the press system (with free and paid-for press)	79
5.11	Versioning and media markets	82
6.1	Economies of scale and entry barriers	90
6.2	Cycles of concentration	92
6.3	Concentration trends, with continuously rising scale economies and declining entry barriers	93
6.4	Convergence of concentration of overall information sector and mass media sector	94
6.5	Information industry total, 1983–2005	96
6.6	Concentration trends by subsectors (HHI)	98
6.7	Concentration trends of various mass media industries	99
6.8	Total share for companies ranked 1–5, 6–10, and 11–25 in the mass media sector (1984–2005)	103
10.1	The shape of a value function, and the shape of a probability weighting function	158
10.2	Current levels of payment for Internet access and mobile phones	160
10.3	Choice between flat rates and measured rates	161
10.4	Comparison of trade-off points	164
11.1	Distribution of *Unitrate* among 46 programmes	177

11.2 Relationship between PPI and PPI-HHI for the case of two products   181
14.1 The impact of technologies on socioeconomic phenomena in time dynamics   221
14.2 Dynamics of knowledge, measurements, models and interpretations   222
14.3 Present world system and normative system   223

List of Tables

2.1	Percentage of population living on less than $2 per day	19
2.2	Approximate literacy rates by continent	21
2.3	Selected comparative costs for a three-minute phone call to the USA	22
3.1	Description of the start-ups involved in the study in 2007	33
3.2	Summary of the business models of the start-ups in 2007	37
3.3	Summary of the Business Models of the largest Internet based companies (based on ComScore Media Metrix release for August 2007)	38
5.1	Number of visits to the internet sites of French media groups (20 largest numbers)	83
6.1	Top company shares (over 60 per cent)	101
8.1	The main titles and groups of the French press	132
8.2	CR4 and HHI concentration indexes for the French press industry	134
8.3	Evaluations of HHI and of NI on the French national daily press (2008 figures)	135
8.4	Various concentration and diversity indexes for the French daily press in 1997, 2000, 2004, 2006 and 2008	136
8.5	Evaluations of HHI and of NI in the case of the regional daily newspapers in two regions where there is more than one title (Alsace and Lorraine)	137
9.1	Estimations of the explanatory models for margin (N = 77)	147
9.2	Estimations of the explanatory models for ROE (N = 70)	148
9.3	Estimations of the explanatory models for ROA (N = 38)	149
10.1	Basic attributes of the respondents	160
10.2	The choice between measured and flat rates for Internet access and mobile phones	162
10.3	Actual usage of tariff and the choices stated in the answers (the cross-tabulation)	163
10.4	Comparison of trade-off points between the media	165
10.5	The factors of preferences	166
10.6	Comparison of preference factors contributing to the choice between flat rates and measured rates	167

x List of Tables

10.7	Relative contributions of the factors: the case of mobile access	168
11.1	*AdAge.com* and Simmons product categories	179
11.2	Descriptive statistics of variables	184
11.3	Demographic and PPM regressions (variables PPM1 and PPM2) for *InUnitRate*	185
11.4	PPM regressions for *InUnitRate* (Variable PPM3 and PPM4)	186
12.1	Complete list of explanatory variables	201
12.2	Determinants of total logged advertising expenditure	202
12.3	Determinants of advertising media usage	203
12.4	Correlation matrix of residuals	204
13.1	Results of regressions	214
13.2	DPD regression (bootstrapped standard errors, 1,000 iterations)	216

Acknowledgements

Most of the work reported in this volume has been presented during two international conferences that took place in November 2007: the International Conference of the Applied Econometric Association at Paris-Sorbonne University, Paris, and another International Conference held at the Université de la Méditerranée in Marseille. Invited conferences presented in Paris by Hitoshi Mitomo (Waseda University, Tokyo, Japan) and by Eli M. Noam (Columbia University, New York, United States), and the invited conference presented in Marseille by Robert Picard (Jönköping International Business School, Jönköping, Sweden), which led to three chapters of this volume, are gratefully acknowledged. We also acknowledge the helpful comments from participants in both conferences which have greatly benefited this work.

P.-Y. Badillo
J.-B. Lesourd

Notes on the Contributors

Juan Pablo Artero is an Assistant Professor of Media Management and Structure of Media Industries at the School of Communication of University of Navarra, Spain.

Patrick Badillo is a Professor at Aix-Marseille University, France; formerly Director of the School of Journalism and Communication of Marseille; Director and Founder of the Research Institute on Information and Communication; Project Manager, French National Research Agency.

Dominique Bourgeois is a Professor at the University of Fribourg, Switzerland, Chair of Communication and Media Sciences.

Orietta Dessy is a Lecturer at the Institute for Industrial and Labour Economics, Catholic University, Milan, Italy.

Caroline Elliott is a Senior Lecturer at the Department of Economics of the University of Lancaster.

Cristina Etayo is a Lecturer at the School of Communication of the University of Navarra, Spain, Department of Media Management.

Suzana Zilic Fiser is an Assistant Professor at Faculty of Electrical Engineering and Computer Science, Institute of Media Communications, University of Maribor, Slovenia.

Wayne Fu is an Associate Professor at the Wee Kim Wee School of Communication and Information, Nanyang Technological University.

Marco Gambaro is a Professor of Media Economics at Department of Economics and Business (DEAS), Università degli Studi di Milano, Italy.

Christophe Garonne is a PhD candidate in Management, Queensland University of Technology, Brisbane, Australia, and an Associate Researcher, Euromed School of Management, Marseille, France.

Orhan Güvenen is a Professor at Bilkent University, Ankara, Turkey, as well as Founder and Director of the University's Institute of World Systems, Economic and Srategic Research.

Mónica Herrero is an Associate Professor of Media Management and Dean of the School of Communication, University of Navarra, Spain.

Notes on the Contributors xiii

Dr Petros Iosifidis is a Reader in Media and Communications Department of Sociology at the School of Social Sciences, City University of London, Northampton Square, London, United Kingdom.

Jean-Baptiste Lesourd is a Professor at Aix-Marseille University, France.

Hairong Li is a Professor in the Department of Advertising, Public Relations, and Retailing at Michigan State University.

Mercedes Medina is a Professor at the University of Navarra, Spain.

Hitoshi Mitomo is a Professor at Graduate School of Asia-Pacific Studies, Waseda University, Japan.

Eli M. Noam is a Professor, Columbia University Business School, Columbia University, New York, and Director of the University's Columbia Institute for Tele-Information (CITI).

Tokio Otsuda is an Assistant Professor, at Shumei University, Japan.

Robert G. Picard is a Professor at the Media Management and Transformation Centre, Jönköping International Business School, Jönköping, Sweden.

Alfonso Sánchez-Tabernero is Vice-President of the University of Navarra, Spain, and Professor of Media Management at the university's School of Communication.

Rob Simmons is a Senior Lecturer at the Department of Economics of the University of Lancaster.

Dr Félix Weygand is an Associate Professor at Ecole de Journalisme et de Communication, Université de la Méditerranée and Euromed School of Management, Marseille, France.

Steven S. Wildman is a Professor at the Department of Telecommunication, Information Studies and Media of Michigan State University, East Lansing, Michigan, and co-director of the university's Quello Center for Telecommunication Management and Law.

Foreword

Dominique Roux*

The work of Patrick Badillo and Jean-Baptiste Lesourd on the economics of the media industries, relying on quantitative and statistical methods, is both timely and original. As the editors of this book, they present some of the best and most recent work on the economics of the media and information sectors, and on the management of enterprises of these sectors. They also provide some of their own recent and original analyses of these topics. Moreover, this volume is an international pursuit as it includes contributions from several European countries, Japan, and the United States.

The media sector is an industry that can be an object of study from the points of view of information and communication science, economics and management, often from a cross-disciplinary standpoint. It is also an industry that cannot be studied without taking into consideration other related industries, such as the telecom industry. However, at least to our knowledge, there existed no updated and recent book in this field devoted to quantitative studies with a firm grounding in modern statistical and econometric methods. This work thus bridges a gap. It is concerned with all media, including the press, radio, TV, cinema, and the Internet, as well as with the related telecom sector. It is also concerned with many aspects of the subject, including business strategy, entrepreneurship, supply and demand. It includes publicity-related audience measurement and marketing studies. This is important, since for most media organisations, advertising and publicity directed to their readerships and audiences is a major source of income. This book also highlights the importance of technological advances and innovations related to content digitalisation processing and transmission. These are leading to the emergence of new media such as the Internet, and to a convergence between the media sectors, and other neighbouring sectors such as the information and telecom sectors. Whether contemporary societies are so-called 'information societies', dominated from an economic standpoint by information-related goods, is discussed in the book. Some of its quantitative studies show that this is a questionable assertion, especially

*Dominique Roux is both a Professor of Management at the University of Paris-Dauphine, and the President of a telecom company (Bolloré Telecom, which is a part of the Bolloré group, involved in different media – especially television and newspapers, and also in the Havas advertising group).

because of the so-called 'digital divide' whereby most people in some less advanced economies are deprived of access to new digital technologies. Finally, other important debates such as the debate on concentration in the media and information sectors are well documented in this book. In particular, its discussions on concentration-related quantitative data and indicators are welcome.

I believe that this unique work will be of great interest for scholars and researchers in areas such as information and communication science, as well as media and information economics and management. I also strongly recommend this book to practitioners of the media and information industries.

1
Introduction

Patrick-Yves Badillo and Jean-Baptiste Lesourd[1]

1.1 Information, information society, and the media

Information is a word which has a number of meanings. In a comparatively limited sense, it can be defined as any structured set of data that can be interpreted by human beings and is useful for human action.

From an economic standpoint, information, as defined in the above limited sense, is a scarce resource which is fundamental in market economies, for all economic agents, for businesses as well as for the general public. It can be decentralised and partly private information, but we are concerned here with public information (or information with the characteristics of public goods). Such public information is produced and transmitted by the media. But, as we shall see, information in this limited sense is far from being the only good to be produced, processed, or transmitted by the media.

In a much broader sense that includes the previous sense as a particular case, information can be defined (Shannon and Weaver, 1948) as any set of signs or data accessible to our senses. The transmission from one individual to another of such information generally involves a message, that is, a set of signs, going from an individual called the transmitter to one or more other individuals called receivers.

The occurrence of digitising allows for an equivalent definition of this broader definition of information, which is due to Shapiro and Varian (1999, p. 3): '*Anything that can be digitized – encoded as a stream of bits – is information*'.

A book, an article in a newspaper or in a magazine, a telephone conversation, a television programme, a film are examples of information in this generalised sense. The transmission and processing of information necessarily involve some kind of material data carrier, that is, a device capable of containing this information (human memory, paper, computer disc…). In this instance we are discussing only meaningful information, that is, information which is understandable to human beings, only a particular case of the most general meaning of this term. In addition, any meaningful information is not necessarily useful for a given audience.

We will define a *content* (or the information contained in some material device) as information which is both meaningful and useful in the economic sense of the word, to some audience, that is, a group of receivers to which the information is directed as a message.

Finally, a *medium* can be defined as some kind of a transmission technology. Paper dailies, paper weekly magazines, radio and television, as well as the Internet, are examples of media. Marshall McLuhan (1964) considers that the information message cannot be dissociated from the media that carries it ('the medium is the message'). Following the emergence of the digital revolution, it is clear that the possible digitising of contents can lead to a technical and economic separation of the contents from the underlying media. This leads to a stand-alone existence of contents which raises new problems, especially from the economic point of view and from the point of view of media enterprises.

Having proceeded so far the concept of a *media enterprise* can now be defined. A media enterprise is an enterprise or firm that uses one or several media to distribute contents to a specific audience after having either purchased it from vendors (for example, a TV channel who buys a movie to a producer), or produced it. Media firms different from those found in most other sectors. More precisely, media companies products have two original characteristics. Firstly, these companies require a quick and constant renewal of their products; they rely on a high degree of creativity. Secondly, they fall within what can be described as project production, that is to say that their product is a single, non-repetitive product, and unique of its kind.

It is clear that media companies sell products that very rapidly become outdated, and whose novelty is an essential aspect of their attractiveness to their audiences, and thus to demand. Accordingly, one can talk in terms of a process of continuous innovation. For example, in the case of news printed in daily press articles, or broadcast by a television channel, novelty is an essential element, and any new information will remain in the news only for a certain period of time, and then will be outdated when more news take over. A television channel will generally broadcast either new films, or older films that are little known or forgotten. And what is true of news or films is also true of almost all content. The media industry is an industry in which a product often loses virtually any interest as soon as it is out of date. Indeed, many industrial activities are characterised by the constant renewal of their products, but the life cycle of a product can very often be longer than is the case in the media industry (for example, in the case of the automotive industry, the lifetime of a particular brand of car is generally of the order of seven to 10 years, which is much longer than in the case of most contents sold by the media industries). Thus, the media industries, by the very nature of their products, require daily rapid innovation and a high degree of creativeness. Contents produced by the media share this feature with a certain number of goods and, in particular with artistic and cultural goods, many of which can in any event be produced and/or sold by the media industries. Artistic and cultural goods share these characteristics with virtually all other contents of media, whether such contents are knowledge-oriented, technical literature, advertising, or leisure-oriented contents.

As will be discussed in several parts of this book, the recent evolution of the media industry is related to the dynamics of the so-called *knowledge-information society*, or *information society*. As early as 1933 Machlup (1962) was developing some of the earliest analyses of this concept. More recent studies have been carried out by authors such as Downes (2000) and Webster (2006). Clearly, we are dealing with evolutions that can be rather different in various developed economies, emerging economies, and developing economies. Globally, a number of common features can be observed, as this evolution tends to be *global*. However, as will be discussed by Robert Picard in Chapter 2, there are obstacles to the establishment of a global information society, which leads to the formation of some kind of 'digital divide' between the comparatively affluent societies of the developed and emerging economies, and the less developed economies.

This book is devoted to the econometric and quantitative analyses of the media industries and their markets from both an economic and a management point of view, a field that has apparently been investigated less extensively than more qualitative analyses. Following this introduction, our book is organised into three distinct parts, followed by some conclusions.

Firstly, we will discuss the general features that characterise the media industries, including their relation to the concept of an information society, and the original aspects of what might be called their business models.

Secondly, we will discuss the media industries from the point of view of supply. Since media enterprises are characterised by both economies

4 The Media Industries and their Markets

of scale and economies of scope, there are strong incentives towards increasing the levels of concentration in the media sector. Therefore, one important supply-related problem that will be discussed here is the problem of concentration in the media industries.

Thirdly, we will discuss the media industries from the point of view of demand. As far as demand is concerned, media enterprises are characterised by dual markets, meaning that they are operating on two markets that are complementary to one another: the markets for information, as well as the markets for advertising. Consequently, there are some media markets that are mainly dependent on audiences, and there also media markets that depend mainly on advertising.

Finally, we analyse the concluding remarks by Orhan Güvenen, which constitute the last chapter of the book.

1.2 The media industries: general economic environments, business models and strategies

One fundamental problem that has to be addressed in any media study is whether or not the information society is a global phnenomenon. In Chapter 2, Robert G. Picard shows that there are enormous impediments to the creation of a global information society. Because of the so-called *digital divide*, the information society is *not* a global phenomenon, and it concerns mostly developed economies. In less developed countries, the majority of the population have no access to the infrastructures that are essential for access to the new media such as the Internet, including electricity and fixed telephony, are lacking to a majority; the oldest media, such as the written press, radio and television, are not available to everybody. Among other factors contributing to this situation are illiteracy and the very low levels of income in these countries. Even in the most developed regions such as Europe, North America and the highly developed nations of Asia, such as Japan and South Korea, poverty excludes some people from the benefits of the information society. In emerging countries such as India and China, despite the fact that these are countries with high technological and scientific levels, people with very low incomes usually have less (or no) access to the newest developments of the information society. Finally, Robert G. Picard concludes by showing that, even if increasing numbers of people are participating fully in the global information society, 'social, economic and technical factors make global information society merely a dream, not a reality', even in developed nations. This is a problem that has to be taken into account in the strategy of many companies, such as telecommunication and other high-technology companies, as well as by national governments and by international development institutions.

The remainder of this part of the book is devoted to some general economic, management and strategic questions. In chapter 3, Christophe Garonne and Félix Weygand discuss the adaptation of Internet-based companies' business models to changes in the global economic and technological environment after the so-called 'dot.com burst'. Their discussion concerns both companies that survived the Internet bubble of the decade from 1990 to 2000, and new companies, in particular start-ups and ventures that appeared after this time. Taking into account the specificities of E-Business models, the authors examine the evolution of business models using as a guideline a classification developed by authors such as Mahadevan (2000). From the empirical point of view, the study is conducted on the basis of several company surveys, including a survey of 10 E-business start-ups in Southern France, and an international survey of several companies that survived the 1998–2001 period and are included in the Top 10 list published by ComStore Inc. This second set of companies includes Internet giants such as Yahoo!, Google, eBay, Amazon, Ask Network and Wikipedia. The discussion shows that the business models of some of these companies, including Yahoo! and Google, still derive the majority of their revenues from advertising, while most start-ups have diversified their revenue acquisition schemes. The same is true in the case of Amazon, a company which has diversified from its initial service provider model to a more diversified model, including being a market-maker. This move towards the diversification of business models seems to be a response to a more risky, and more competitive environment, and, as will be discussed later, similar trends may be observed in the case of many media groups.

In chapter 4, Suzana Zilic Fiser also discusses some business model issues in the case of public service television companies. Many of these companies have both profit-maximising objectives and public service social responsibility objectives. This is true in the case of the UK company Channel 4, which is used as a case study. More precisely, Channel 4 is a public service television channel, but (in contrast to the BBC, which is also a British public service company) it has adopted a hybrid business model relying on both commercial incentives (especially on advertising), and also public service objectives. It is therefore an interesting case. Furthermore, Channel 4 competes with other British terrestrial television channels, including the BBC, ITV and Channel 5. Channel 4 has been given public service objectives such as supporting British independent production, together with developing educational and innovative programmes. In the final analysis, Zilic Fiser concludes that Channel 4 has achieved a good compromise between its commercial and its public service objectives.

The final chapter in this part of the book, chapter 5 by Patrick-Yves Badillo and Dominique Bourgeois, discusses some more long-term and strategic issues in the management of media companies, especially in relation to the daily and periodical press industry. In particular, the authors examine the implications of the development of Internet media on the long-term evolution of the business models adopted by press companies. If a business model is defined as the management implications of the combination of activities and financial flows in a business company, it should be recognised that, historically, the business models of newspapers have undergone significant evolutions, resulting from technological advances and the development of advertising as one of the main sources of revenue for these companies. The evolution from comparatively high-cost newspapers with small readerships and with little or no advertising as a source of income to low-cost newspapers with large readerships was an essential long-term historical evolution over the nineteenth and most of the twentieth centuries, but it has now come to an end. Since the decade from 1990 to 2000, another long-term evolution appears to be taking place, with the development of new Internet-based media. These new media appear, in some respects, to be both competitors and substitutes to the written press, but, as is shown by Badillo and Bourgeois, they are also to some degree complements to the written press. They are characterised by several fundamental features. Firstly, Internet-based media have comparatively low variable costs, so that they are almost completely dependent on advertising as their main source of income. In the case of the written press companies, the authors find that the evolution of their business models will probably not result in the replacement of the older paper press media by the so-called new, Internet-based media. According to the authors, the written press media are more likely to a change towards blended or mixed business models in which the press companies will achieve an optimal combination of both their paper versions and their online versions.

1.3 Concentration in the media industries and supply studies

The second part of our book is devoted to supply studies of the media industries, which are characterised by a strong movement towards concentration. It opens with chapter 6 by Eli M. Noam, who is interested in the dynamics of media concentration, focusing on the US experience. The author shows that concentration in the media industry is a global phenomenon, concerning a number of countries such as Australia, Brazil, Germany, Italy, Mexico, and, of course, the United States. However, views differ widely as far as the interpretations and implications of this phenomenon are concerned. In the US case, a distinction can be made between what one might call 'media-pessimistic' and 'media-optimistic' authors who hold conflicting views. According to 'media-pessimistic' authors, there is a cartel or a quasi-monopoly of media companies that is causing damage to diversity, and, hence, to democracy (Bagdikian, 2004). By contrast, according to 'media-optimistic' analyses, especially those advanced by free market advocates, libertarian circles, especially the libertarian Internet communities, free market forces and technological advances such as the Internet are essentially beneficial to our societies. Chapter 6 aims to provide a clearer picture of this situation through a detailed and quantitative analysis that is often absent from these conflicting analyses. The author shows that, firstly, as already noticed in the above general discussion, media enterprises are characterised by strong *economies of scale*, because of low variable costs, as compared to the costs of production of information. Secondly, *barriers to entry* in the media industries have been lowered because of new technologies that enable comparatively small innovative companies to enter the media industry. Thirdly, the digital revolution enhances economies of scale and also leads to economies of scope and to *digital convergence* between different media that were previously distinct industries. The effect as a result of lower barriers to entry is distinct from the economies of scale and economies of scope effects, and its effects on concentration are ambiguous. In some circumstances, the effect of lower entry barriers in the media and information industries can lead to more competitive markets, while under different circumstances, they can lead to more concentration in these industries. Consequently, concentration is not increasing steadily and cycles can take place with three stages: an early stage during which there is a decrease in the level of concentration resulting from lower entry barriers that introduce new competitors, an instability stage during which these antagonist forces are compensating each other, and a final consolidation stage during which concentration increases again. Quantitative analyses follow these theoretical considerations using quantitative data for the USA on the information sector, including the conducting of a survey into subsectors such as broadcast TV, cable TV, cinema and TV film production and distribution, the telecom and the Internet industries, and several other subsectors. These analyses lead to the determination of the usual concentration indicators such as the total market shares of the largest firm and of the four largest firms, and the Herfindahl–Hirschman Index (HHI) in the US case. These calculations show that the 1983–2008 historical evolution of concentration in this aggregate information sector is clearly not one of steadily increasing concentration, and a cycle seems to take place along the lines previously discussed. As far as the various subsectors of this enlarged information sector are concerned (the mass media, telecom, information technology and the Internet), they seem to converge in terms of concentration measurement indexes since the beginning of the twenty-first century: their HHI, for instance, all converge to values between 1,000 and 2,000 with a decrease in concentration for some industries (telecom and mass media) and, by contrast, increased concentration for the two other industries (the information technology and Internet industries).

Chapter 7 by Petros Iosifidis offers a discussion of various measures of concentration and diversity for the purposes of assessing pluralism and democracy, which is a public concern and therefore requires quantitative indicators. With Hoffmann-Riem (1987) the author distinguishes four dimensions in pluralism that are media-specific and that complete the economic concept of concentration on a given market: *diversity of formats and issues*, meaning that all the various sorts of contents (information, entertainment, education and culture), are present in the media; *plurality of contents*, meaning that the various opinions that prevail are factually covered; *person and group diversity*, meaning that contents take into account the various interests of various groups existing in the audience, and, finally, *geographical diversity*, meaning that local, regional, national and international contents are present. Other classifications of diversity are also discussed. The methodologies for measuring these diversity concepts are discussed and several concentration and diversity indicators are presented. Concentration indicators are first presented, including the sum of market shares of the four largest firms present on a given market, and the Herfindahl–Hirschman Index (HHI), which is defined as the sum of the squares of the above market shares). Measurements of the shares of political and cultural contents are also discussed. The relationships between economic market power and diversity is discussed. The positions of the UK government, and of the European Union, are also presented.

In chapter 8, Patrick-Yves Badillo and Jean-Baptiste Lesourd aim to analyse the drivers and the indicators for concentration in the media industry. After describing the economic and technological environments which are driving concentration phenomena in the media industry, we survey the various indicators of concentration in a media-specific context. More precisely, we apply these indicators to the case of the concentration of the French press using various measurements, including the traditional Herfindahl–Hirschman Index (HHI), and a new concentration index proposed by Eli Noam, which is specific to the media industry. It appears that HHI as calculated for the entire French daily press industry is equal to 791.4, leading to the conclusion that the concentration in the whole French press industry is still low. In the case of French national dailies, we find a much higher figure of 2,365.4 as the mean value of HHI over the period from 1997 to 2008, which corresponds to a high level of concentration. Finally, as far as provincial daily newspapers are concerned, we find very high HHI figures, because of local monopoly or quasi-monopoly situations. Diversity Indexes, and the new Noam index are also calculated for all these cases, and are found to increase significantly over the 1997–2008 period, showing that diversity decreased significantly in the case of the French daily press, which is, however, a declining sector.

Finally, this second part of the analyses reported in our book ends with chapter 9 by Juan Pablo Artero, Cristina Etayo, Mónica Herrero, Mercedes Medina and Alfonso Sánchez-Tabernero. These authors are concerned with the effects of competition on the levels of profitability of European TV channels. The authors show that quantitative studies of television economics in Europe can be of great interest from several points of view, including markets for ideas and cultural diversity, the management of advertising, the management of public service television channels as well as pay television channels, and technological aspects of the economics of TV channels. Their study is an econometric study of the profitability of 11 TV channels drawn from five European countries: Spain, France, the United Kingdom, Germany and Portugal. The dependent variables are essentially profitability indicators, including the profitability margin on sales, the return on equity (ROE), and the return on assets (ROA), while the explanatory variables are audiences, the number of channels per household, the average daily TV viewing time for the inhabitants of a given country, and the seniority of the network. As expected, audiences are a very important positive determinant of the profitability of the industry, while the number of channels available has, as might also be expected, a negative effect, a quite logical conclusion that highlights the competition between channels. The average watching time is not very significant as an explanatory variable, and seniority of the network negatively impacts on profitability.

1.4 Media markets and demand studies

The third part of our volume is focused on media markets and demand studies. It begins with chapter 10 by Hitoshi Mitomo and Tokio Otsuka, who investigate, from the point of view of experimental and behavioural economics, the demand for mobile phone and Internet access. More precisely, the authors investigate the existence of users' preference for flat-rate media access fees and identify the factors that influence such preferences. The authors explore consumer preference for flat-rate pricing plans, defined as 'flat-rate preference'; such a preference for flat-rate tariffs contradicts traditional expected-utility theories and is more in line with general theories such as the behavioural economics approach of Kahneman and Tversky (1979). Consumers' psychological factors employed from behavioural economics are used to explain the preference for flat rates and measured rates. The result from statistical tests based on the questionnaire survey strongly suggests the existence of flat-rate preferences in both Internet access and mobile access services. The survey was conducted on a sample of 400 mobile phone users aged between their teens and their forties. Several preference factors are found to be statistically significant, including choice by habit, aversion for ambiguity, a misunderstanding of tariff schemes, the level of usage, the aversion to loss and the overvaluation of low probabilities, mental accounting, and, finally, 'other' external factors.

Chapter 11, by W. Wayne Fu, Hairong Li, and Steven S. Wildman, is concerned with the demand for TV advertising time, and in particular with providing an explanation of the prices for TV advertising time. Measures of the demographic composition of media audiences have been used traditionally to explain prices paid for ad time in broadcast programmes as well as the advertising possibilities available in other media. Advertisers, on the other hand, are not interested in an audience's demographic composition per se. Rather, they combine demographic measures with information from other sources to estimate the numbers of potential customers in an audience generated by television programmes and other media products. The results presented here use the model in Wildman (2003) which introduces an economic model showing how markets aggregate individual advertisers' demands for television advertising time. This study introduces the purchasing profile, a measure of the mix of products purchased by the members of a programme's audience, as a variable that can be used to construct empirical models that incorporate the critical elements of the above model. Using data on prices paid for network commercial time in the USA in 1997, we show that regression models incorporating two variables related to purchasing profiles, a measure of the profitability of ad-generated sales for different types of advertisers, and a proxy for the effectiveness of television ads for promoting different type of products, do about as good a job of explaining observed variation in prices paid for ad time in prime time programmes as do traditional demographics-based models. They also reveal how variation in the sets of products purchased by programmes' viewers interacts with heterogeneous advertiser demands to determine the process of ad time.

Chapter 12, by Caroline Elliott and Rob Simmons, is devoted to the demand for another product of an important media industry – film production. It is devoted to advertising for films in various media in the context of the UK film production industry. The primary aim of the authors is to identify statistically the multiple determinants of film advertising expenditures in four important media, namely television, press, outdoor and radio, using the seemingly unrelated regression estimation (SURE) method. Prior to this they have also conducted an analysis of the factors that determine the total amounts spent on advertising films when they are first released in the UK. The results highlight the importance of potential film quality signals in determining advertising expenditures, with major distribution companies having differing preferences for the use of the alternative advertising media. The results indicate that additional factors, such as production inputs and the genre of film, have differing impacts on the choice of advertising media used to market films.

Finally, Chapter 13, by Orietta Dessy and Marco Gambaro, is also devoted to the movie industry, but from the point of view of film distribution in public movie theatre venues. Cinema is still a very important medium, but public movie film attendance in the USA as well as in other developed countries reached a peak some time after the Second World War, and declined sharply thereafter, as a result of competition with TV film watching and, more recently, with home cinema viewing in the form of DVDs. In this context, a comparatively recent innovation in the context of public movie theatre film distribution has been, since 1957, the development of multiple-screen facilities such as multiplex and megaplex movie theatres. It is important to assess the effect of multiplex diffusion on the demand for films, and therefore the authors of this chapter aim to achieve an assessment of the role of multiplex facilities on the demand for movie films in Europe. The authors conduct an econometric study of the demand for public theatre movie film, and, more precisely, for public movie theatre attendance in 15 European countries

(Austria, Belgium, Denmark, France, Finland, Germany, Greece, Ireland, Italy, Luxembourg, Norway, the Netherlands, Portugal, Sweden and the UK) over a 15-year period (1989–2003). GDP per capita appears, as expected, to be a significantly positive determinant of demand, while the price elasticity of demand is negative as expected, but small. Finally, multiplex facilities appear not only to attract demand for movie theatre watching from traditional theatres, but also to be a positive determinant for the growth of overall demand.

1.5 Concluding analyses

Chapter 14 by Orhan Güvenen offers some concluding comments. This final chapter stress technological advances, and the dynamics of the changes driven by advances in information and communication technologies, which are considered by the author as leading to a second industrial revolution. This chapter shows that the quantitative statistical and econometric studies developed in this volume are an invaluable tool for both applied and theoretical research of all aspects of the economics of the media industries, as well as for applications in the management of media enterprises.

Note

1. Patrick Badillo is a Professor at Aix-Marseille University, France; formerly Director of the School of Journalism and Communication of Marseille; Director and Founder of the Research Institute on Information and Communication; Project Manager, French National Research Agency; Jean-Baptiste Lesourd is a Professor at Aix-Marseille University, France.

References

Bagdikian B. 2004. *The New Media Monopoly*, Boston, MA: Beacon.
Downes D.M. 2000. The medium vanishes? The resurrection of the mass audience in the New Media Economy, *Media/Culture: A Journal of Media and Culture*, 3(1), http://dx.doi.org/10.3998/3336451.0007.305.
Hoffman-Riem, W. 1978. National identity and cultural values: broadcasting safeguards, *Journal of Broadcasting*, 31(1), 57–72.
Kahneman, D., and Tversky, A. 1979. Prospect theory: an analysis of decision under risk, *Econometrica*, 47(2), 263–91.
McLuhan, M. 2003[1964]. *Understanding Media: The Extension of Man*, Corte Madera, CA: Gingko Press.

Machlup, F. 1962. *The Production and Distribution of Knowledge in the United States*, Princeton: Princeton University Press.

Mahadevan B. 2000. Business models for Internet-based eCommerce: an anatomy, *California Management Review*, 42(4), 55–69.

Shannon, C.E., and Weaver, W. 1963. *The Mathematical Theory of Communication*, Chicago: University of Illinois Press.

Shapiro, C. and Varian, H.R. 1999. *Information Rules: A Strategic Guide for the Network Economy*, Cambridge, MA: Harvard Business School Press.

Webster, F. *Theories of the Information Society*. 3rd edition. London: Routledge, 2006.

Wildman, S.S. 2003. Modeling the ad revenue potential of media audiences: An underdeveloped side of media economics, *Journal of Media Economics and Culture*, 1(2), 7–37.

Woodward, J. 1980. *Industrial Organization: Theory and Practice*, 2nd edn, Oxford: Oxford University Press.

2
Impediments to a Global Information Society

Robert G. Picard[1]

2.1 Introduction

The proponents of information and communications technologies and development are promoting the vision of a global information society in which information flows throughout the world improving lives, promoting sustainability, reducing conflict, and advancing the human condition. National and regional economic policies have been put in place around the world to support information and communications initiatives as a means of boosting economic growth and development. In doing so, a lovely vision of a better world is asserted: By using more communications products and services, distances disappear in the wired world, information becomes universally available, global interaction becomes the same as local interaction, and human needs will be satisfied with non-material products and information.

Even without debating the ability of communications to produce peace, prosperity, and sustainable development, however, widespread differences in the availability of and ability to use information and communication technologies and systems globally – and within nations – produce enormous impediments that make the vision of global information society an impossible dream for many decades to come. These impediments keep the majority of the world's population from becoming active in the information society or even hoping to become part of it during their lifetimes. Extensive resource and socio-economic limitations hinder information use and, consequently, policy uses of information technology to create economic growth and promote the claimed benefits of information society are defective.

Limitations on the abilities of persons to use information technologies have generally been referred to as the 'digital divide', which

Rice (2002) defines as 'differential access to and use of the internet according to gender, income, race, and location' and the Digital Divide Network (2006) says is the 'gap between those who can effectively use new information and communication tools, such as the internet, and those who cannot'. In the developed world the 'digital divide' is discussed in terms of issues related to class, race/ethnicity, income, gender, and age and at the global the terms is discussed in terms of the divide in technology availability and use in wealthier, developed nations compared with other nations.

If one considers this concept more broadly, however, it becomes evident very rapidly that the divide is not merely digital but is far more fundamental and profound. Information haves and have nots existed long before contemporary information and communications technologies and the divide involves much more than technology. The factors in this broader divide that must be addressed before the digital divide can be effectively spanned because they affect both the availability and use of information products and services.

2.2 Factors influencing the availability of information products and services

The general availability of information and communications products and services is affected by urbanisation, required infrastructures and services, and income and desire to acquire hardware and services. Each of these creates significant challenges in creating global information flow.

2.2.1 Urbanisation

Urbanisation is a critical factor because it is a necessary component in the development of the wage-earning system that ultimately generates the disposable income that can then be used to purchase or use communications products and services. It is also necessary because it produces the densities of population that are necessary to make the infrastructures required for modern communication systems economically efficient and to provide the necessary financial support. Urbanisation is related to nearly every variable of economic development and is a critical factor in creating and maintaining post-modern society. Today only about 47 per cent of the world's population live in urban areas, illustrating that there exist significant economic and social hurdles for communications infrastructures and social development.

Persons living in rural areas have significant unmet needs relating to the general quality of life (nutrition, housing, health, longevity, and so on), education and training opportunities, ability to earn cash for goods they produce or to earn wages rather than living in a subsistence economy, medical and other social services. Clearly, the replacement of many physical products/services with digital services may help to overcome some transportation and acquisition issues, permitting rural residents to gain broader perspectives on life and the world, and provide them with the ability to convey their ideas, aspirations, worth, and contributions to life. However, the achievement of these benefits will first require enormous social and infrastructural improvements.

This is not to say that urbanisation is a panacea for underdevelopment and it is clear that urbanisation itself creates its own set of social and economic problems. But without urbanisation the necessary requirements for communication and information systems cannot exist.

Patterns of urbanisation vary widely across the world. The population of Europe, for example, is around twice as urbanised as that of Africa and North America is about twice as urbanised as Asia. Such differences affect the basic ability to support communications infrastructures and create information societies.

2.2.2 Electrification

A crucial resource and service infrastructure for information society is electricity, which is obviously required for the operation of all electronic equipment. This resource – which tends to be ignored and taken for granted in western nations – must be in place and readily usable in order for the vision of a connected world to be pursued. Today, however, more than two billion people worldwide have no access to electricity (World Bank, 1996). This means that about one-third of the world's population are unable to turn on a light, charge mobile phones, or power up a computer. This impediment is particularly acute in some regions. In Africa and Asia, for example, almost two-thirds of the population lives without electricity.

Even where electricity exists, the amounts available and the times at which it is available are often limited because of the poor capacity of infrastructure or the costs of generation. As a result, in 2007, the inhabitants of OECD countries, mostly developed countries, used about 15 times as much electricity as Africans and Americans about 20 times as much as Asians (International Energy Agency, 2009). In that year Africans, for example, only used an average of 578 kilowatt hours per capita, just enough to power one or two light bulbs for only part of the day.

2.2.3 Telecommunications

Telephony is also a critical infrastructure for digital communication products and services. It provides a means of overcoming time and distance through telephone services, fax, data transmission, and Internet access and operation.

The global structure of telephony is undergoing a process of rapid change because of the privatisation of state monopolies, the reduced regulation of private firms, and increased competition from new telephone companies and companies from other countries entering domestic markets. Mobile telephony is increasingly challenging fixed telephony as the major player and there is a move from conceptualising telephones as providing household service to one providing individual service.

Nevertheless, the availability of telephony varies widely around the globe and most of the population has no access to such a service. Indeed, there are only 12 fixed lines and 17 mobile phones for every 100 inhabitants worldwide (International Telecommunications Union, 2008). This is compounded by the fact that the majority of the world's population lives more than three kilometres from the nearest telephone. These and other social factors combined produce a milieu in which two-thirds of the world's population have never made a phone call.

This is caused in part by the huge disparities in the availability of telephones. Western Europe, the United States/Canada, and Japan, for example, account for 75 per cent of all phone lines. Africans have only three fixed lines for every 100 inhabitants, compared to 74 for Sweden. Haiti has just three mobile phones per 100 inhabitants, compared to 90 per 100 in Finland (International Telecommunications Union, 2008). And even if telephones are available and one has the money to purchase one, this may involve a long wait: at the turn of the millennium the average waiting time between the placement of an order for a phone and its installation was about eight years in Cameroon, five years in Bangladesh, three years in the Philippines, and one year in Panama (World Bank, 2000).

Even where telephony systems exist, there are wide variations in terms of their capabilities. This occurs because the capabilities are related to the amount of use and high-use systems tend to have greater capacity, higher speeds, and more up-to-date equipment. Capabilities are also related to population densities and telephone companies provide different levels of systems capabilities within their service areas depending upon those densities. Capabilities are also related to the levels of competition because companies will make investment in their systems when they are under the pressure of competition.

The availability of telephony and the capabilities affect the ability to provide universal levels of service, the ability of less-developed nations to take part in the global information society, and the ability of the rural and less-developed regions of developed nations to participate on an equal footing with urban developed areas. Even in Europe there are wide differences in telephone systems both among nations and within nations and significant subsidies and public investments are being undertaken to reduce some of the variance.

The disparities in telephone availability and use are seen in the figures for international telephone traffic. Asia, with about two-thirds of the world's population, accounts for only about 20 per cent of international phone calls. Europe accounts for more than 40 per cent and the USA and Canada, which together have only 5 per cent of the world's population, make one-third of all international calls.

Although improvements in telecommunications systems and availability are taking place worldwide, the overwhelming majority of the world's population still has no access to either fixed or mobile services through which to become part of the global information society.

2.2.4 Income

Personal and household incomes are a critical factor for information and communications technology and use because of the costs of the acquisition of equipment and services. Income is limited and any spending on communications must be balanced alongside the other needs of life. This problem of income is particularly important because the costs for the acquisition and use of media and communications are increasing in post-industrial society. Individuals are being asked to absorb increased hardware and content costs, and to acquire a wider range of communication devices. The content costs are being shifted increasingly to consumers as there is a diminution in the level of media subsidisation by the government and advertisers.

Worldwide, of course, there are wide levels of variation in income levels. In Malawi, for example, GDP per capita is about $596 compared to $30,617 per capita in Japan. Even in Europe there are significant differences in income. Luxembourg, for example, has a GDP per capita of $69,800 compared to $30,436 in the United Kingdom. A person living on $3 a day in Bangladesh is not going to spend as much on communications as a person in France living on $50 a day. Similarly, a person living on $20 in Wales is not going to spend as much as a person living on $45 a day in London.

Three billion people (half of the world's population) live on incomes of less than $1 (€.70) per day and together they account for only 1 per cent of the world's wealth. Their ability to acquire and pay for the use of information and communications technologies and services is thus an enormous challenge. This impediment is particularly significant because of the disparities in the world's most populous countries (see Table 2.1), where significant development will need to take place to spread the benefits of the information society.

Income affects the consumer acquisition of computers, Internet services, mobile phones, CDs, etc., but so do individual choices. Acquisition and use requires monetary and temporal expenditures that must be balanced within other expenditures in human lives and persons often chose not to equally acquire all media and communication products and services even if they have the financial resources to do so.

If one considers the global spread of information society technologies, there are nearly one billion computers in use, meaning that there are at present around one computer for every six people in the world (Computer Industry Almanac, 2005). These are distributed very unevenly across the globe, however, with just 15 nations accounting for 75 per cent of all computers. About 1 billion persons worldwide use the Internet, 17 per cent of the world's population. However, this use is skewed because 15 nations account for 70 per cent of those users – the USA alone accounts for 18 per cent of the users (Computer Industry Almanac, 2005).

One particular challenge of Internet use is language because the majority of the world's population does not speak a European-based language and services are overwhelmingly provided in those languages. Today 45 per cent of the online population uses English as its native language and another 30 per cent are native users of other European languages. Only

Table 2.1 Percentage of population living on less than $2 per day

	Percentage
China	46.7
India	79.9
Indonesia	52.4
Brazil	22.4
Pakistan	65.6

about 25 per cent of online users employ non-European languages. The level of services in these languages is increasing, but linguistic impediments will continue to constrain global information flows for a considerable period.

To help overcome cost and infrastructure challenges, the MIT Media Lab developed a $100 computer for the One Laptop per Child Foundation, but even the costs of this product have now risen to $200. The computer – designed primarily for use with educational programmes and marketed to government ministries of education worldwide – incorporates a hand crank to generate electricity and has no telecommunications link. While it may therefore be useful for some educational and informational activities, it will not link users into a global information society.

2.2.5 Factors influencing the use of information products and services

The use of information and communications products and services is affected by literacy and the costs of use and these create significant impediments to global information flow.

Literacy

Information and communication equipment and software are sophisticated and require the operator to have a certain level of literacy. Even the Internet is primarily a text-based medium, although augmented with visual and audio material, and its use requires some ability to read and write to locate websites, conduct searches, and select and read material. This is a problem for global information society because only around 30 per cent of the world's population are literate, making the potential for them to use information technologies to access information extremely poor. Even those who are literate will have difficulties benefiting directly from online information and communications because fewer than 20 per cent have completed their education at elementary school level. The wide variance in literacy rates are shown in Table 2.2.

Literacy rates are affected by the availability and education systems, differences in the educational opportunities afforded to men and women, and secondary language issues. Even in highly developed nations, literacy issues exist as the result of immigration patterns. All of these are heightened because many information and communication technology services are provided in dominant languages.

Table 2.2 Approximate literacy rates by continent

	Percent literate
Europe	99
U.S.A./Canada	95
Latin America	80
Arab States	80
Oceania	80
Asia	60
Africa	40

Source: UNESCO (2009).

Thus, one must improve the ability to read and write before the benefits of information society can become possible.

Costs of use

The costs of use are also important components in the choice to use media and of the amount of use that is made of them. As noted earlier, the income levels across most of the world are so low that many families are barely able to feed themselves, let alone spend significant amounts on information and communications products and services. But even if their income levels are above the survival level, disparities in the costs of using equipment and services hamper significant use.

This challenge is illustrated clearly by the pricing of telephone services. Telephone use prices are based on individual factors such as the number and duration of calls, the number of services used, and whether one owns or rents equipment, but overall system use is also a factor because average costs fall as the level of use rises, and the type and ownership structure of the system also has an effect on prices.

These factors create advantages for heavy users, developed nations, large nations, and people in urban areas. Conversely, price disadvantages exist for low users, less developed nations, smaller nations and rural areas. Examples of the wide variations in prices are seen in the fact that a three-minute phone call to the USA from the Central African Republic costs 40 times as much as one from Sweden and that a call from Japan – half a world away – costs half of what it costs to call from neighbouring Mexico (Table 2.3).

This problem is also mirrored internally in nations and has an effect on both ownership and pricing for local and long distance access and the amount of use by subscribers. These factors also affect the pricing of Internet services. In Canada, for example, the costs for Internet services

Table 2.3 Selected comparative costs for a three-minute phone call to the USA

	Price ($)
Sweden	0.32
Germany	0.35
Hungary	0.79
Czech Republic	0.83
Portugal	0.93
Finland	1.06
United Kingdom	1.18
Japan	1.67
Poland	1.79
Italy	1.95
Latvia	2.02
Belarus	2.25
Egypt	2.57
Mexico	3.04
Kenya	5.84
India	3.20
Iran	7.70
Central African Rep.	12.93

Source: World Bank (2004).

are relatively low because they involve only a low fixed phone fee and service provider fee; by contrast, they are about seven times higher in Hungary because they include a low fixed phone fee, high phone usage fee, and high service provider fee.

Broadband prices also reflect the cost discrepancies, even among developed countries. The cost of a monthly subscription in Greece is only 40 per cent of what it costs in the Slovak Republic and the cost in the United Kingdom is half what it is in Mexico (Figure 2.1).

Cost factors thus create differences in demand in various countries and produce limitations on use even when services are available.

Need and desirability

The need for desirability of information and communications products and services also affects use. In order to be successful, they must fulfil the wants and needs of people and there must be clear benefits from their use. This is somewhat problematic because most services are designed for persons who live away from their families and friends, have widespread personal, business, and professional contacts, live and have highly mobile lifestyles.

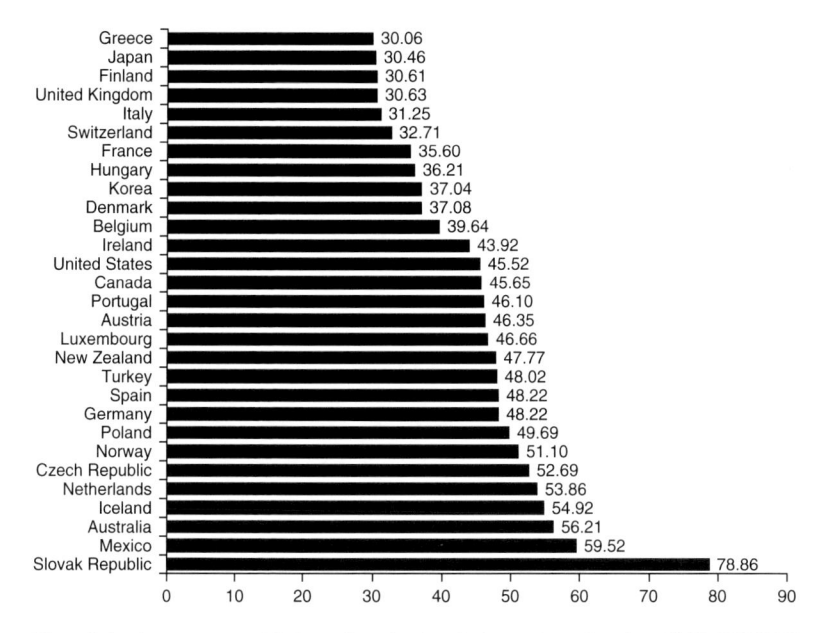

Country	Price
Greece	30.06
Japan	30.46
Finland	30.61
United Kingdom	30.63
Italy	31.25
Switzerland	32.71
France	35.60
Hungary	36.21
Korea	37.04
Denmark	37.08
Belgium	39.64
Ireland	43.92
United States	45.52
Canada	45.65
Portugal	46.10
Austria	46.35
Luxembourg	46.66
New Zealand	47.77
Turkey	48.02
Spain	48.22
Germany	48.22
Poland	49.69
Norway	51.10
Czech Republic	52.69
Netherlands	53.86
Iceland	54.92
Australia	56.21
Mexico	59.52
Slovak Republic	78.86

Figure 2.1 Average monthly broadband subscription prices, October 2008 ($US PPP)
Source: OECD (2009).

These factors tends to be absent among rural populations – half of the people in the world – who tend to share houses and villages with most of their immediate family, know few people outside their neighbourhood, engage primarily in agriculture rather than trade, and tend to travel only infrequently. When new and potentially useful products and services appear, their use is dependent upon them providing improvements on existing media and communications opportunities in terms of both function and price.

Today, most products and services are targeting young, urban dwellers and making limited efforts to adapt to local lifestyles and cultures. These approaches limit the desirability of products to certain groups of consumers and make it less likely that persons outside those groups will use them.

2.3 Discussion

In the majority of the world the requirements for producing a global information society remain undeveloped, or their development is so limited that they can provide only essential or basic services. Social, economic and technical factors mean that the global information society remains a dream rather than a reality.

Even in developed regions such as Europe there are nations and rural areas where inequalities persist in terms of both the access to and the pricing of services. If one actually wishes to move to the achievement of a global information society, efforts must be made to overcome the fundamental impediments to its achievement.

Development institutions and programmes are making significant efforts to improve social conditions and global communication infrastructures. Nevertheless, for many decades to come the majority of the world's population will have to continue to live with less ability to communicate and receive communications than is the case in North America, Europe, and the few highly developed nations in Asia.

Although an increasing number of persons across the globe are becoming able to participate in the global information society, most are being excluded. However, it is not simply a matter of access to computers, mobile phones, or the Internet. Only around 40 per cent have access to radios and only 20 per cent have television sets, thus limiting access to information in more rudimentary forms.

The realisation of a global information society thus remains far away and will not occur within our lifetimes. The existing impediments should not halt our efforts to promote a connected world, but we must be realistic in acknowledging what we can accomplish and we must first pursue fundamental improvements to the basic conditions that most persons in the world encounter in their daily lives.

Note

1. Robert G. Picard is a Professor at the Media Management and Transformation Centre, Jönköping International Business School, Jönköping, Sweden.

References

Computer Industry Almanac Inc. 2005 and subsequent years. *Market Research Reports. Computers In Use By Country*. Arlington Heights, IL, USA: Computer Industry Almanac Inc. http://www.c-i-a.com.
Digital Divide Network. 2006. www.digitaldividenetwork.org.
International Energy Agency. 2009. *Key World Energy Statistics 2009*. Paris: IEA. Available at http://www.iea.org.

International Telecommunications Union. 2008. *Yearbook of Statistics, Chronological Time Series 1997–2006*, Geneva: International Telecommunications Union.
OECD. 2009. OECD Broadband Portal. Organization for Economic Co-operation and Development. Available at http://www.oecd.org/document/54/0,3343,en_2649_34225_38690102_1_1_1_1,00.html.
Rice, Ronald E. 2002. Primary issues in Internet use, in Leah A. Lievrouw and Sonja Livingstone (eds), *The Handbook of New Media*, London: Sage Publications.
UNESCO. 2009. Adult literacy rates. Available at http://www.uis.unesco.org/statsen/statistics/indicators/i_pages/IndLit.asp.
World Bank. 1996. *Rural Energy and Development: Improving Energy Supply for Two Billion People*. Washington, DC.
World Bank. 2000. *World Development Indicators*. Washington, DC.
World Bank. 2004. World *Development Indicators*. Washington, DC.

3
Transformation of Internet-based Companies' Business Models: Ten Years after the Dot.com Burst

Christophe Garonne and Félix Weygand[1]

3.1 Introduction

Since 2004, a new wave of Internet-based companies has emerged throughout the world trying to capitalise on the new technologies that are commonly labelled Web 2.0 (McAfee 2006). 'Web 2.0' or the 'Digital Economy' is the latest terminology in force to describe the new utilisation of digital solutions based on a convergence between technology, economy and public acceptance. The widespread diffusion of the Internet protocol with broadband access and mobile communication (the technological side) is combined with a generalised acceptation, growing interest and utilisation of the eCommerce (the economic side) (Brynjolfsson and McAfee 2007; Brousseau and Curien 2007). As a result, the capitalisation of ventures evolving in the Digital Economy has been growing exponentially in recent years: in 2005 eBay bought Skype for US$3.1 billion and in 2006 Google acquired You Tube for US$1.65 billion. At a first glance, it may appear that this period presents some similarities with the first Internet Bubble (1998–2000). In the first semester of 2007 alone, almost US$500 million have been invested in Web 2.0 new ventures around the world[2] which represents a 6 per cent increase since the 1st semester of 2006. The steepest growth in investments on Web 2.0 has occurred in Europe and Israel, which have seen a 100 per cent increase since the 1st semester of 2006 (US$52 million). The largest part of these investments has been realised in the USA (75 per cent) followed by Europe (12 per cent) and China (10 per cent).[3] On average, global Web 2.0 start-ups have secured US$4.6 million.

Overall, amounts invested in new ventures have been slightly reduced by the global financial crisis hitting the world in the second part of 2008 but have not plummeted (Deloitte, 2009). Moreover, venture capitalists and other institutional investors have not modified their investing strategies in industry sectors (Deloitte 2009). This statement is especially true for the technology industry as investments in Internet based-ventures have continued to grow internationally and have reached in 2009 their highest level since 2000.[4]

These elements raise some questions about the profitability and the modus operandi of companies involved in the Digital Economy, especially on their business models.

The analysis in this chapter, along with the use of the business models' framework developed in Mahadevan (2000), addresses three key questions:

- The first question concerns the evolution of the business models:
  Are the business models of companies evolving in the Digital Economy in 2007 different from the business models of the companies in the previous period?
- The second question concerns the actual positioning of the survivors of the dot-com bust in the Digital Economy in 2007:
  What is the actual positioning of these companies in the framework developed by Mahadevan in 2000?
- The last question examines the positioning in Mahadevan's framework of a number of start-ups involved in the Digital Economy today.

A twofold methodology will be used to address these questions: firstly, the framework developed by Mahadevan in 2000 is to be applied to assess the position and evolution of large Internet-based companies today and then, the same criteria will be applied to a number of nascent start-ups involved in the Digital Economy today.

This chapter consists of five sections. Following this introduction, the second section provides an overview of previous research and empirical studies on business models in the Digital Age from 1998 to the rise of the Web 2.0 phenomenon. Section 3.3 then introduces the case and provides information on data, variables and research methods. Section 3.4 describes the empirical results of the sets of questions and their potential limitations while section 3.5 provides a conclusion on the validity of Mahadevan's framework in 2007 and some recommendations for future research.

3.2 Conceptual framework

Research on start-ups, the eEconomy, and the influences of IS and IT technologies on business have interested both academics and practitioners for a considerable period and, as a result, there is a fairly substantial body of literature available on the subject of business models and/or eBusiness models. However, no widely accepted definition of business models has been delivered so far, especially for business models of the so-called 'Digital Economy' (McAfee 2006; Brynjolfsson and McAfee, 2007; Brousseau and Curien, 2007). On the other hand, there is a growing general literature on business models, with a focus on the links between business models and the Internet (Afuah and Tucci, 2001; Gordijn and Akkermans, 2001a 2001b; Papakiriakopoulos et al., 2001; Petrovic et al., 2001; Weill and Vitale, 2001; McGann and Lyytinen, 2002; Ostwalder and Pigneur, 2002; Rappa, 2003; Vasilopoulou et al., 2002; Pateli and Giaglis, 2004; Lambert 2006; Garonne and Weygand, 2007). The literature on business models may be classified into the following four broad categories:

- studies focusing on defining the business models by describing its components
- studies explaining the specificities of the eBusiness models
- typologies
- studies exploring the reasons behind the first dot-com bust in 2001 and research describing the key success factors to be implemented when developing a business model for an Internet-based new venture.

Mahadevan's work (2000) used in this study is included in subsection 3.2.1 as it describes the components of the business models and also in subsection 3.2.3 as it provides one of the earliest typologies of the Internet business models.

3.2.1 Components of a business model

The first studies realised at the end of the 1990s described the elements to be included in a business model to provide a preliminary definition of the concept. According to Timmers (1998), the business models of Internet-based companies rely on three elements: the IT architecture enabling the exchange of information, products and services; the benefits that can be retrieved by the different actors involved; and the sources of revenue. Many researchers have capitalised on Timmers's work and have included other elements in the business model, including the role of IT (Bagchi and Tulksie, 2000; Klueber, 2000), and finance, product innovation and customer relationships (Osterwalder and Pigneur, 2002). Then, Weill and Vitale defined a business model as 'a description of the roles and relationships among a firm's consumers, customers, allies and suppliers that identifies the major flows of product, information and money, and the major benefits to participants' (Weill and Vitale, 2001).

Different authors have provided their own definition of business models emphasising on specific components such as Rappa (2003) who mentioned the value chain or Amit and Zott (2001) who focussed on the governance of transactions to create value.

Finally, several definitions of business models have also been provided without mentioning their core elements by Linder and Cantrell (2000), Klueber (2000), Applegate (2001), Petrovic et al. (2001) and Magretta (2002). They describe the business model as a system or as 'a story that explains how an enterprise works' (Magretta 2002).

Mahadevan (2000) described the different market structures a company may choose to operate on the Internet.

3.2.2 Specificities of the e-business models

In the Digital Economy, innovative products and/or services using cutting-edge technologies are launched into the market without extensive testing leading to high risks and uncertainty. In addition, markets for these innovations are largely unknown and so are the expected revenues (Aldrich and Fiol, 1994; Amason et al., 2006; Knight 1921; Loch et al., 2005; Shane and Stuart, 2002). As a result, business models established at the nascent stage are based on unreliable estimates (Champion and Carr, 2000; Drucker, 1985; Druilhe and Garnsey, 2004; Porter 2001; Stoica and Schindehutte, 1999). Those 'beta' business models should be modified to closely fit with the economic environment newly discovered as the product/service is adopted – or not – by the market. The company is then engaged in a constant trial-and-error process to develop the best business models. From this situation derive many pitfalls: continuous change of business models, increasing difficulties to retrieve funds from potential investors or customer deception.

Moreover, those first models may have a strong impact – either positive or negative – on the future of the company and may be bundled with the first mover advantage – or disadvantage (Porter, 2001): a less efficient business model may impact the development of the firm on the long run by acting as an impediment to investment in R&D, to create barriers to entry, or to size new opportunities or markets. In addition, the trial-and-error model may send wrong signals to the stakeholders and investors (that is, continuous change of Business Models + Digital Economy + start-ups + high tech = highly risky investment) (Andries et al., 2005).

Several authors have specifically described the eBusiness models and their relationships with technology (Gordjin and Akkermans, 2001b; Papakiriakopoulos et al., 2001; Weill and Vitale, 2001; McGann and Lyytinen, 2002; Osterwalder and Pigneur, 2002; Vassilopoulou et al., 2003).

Another specific aspect of the Digital Economy is that many services are offered on the Internet at no cost, at least for the final user. The main challenge for the start-ups of the Digital Economy is to transform their use value into monetary terms. However, convincing the final user to pay a fee for a service that may be available free of charge elsewhere on the network is only possible if the final user perceives that a new and specific value is added to the service. As the willingness of the final user to pay for a service provided through the Internet is low,[5] companies engaged in business have looked for alternative revenue streams such as advertisement, click per use, click per thousand, sale of customer data, intermediary ... As a result, these companies may offer free services to the final user on a continuous basis while retrieving some revenues from diverse sources and by doing so, developing a profitable business (Dang Nguyen and Penard, 2004).

3.2.3 Typologies

Classifications of business models by using different criteria have been developed since the beginning of the Internet Bubble in 1998. Timmers, the first to propose a typology of the business models used on the Internet, was followed by Mahadevan (2000); Tapscott et al. (2000); Linder and Cantrell (2000); Kaplan and Sawhney (2000); Alt and Zimmermann (2001); Applegate and Collura (2001); Rappa (2003); Weill and Vitale (2001); Pateli and Giaglis (2004). Other business models typologies have been elaborated with a specific emphasis on software industry (McKelvey 2001) or biotechnologies (Bigliardi et al., 2005; Mangematin et al., 2003; Willemstein et al., 2007).

Three different models can be derived from these typologies (McKelvey 2001):

a. A model which is based on the ownership of the technical solution and on the total control of the knowledge and economic values created.
b. The second model is a hybrid where the company commercialises a product and/or service and as a result has a control over the economic gains but the development and the knowledge created are done in association with the company and the communities of practice.

c. In the third model, all the knowledge and the development are elaborated by the network members. This business model is an 'ideal business model' for developers do not benefit economically from the innovative product/service developed.

Companies that operate in these three different models may be classified in two groups:

1. Companies created in R&D laboratories that developed an innovation protected by a patent. They use their patent and their temporary monopoly situation to exploit economically their innovation. (ex: biotechnology, micro electronic industries…) (Model A)
2. Companies created on an open source innovation where no patent exists but where the innovation developed meets a high degree of interest in the public. These companies will have trouble defining an economically viable business model (Models B and C). By trial and error, they develop hybrid business models. Generally speaking, Web 2.0 new ventures belong to this group, and this is the case for the sample of companies we intend to study in this article.

With the notable exception of the biotechnologies, no further work seems to have been done on this theme since 2001, inducing that typologies or taxonomies are no longer on the research priorities agenda or that no significant changes has occurred in this research area. Mahadevan's typology was also selected for this reason and we intend to study the validity of this model in 2007.

3.2.4 Reasons for the dot-com failure in 2001 and key success factors

Preliminary studies realised during 'the Internet Bubble' period (1998–2001) (Applegate 2000 and 2001; Champion et al., 2000; Porter 2001) focused on an examinination of the reasons behind success or failure of companies during this unique period.

The literature on eBusiness models suggests that authors tried to identify the most important key success factors for companies engaging on eBusiness such as technology (Barua et al., 2001); management (Wathne et al., 2001); network (Doyle and Melanson 2001) and wealth creation (Bouwman and van Ham 2003). Some studies considered the key success factors from a holistic point of view (Vasipoulou et al., 2002; Amit and Zott 2001; Duh et al., 2001; MacInnes 2005) while some considered the influence of the marketing strategy on the business model

(Maitland et al., 2005). However, new technological phenomena such as Web 2.0 have not yet been the subject of much academic research (Floyd et al., 2007), with the article from Brynjolfsson and McAfee (2007) being a notable exception.[6] As a result, it appears that at the time of writing almost no academic research has been published on the business models of the companies using technologies based on Web 2.0.

3.3 Data and research methods

3.3.1 Data and research population

To answer the questions, two datasets were examined. The first dataset was collected through an online survey among 10 start-ups involved in eBusiness located in Southern France. These start-ups have been operating for a few years, but are regarded as being representative of a second generation of entrepreneurs involved in the Digital Economy. As this study is exploratory in nature, these firms are not representative of all start-ups; rather, they are representative of those created in the multimedia industry at the time of the study. Authors have selected these companies according to the following variables: the companies (i) are involved in eBusiness; (ii) invest a significant part of their revenue in R&D; (iii) have developed a hybrid business model; and (iv) have to be located within the 'Secured Communication Solutions' cluster.[7] These companies are representative of the Multimedia/High technology industries as defined by the local Chamber of Commerce in 2005.[8] Those companies have: between one and forty employees, have been in business for one to six years and had annual revenues of between €100,000 and €3.4 million in 2006. The survey was realised during the second half of October 2007. As companies were selected by the authors, the response rate was 100 per cent.

The second dataset was chosen according to the following criteria: companies have to have been in continuous operation since the first Digital Economy (1998–2001) and have to be on the Top Ten list elaborated by ComScore Inc., Mediametrix regarding their traffic volume in August 2007. The objective is to study companies which have shown flexibility and strategy since the 2000s in order to secure a position among the top websites today. As some of those companies are listed on the stock exchange, the composition of their business models was also examined using Annual Reports for FY 2006. The companies chosen are: Yahoo! Sites, Google Sites, eBay, Amazon Sites, Ask Network, and Wikipedia sites.[9]

Table 3.1 Description of the start-ups involved in the study in 2007

Name of Company	Description of the company	Modes of Business	Changes in Business Models since the Creation of the Company	Market Structure
A	Anti-spam solution	B2B B2C	No	Product/service provider
B	Open source software developement	B2B	Yes	Product/service provider
C	Webcity magazine	B2C	Yes	Portal
D	Mobile applications	B2B B2C	Yes	Product/service provider // Market maker
E	Online music learning tool	B2B B2C	Yes	Product/service provider
F	Open source software developement	B2B	Yes	Product/service provider
G	Mobile communication services	B2B	Yes	Product/service provider
H	Virtual mobile desktop	B2B B2C B2G	Yes	Product/service provider
I	Web agency	B2B	Yes	Product/service provider
J	Mobile applications	B2B B2C B2G	Yes	Product/service provider

Other companies listed on the Top 10, including Time Warner Network, Microsoft Sites, Fox Interactive Media and Viacom Digital, have been excluded from this research for the reason that they are not 'Internet pure players' since they are traditional mass media companies who are using the digital economy as an extension of their traditional businesses. However, a shift in power between the traditional and digital branches of the media industry occurred in the period between 1995 and 2000. Future research may investigate how this change has impacted the business models of the mass media industry.

We have purposely chosen to compare well-known and 'experienced' Internet companies with young and nascent locally-based start-ups to detect similarities or differences in their business models (that is, do the young start-ups copy the top companies or are they developing and trying new models based specifically on the Web 2.0 phenomenon?)

3.3.2 Variables and research method

Mahadevan's framework (2000) was chosen in order to compare the largest Internet-based companies by consumer activity (that is, the number of unique visits) with recent start-ups for the following reasons: it is one of the most comprehensive frameworks developed during the first Digital Economy (before the burst) and many later authors capitalised on its work; it provided some insights and recommendations that may be interesting to test today with the surviving companies of the period and with the nascent companies to determine if changes have occurred in the way companies are using Internet to do business. Mahadevan's article was followed by the burst of the Internet bubble in 2001 and a four-year period described by the Yankee Consulting Group as the 'Telecom Nuclear Winter' when Internet-based companies experienced extreme difficulties finding securing financing. Since 2005, there has been an increase in the level of investment in new Internet ventures. As a result, Mahadevan's framework may be a convenient tool to better understand the new situation: If the new surge in investments and companies development relies on principles similar to those in the 1998–2000 period, then, Mahadevan's framework is still effective to describe the business models; if the reasons are different, then, the new models will not be mirrored by Mahadevan's framework and a new grid will have to be developed.

Since 2001 crucial changes have occurred in the Digital Economy at the macroeconomic level:

- New technologies have emerged such as the wireless and mobile Internet.
- Diffusion (more people have access to the Internet around the world) and appropriation (people have a better understanding on how to use the Internet) of these new tools and techniques are much higher in 2007. As a example, Internet users worldwide were 384 million in 2000; 725 million; 1 billion in 2005; 1,2 billion at the end of 2006.[10]
- People are now using the Internet for both their leisure and their professional activities.[11]
- People use technologies called Web 2.0 primarily for leisure activities or during their free time.

Mahadevan distinguishes three types of 'market structures' in which the company may operate on the Internet: 'portals, market maker and product/service providers'.

1. Portals act as a path to direct customer to specific websites and, as such, portals have a direct link with product/service providers. 'A portal engages primarily in building a community of consumers of information about products and services' (Mahadevan, 2000). Portals can be either B2B or B2C.
2. Market Maker is similar to a portal regarding the creation of a community of customer/suppliers of products and services but has also some specific characteristics: they act as a facilitator of business transactions between the buyer and the seller; they have to provide a 'value to suppliers and customers through a system of implicit or explicit guarantee of security and trust in the business transaction' (Mahadevan 2000). As a result, market makers are predominantly oriented B2B.
3. Product/service providers may be defined as online boutiques that sell product/services to customers. They are B2B or B2C.

Those three types of market structures are then combined with the following three interlinked critical streams that form the business models: the value, the revenue and the logistical streams. Value stream includes the following elements which create 'the value' for the companies operating on the Internet: virtual communities (they generate knowledge, value and share them with the other group members), dramatic reduction in transaction costs (the cost of providing product and price comparison on a website is almost zero), gainful exploitation of information asymmetry, value-added market making process (such as security and trust). According to Mahadevan, those value streams are not mutually exclusive but organisations develop a business model based on a dominant value stream (see Table 3.2).

Mahadevan distinguishes six revenue streams which can be defined as 'the realisation of the value proposition in the short term' (Mahadevan 2000): 'Increased margins over brick and mortar operations, revenue from online seller communities, advertising, variable pricing strategies, revenue streams linked to exploiting information asymmetry, free offerings.'

Finally, logistic streams deal with the position of the Internet-based company on the supply chain. Three types of logistic streams exists: Dis-Intermediation (a dramatic reduction in the supply chain to deliver a better responsiveness to customer while decreasing the costs); Infomediation (a search engine is necessary to conveniently use the always increasing volume of information accessible on the Internet); meta-mediation ('the process that goes beyond aggregating vendors and products and includes additional services required for facilitating transactions').

3.4 Results, discussion and limitations

For each dataset, a framework based on Mahadevan's article was designed and companies were positioned on the grid according to their business models and market structures in 2007. Table 3.2 presents the grid for the 10 selected start-ups while Table 3.3 displays the positions of the largest Internet-based companies by unique visitor in August 2007. Business models of the two sets of firms are presented in separate groups before providing an analysis of the common characteristics.

According to Mahadevan, the logistical stream was a clear division between the three market structures. However, this division does not seem that clear anymore either for the start-ups or for the largest companies. Both start-up D and Wikipedia capitalise on dis-intermediation by providing information on mobile phone/online encyclopaedia (respectively) and infomediation by offering a search engine on their own website that can retrieve and filter information on a particular topic for the customer at the same time (for both start-up D and Wikipedia). Amazon utilises both dis-intermediation (by shrinking the supply chain in its traditional business of delivering culture products) and meta-mediation (by offering a secure marketplace where transactions between sellers and buyers are facilitated).

Table 3.2 Summary of the business models of the start-ups in 2007

Business Model Building Blocks	Market Structures		
	Portals	Market Makers	Product/Service Providers
Value Streams			
Virtual Communities	C	D	A B D E F G I J
Dramatic Reduction in Transaction Costs		D	D H
Gainful Exploitation of Information Asymmetry			
Value-Added Market Making Process		D	
Revenue Streams			
Increased Margin over Brick and Mortar Operations			D E H I J
Revenue from Online Seller Communities		D	B D F G
Advertising	C	D	J
Variable Pricing Strategies	C		A B D E F I J
Revenue Streams Linked to Exploiting Information Asymmetry			
Free Offerings	C	D	B D E F J
Logistical Streams			
Dis-Intermediation			A B D E F G J
Infomediation	C		H I
Meta-Mediation		D	

Source: Adapted from Mahadevan (2000).

The shift towards a consolidation of the market structure is apparent and business borders are no longer well defined between the main players on the market.

End-users' pressure to benefit from state-of-the-art online services without the willingness to pay for them has dramatically affected the Internet landscape since 2001. Internet players have been forced to change their business models to include more free options or to offer their entire services for free. As a result, advertising revenues have become the keystone of their business models. This shift in paradigm has had two major effects:

a. The fierce competition between the different actors led them into a pursuit to gather the largest 'virtual communities'.[12] This is the first step to increase the notoriety of the company in order to

Table 3.3 Summary of the Business Models of the largest Internet based companies (based on ComScore Media Metrix release for August 2007)

Business Model Building Blocks	Market Structures			
	Portals	Market Makers		Product/Service Providers
Value Streams				
Virtual communities	Yahoo! Sites / Google Sites / Ask Network	eBay / Amazon Sites		Ask Network / Wikipedia sites / Amazon Sites
Dramatic Reduction in Transaction Costs	Yahoo! Sites / Google Sites / Ask Network	eBay / Amazon Sites		Ask Network / Wikipedia sites / Amazon Sites
Gainful Exploitation of Information Asymmetry	Yahoo! Sites / Google Sites / Ask Network	eBay / Amazon Sites		
Value-Added Market Making Process	Yahoo! Sites / Google Sites / Ask Network	eBay / Amazon Sites		Ask Network
Revenue Streams				
Increased Margin over Brick and Mortar Operations				Ask Network / Wikipedia sites / Amazon Sites
Revenue from Online Seller Communities		eBay / Amazon Sites		

Advertising	Yahoo! Sites / Google Sites / Ask Network	eBay / Amazon Sites	
Variable Pricing Strategies			Ask Network
Revenue Streams Linked to Exploiting Information Asymmetry	Yahoo! Sites	eBay / Amazon Sites	
Free Offerings	Yahoo! Sites / Google Sites / Ask Network	eBay / Amazon Sites	Wikipedia sites
Logistical Streams			
Dis-Intermediation		Amazon Sites	Ask Network / Wikipedia sites / Amazon Sites
Infomediation	Yahoo! Sites / Google Sites / Ask Network		Wikipedia sites
Meta-Mediation	Yahoo! Sites / Ask Network	eBay / Amazon Sites	

Source: Adapted from Mahadevan (2000).

generate an important traffic to attract potential advertisers. This traffic may then be converted into revenue and thus limiting the potential loss due to the abandonment of subscription fees;
  b. Market Structures definitions have become blurred. Amazon, for example, capitalises on its notoriety as a product/service provider to develop a large traffic which in turn, has enabled Amazon to develop a marketplace to offer value added to their final customers and to other resellers. As a result, differences between Portal and Market Makers and the definitions of the market structures components are no longer clear.

Questionnaire (for start-ups) and annual reports (for the largest companies, FY 2006) were utilised to answer the three questions formulated in Part 1.

  1. The evolution of the business models: Are the business models of companies evolving in the Digital Economy in 2007 different from the business models of the companies in the previous period?

It is interesting to note that while all of the largest companies provide free offerings for their customers only six out of ten start-ups are doing this. The reasons for not doing this are 'large infrastructure and R&D costs and the customer's willingness to pay for an efficient anti spam solution' for start-up A; a 'B2B only service oriented' for start-ups G and I. No answer to this question was provided by start-up H. A similar distortion appears in the advertising revenue which is used by all the largest companies except Wikipedia, but only by start-ups C, D and J. Start-up A offers a spam control solution and for ethical reasons cannot use advertising fees. A B E F G H I are all B2B product/service providers in rather specific areas and for a range of reasons they do not want to provide third party advertisements on their websites.

All revenue streams described for the Market Makers such as revenue from online seller communities, advertising and revenue streams linked to the exploitation of information asymmetry (with the auctions) are utilised by eBay and Amazon sites while start-up D retrieves revenue only from online seller communities and advertising.

In 2007, advertising constitutes the largest part of the revenues of portals such as Yahoo! Sites; Google Sites; Ask Network and start-up C. Yahoo! Sites is also able to collect some revenue through exploiting the information asymmetry on its Yahoo! Properties websites dedicated to travel and shopping. Google is the only portal in this study to retrieve almost 100 per cent of its revenues from advertising fees. Advertising revenue stream is usually divided between 'impressions' when an advertisement appears in pages viewed by users and 'click-through' when a user clicks on an advertiser's listing. On the other hand, Google Sites experience a 'dramatic reduction in transaction costs' by delivering online scientific documentation such as the service provided by Google Scholar or the digitisation of books.

Globally, the start-ups identified in our dataset have a more diversified model of revenue acquisition, in particular the Product/Service providers. Start-ups A B C D E F I J have implemented variable pricing strategies, meaning that they deal with different kinds of actors across different markets. Start-ups B D F G benefit from online seller communities revenues. However, only start-ups C D and J retrieve revenue from advertising when this segment is the most lucrative and the most represented in all the largest companies. However, since the difference in traffic with the largest companies is colossal, the diversification of revenues is crucial for the sustainability of the start-ups even if this diversification is by itself time consuming and may constitute an obstacle to further growth by dispersing the start-up resources and core activities.

Wikipedia is an awkward case as it is a not-for-profit association. However, Wikipedia was included in this study because of its ranking of ninth on the ComScore ranking and its uses of numerous items in Mahadevan's framework. Wikipedia is the first not-for-profit association ever to reach this audience level on the web and it may also constitute a totally new form of business model or it may prefigure the future of the free trend on the Internet (based on the involvement of the virtual communities at its strongest and on the open source software development). The company is funded by donations in cash and in kind.

2. The second question concerns the actual positioning of the survivors of the dot-com burst in the Digital Economy in 2007: What is the actual positioning of those companies in the framework developed by Mahadevan in 2000?

For the largest companies, the positioning is more complex: Yahoo! Sites, Google Sites and Ask Network are classified under Portal; eBay and Amazon Sites under Market Makers; Ask Network, Wikipedia and Amazon Sites under Product/Service providers. As a result, two companies are listed under two different market structures: Ask Network as a Portal and a Product/Service provider; Amazon as a Market Maker and a Product/Service provider.

Ask Network (formerly Ask Jeeves) was listed as a Portal by Mahadevan in 2000. In 2007, Ask Network is also a Product/Service provider for it sells different types of products (shoes, electronics, cosmetics, etc.) over the Internet through several websites. The combination of portal and product/service provider allows economies of scale and a diversification of the sources of revenues.

Amazon was also listed as a Portal by Mahadevan in 2000 but since this time, Amazon has created a marketplace where there is an interaction between buyers and sellers. This marketplace fits the two elements of a Market Maker as described by Mahadevan: Amazon has a 'high degree of domain knowledge' of the culture products and this marketplace 'provides value to both suppliers and customers through a system of implicit or explicit guarantee of security and trust in the business transaction'.

The competitive environment has changed since 2000. All of the larger companies in this study compete again each other to increase their traffic and their revenue. They also try to extend their scope. Yahoo! Sites compete against AOL, Google and Microsoft on the portal segment but also with Amazon and eBay in terms of e-commerce operations (Yahoo Annual Report 2006, p. 14). Amazon is not only a product/service provider, but has also shifted towards becoming a Marketplace. As a result, Amazon Sites is a competitor for both eBay and Yahoo! Sites.

3. The third question concerns the positioning in Mahadevan's framework of a number of nascent start-ups involved in the Digital Economy today.

According to Table 3.2, eight start-ups are defined as Product/Service providers (A B D E F G I J H), one as a Portal (C) and one as both a Market Maker and a Product/Service provider (D).

Nine out of the ten start-ups capitalise on virtual communities to do their business and none exploit the asymmetry of information. Their revenue streams are evenly spread between revenue from online seller communities and variable pricing strategies, with the exception of advertising which is underutilised as explained above. Seven start-ups have tried different business models since their creation. Half of the start-ups studied have an increased margin against brick and mortar operations and, as a result, disintermediation is the most cited logistical stream.

3.4.1 Specific features

Some start-ups are strictly pure Internet players – for example, start-up A caters only for the online community through the web. As a result, start-up A cannot benefit from a dramatic reduction in transaction costs nor can it have an increased margin over bricks and mortar operations.

Start-up B capitalises on virtual communities to further develop its open source software and as such B offers a part of their services free of charge.

According to the survey, D is classified as a Market Maker and a Product/Service Provider. They create added value for the manufacturers of electronic devices and also for the final user. D does not exploit information asymmetry; rather, it increases its margin over bricks and mortar operations by selling its software and solutions online (through downloading).

E offers a product combining online and offline support (a CD bought online is delivered to the final client who can then either use this product alone or in conjunction with a dedicated website).

The limitations of these exploratory results may be divided into two categories: the model utilised and the creation of the sample. This research was based on the sole model developed by Mahadevan. An in-depth analysis of the business models may be realised by future research, combining descriptive and evaluation frameworks to measure the performance of the business models of Internet-based companies. A broader dataset should then be collected in order to extend the scope of this study and to verify, using quantitative methods (through multivariate analysis for example), the preliminary and largely exploratory results exposed in this chapter. Besides, the Digital Economy is by definition an industry in perpetual change so any conclusions should be considered as tentative and not definitive.

3.5 Conclusion

This chapter investigated the business models of the six largest Internet firms by traffic in 2007 along with ten Internet-based new ventures located in Southern France. The business models' framework elaborated by Mahadevan (2000) was used to compare and analyse the business models and market structures of these companies. As a whole, Mahadevan's framework is still a valid and useful tool to describe the business models of the companies operating on the Internet. However, the study shows that the differentiation elaborated in 2000 between the market structures does not entirely reflect the reality of the Internet business in 2007. Some mergers have appeared, especially those between Portal, Market Makers and Product/Service Providers. Portals capitalise on all the value streams and, as such, deliver a larger value to the user in 2007 than they did in 2000. A new category may be included in the Mahadevan framework to fit the hybrid model developed by Google. In this study, Google was categorised as a portal, but this definition is not entirely accurate. Google acts as an efficient search engine and retrieves almost all of its revenues from advertising while providing a totally free service to the final user. New trends have also been noticed for the main players and the start-ups alike, such as the key role played by the advertising as a source of revenue for the main players while the start-ups have a hybrid business model, combining different sources of revenues. An actualisation of Mahadevan's framework would better mirror the Digital Economy in 2007.

The research findings of this study provide some new insights to the literature on business models. Academic papers have focussed on the description of the components of the business models, the specificities of the e-business models, the typologies and the key success factors. We chose to apply the existing research framework to two different sets of companies (new ventures and large companies that successfully went through the Internet burst) operating today on the Internet to determine if a change in modus operandi has occurred since 2001 in the 'experienced companies' and, if yes, was this change integrated by the new ventures? The answer is ambiguous. Changes have certainly occurred and the largest companies on the Internet today have increased their scope of action as stated in the chapter. Start-ups have integrated these changes by a willingness to implement risk mitigation strategies by choosing hybrid business models. Larger-scale research is needed to verify this hypothesis with an ad hoc methodology.

Notes

1. Christophe Garonne is a PhD candidate in Management at the Queensland University of Technology, Brisbane, Australia, and an Associate Researcher, Euromed Management, Marseilles, France; Dr. Félix Weygand is an Associate Professor at Ecole de Journalisme et de Communication, Université de la Méditerranée and Euromed Management, Marseilles, France.
2. http://www.journaldunet.com/ebusiness/internet/actualite/0709/070921-investissements-societes-web-2.0.shtml accessed on 21 September 2007.
3. Ibid.
4. http://www.chaussonfinance.com/indicateur/indicateur.htm. Accessed on 9 April 2010.

5. The final user has a low willingness to pay for a service that may be freely provided by other companies on the Internet. This is especially the case for the media industry. Ex: *The New York Times* ended online subscriptions in September 2007 and offers the entire content of the journal freely on the web. A similar move was taken by the *Financial Times* in 2007. The *NYT* expects to compensate the loss of US$10 million a year provided by the 227,000 paying subscribers by generating more traffic through its website to increase advertising revenue. www.nytimes.com/2007/09/18/business/media/18times.html.
6. On 3 August 2007, research carried out on Ebsco Host (limited to academic journals) with Web 2.0 as part of the title has produced 24 hits only ... with no top-tier journals on the list (except the MIT Sloan and the articles of Brynjolfsson and McAfee).
7. Clusters such as Secured Communication Solutions were decided and launched by the French Government in 2005 to increase the R&D and the cooperation between large and small companies. This cluster's ambition is to be active and influent internationally. www.pole-scs.org.
8. www.pacac.cci.fr accessed on 12 March 2007.
9. Companies such as Yahoo! Sites are composed of different companies. The ranking elaborated here takes into account all those parent companies.
10. *Information Economy Report 200: The Development Perspectives*, United Nations Conference on Trade and Development, United Nations, New York and Geneva, 2006.
11. For instance, ComScore Inc., one of the largest companies measuring activity on the Internet, does not differentiate between Home, Work and University Internet users anymore.
12. Aaron Kessler of Piper Jaffray, an investment bank, said Internet companies 'are buying users instead of revenue and profitability', 'Dot-com fever stirs a sense of déjà vu', *International Herald Tribune*, 16 October 2007.

References

Afuah A., and Tucci C. 2001. *Internet Business Models and Strategies*, New York: McGraw-Hill International Editions.
Aldrich, H.E., and Fiol, C.M. 1994. Fools rush in? The institutional context of industry creation, *Academy of Management Review*, 19(4), 645–70.
Alt, R., and Zimmermann, H. 2001. Introduction to special section – business models, *Electronic Markets*, 11(1), 3–9.
Amason, A.C., Shrader, R.C., and Tompson G.H. 2006. Newness and novelty: Relating top management team composition to new venture performance, *Journal of Business Venturing*, 21, 125–48.
Amazon Sites, Annual Report, FY 2006.
Amit, R., and Zott, C. 2001. Value creation in E-business, *Strategic Management Journal*, 22(6–7), 493–520.
Andries, P., Debackere K. and Verbeeck, D. 2005. News ventures on the search for viable business models: taking into account levels of uncertainty/ambiguity, *Wharton Entrepreneurial Programs Research Paper No. 335*.
Applegate, L.M. 2000. Thought leaders: an interview with Lynda Applegate – E-business lessons from Planet Earth, *Strategy and Business*, 18, 141–9.

Applegate, L.M., and Collura, M. 2001. Emerging networked business models: lessons from the field. Harvard Business School No. 9-801-172 *Harvard Business School, Boston*, In: A. Pateli and G. Giaglis. 2004. A research framework for analysing eBusiness models, *European Journal of Information Systems*, 13, 302–14.

Applegate, L.M. 2001. *E-Business Models: Making Sense of the Internet Business Landscape, Information Technology and the Future Entreprise* (eds Dickson and DeSantis), New York: Prentice-Hall.

Ask Network, Annual Report FY, 2006.

Bagchi, S. and Tulskie, B. 2000. E-business models: integrating learning from strategy, development experiences and empirical research, 20th Annual International Conference of the Strategic Management Society, 15–18 October, Vancouver. In MacInnes, I. 2005. Dynamic business model framework for emerging technologies, *Int. J. Services Technology and Management*, 6(1), 3–19.

Barua, A., Konana, W.A., and Yin, F. 2001. Driving E-business excellence, *Sloan Management Review*, Fall, 43(1), 36–44.

Bigliardi, B., Nosella, A., and Verbano, C. 2005. Business models in Italian biotechnology industry: a quantitative analysis, *Technovation*, 25, 1299–306.

Bouwman, H. and Van Ham, E. Business models and eMetrics, a state of the art. In Preissl, B., Bouwman, H., and Steinfield, C. (eds). 2003. *Elife After the Dot.com Burst*, Berlin: Springer Verlag.

Brousseau, E., and Curien, N. 2007. *Internet and Digital Economics*, Cambridge: Cambridge University Press.

Brynjolfsson, E. and McAfee, P. 2007. Beyond enterprise 2.0, *MIT Sloan Management Review*, 48(3), 50–5.

Champion, D. and Carr, N.G. 2000. Starting up in high gear. *Harvard Business Review*, July–August, 93–100.

ComScore Media Metrix Releases Top 50 rankings for August 2007, http://www.comscore.com/press/release.asp?press=1731 (permanent link).

Dang Nguyen, G., and Penard T. 2004. La gratuité à la croisée des nouveaux modèles d'affaires sur Internet, *Réseaux*, 124, 2.

Deloitte. 2009. Global trends in venture capital 2009 global report. http://www.fast50france.com/downloads/publications/GlobalTrendsVentureCapitalReport2009.pdf (accessed 9 April 2010).

Doyle, T., and Melanson, J. 2001. B2B web exchanges: easier hyped than done, *Journal of Business Strategy*, 22(3), 10.

Drucker, P.F. 1985. *Innovation and Entrepreneurship: Practice and Principles*, New York: Harper and Row.

Druilhe, C., and Garnsey, E. 2004. Do academic spin-outs differ and does it matter?, *Journal of Technology Transfer*, 29, 269–85.

Duh, R., Jamal, K., and Sunder, S. 2001. Control and assurance in e-commerce: privacy, integrity and security at eBay, *Sloan Management Review*, 43(1), 17.

Ebay Inc, Annual Report FY 2006.

Floyd, I., Jones, C., Rathi, D. and Twidale, M. 2007. Web mash-ups and patchwork prototyping: user-driven technological innovation with Web 2.0 and Open Source Software, in *Proceedings of the 40th Hawaii International Conference on System Sciences*.

Garonne C., and Weygand F. 2007. Modèles d'affaires composites des start-ups TIC. Problématique et typologie. In *Proceedings of 'Entrepreneuriat: nouveaux enjeux, nouveaux comportements'*, June, Paris.

Google, Annual Reports, FY 2006.

Gordijn, J., and Akkermans, J.M. 2001a. A conceptual value modelling approach for eBusiness development. In *Proceedings of First International Conference on Knowledge Capture (K-CAP 2001), Workshop WS2 Knowledge in eBusiness*, 27–34.

Gordijn, J. and Akkermans J.M. 2001b. Designing and evaluating eBusiness models, *IEEE Intelligent Systems*, 16(4), 11–17.

Kaplan, S. and Sawhney, M. 2000. E-hubs: the new B2B marketplaces, *Harvard Business Review*, 70(1), 71–9.

Klueber, R. 2000. Business model design and implementation for eServices, *Americas Conference on Information Systems*, Long Beach, CA.

Knight, F.H. 1921. *Risk, Uncertainty and Profit*, New York: Houghton Mifflin.

Lambert, S. 2006. A business model research schema. In *Proceedings of the 19th Bled Electronic Commerce Conference*, 5–7 June.

Lazonick, W. 2006. Evolution of the New Economy Business Model, Business history conference. http://www.thebhc.org/publications/BEHonline/2005/lazonick.pdf (accessed on 15 June 2007).

Linder, J.C. and Cantrell, S. 2000. *Changing Business Models: Surveying the Landscape*, Working Paper, Accenture Institute for Strategic Change.

Loch, C.H., Solt, M.E. and Bailey, E.M. 2006. Diagnosis and managing unforeseeable uncertainty to improve venture capital returns. Working paper. In Andries P., Debackere K., 2006. Adaptation in new technology-based ventures: Insights at the company level, *International Journal of Management Reviews*, 8(2), 91–112.

MacInnes, I. 2005. Dynamic business model framework for emerging technologies, *Int J. Services Technology and Management*, 6(1), 3–19.

Magretta, J. 2002. Why business models matter, *Harvard Business Review*, May, 86–92.

Mahadevan, B. 2000. Business models for Internet-based eCommerce: an anatomy. *California Management Review*, 42(4), 55–69.

Maitland, C.F., Van De Kar, E., Wehn De Montalvo, U. and Bouwman, H. 2005. Mobile information and entertainment services: business models and service networks. *Int. J. Management and Decision Making*, 6(1), 47–64.

Mangematin, V., Lemarié, S., Boissin, J.P., Catherine, D., Corroleur, F., Coronini, R. and Trommetter, M. 2003. Development of SMEs and heterogeneity of trajectories: the case of biotechnology in France, *Research Policy*, 32, 621–38.

McAfee, P. 2006. Enterprise 2.0: the dawn of emergent collaboration, *MIT Sloan Management Review*, 47(3), 21–8.

McGann, S. and Lyytinen, K. 2002. Capturing the dynamics of eBusiness models: the eBusiness analysis framework and the electronic trading infrastructure. In *Proceedings of 15th Bled Electronic Commerce Conference*, 17–19 June.

McKelvey M. 2001. The economic dynamics of software: three competing business models exemplified through Microsoft, Netscape and Linux, *Econ. Innov. New Tech.*, 10, 199–236.

Osterwalder, A. and Pigneur, Y. 2002. An eBusiness model ontology for modelling eBusiness. In *Proceedings of the 15th Bled Electronic Commerce Conference*, June, Bled, Slovenia, pp. 17–19.

Papakiriakopoulos, D., Poulymenakou, A. and Doukidis, G. 2001. Building eBusiness models: an analytical framework and development guidelines. In *Proceedings of 14th Bled Electronic Commerce Conference*, 25–6 June.

Pateli, A. and Giaglis, G. 2004. A research framework for analysing eBusiness models, *European Journal of Information Systems*, 13, 302–14.

Petrovic, O., Kittl, C., Teksten, R.D. 2001. Developing business models for eBusiness. In *Proceeding of International Conference on Electronic Commerce*, Vienna, 31 October–4 November.

Porter, M. 2001. Strategy and the Internet, *Harvard Business Review*, March.

Rappa, M. 2003. Managing the digital enterprise – business models on the web. Available online at: http://ecommerce.ncsu.edu.business_models.html (accessed on 3 February 2007).

Shane, S. and Stuart, T. 2002. Organizational endowments and the performance of university start-ups, *Management Science*, 48(1), 154–70.

Stoica, M. and Schindehutte, M. 1999. Understanding adaptation in small firms: links to culture and performance, *Journal of Developmental Entrepreneurship*, 4(1), 1–18.

Tapscott, D., Lowi, A. and Ticoll, D. 1998. *Blueprint to the Digital Economy: Creating Wealth in the Era of eBusiness*, New York: McGraw-Hill.

Timmers, P. 1998. Business models for electronic markets, *Electronic Markets*, 8(2), 3–8.

Vasilopoulou, K., Pouloudi, N., Patronidou, S. and Poulymenakou, A. 2002. Business models: a proposed framework. In *Proceedings of the e-Business and e-Work Annual Conference*, Prague, Czech Republic, 16–18 October.

Yahoo Inc, Annual Reports FY 2006.

Wathne, K., Biong, H. and Heide, J. 2001. Choice of supplier in embedded markets: relationship and marketing program effect, *Journal of Marketing*, 65(2), 36–51.

Weill P. and Vitale, M.R. 2001. *Place to Space: Migrating to eBusiness Models*, Boston, MA: Harvard Business School Press.

Willemstein, L., van der Valk, T. and Meeus, M.T.H. 2007. Dynamics in business models: an empirical analysis of medical biotechnology firms in the Netherlands, *Technovation*, 27, 221–32.

4
The Management of a Hybrid Broadcasting Model: Reconciling Public and Commercial Interests

Suzana Zilic Fiser[1]

4.1 Introduction

Television has long been expected to play an important role in social, cultural and political systems. In the past decade, it has been stressed in addition that electronic media have become an increasingly important component of the economic system. To be viewed as a success, television should fulfil the special mission that was given to it at the time that it was established. The economic success of television is connected with its mission to promote the public good, which is central to its functioning. Broadcasting is increasingly becoming one of the main agents of the free market. Accordingly, to function in the public interest of an entire society, television should be guided by a political and social and, particularly over the course of the past decade, an economic rationale (Van Cuilenburg and McQuail, 2003).

Television, as the main national media, follows certain values which contribute to the public welfare (Rozanova, 2007). In addition to public and social welfare, the broadcasting industry contributes to economic welfare. Economic values follow the criteria of the free market and there are no media that can deny the importance of economic development. Economic incentives are the main incentives in commercial media, but even strict public media should respect the rules of the free market. The very difficult question that needs to be addressed is: how can we combine economic interests and the promotion of the public interest.

Today television companies are faced by a unique and rapidly changing environment (Albarran, 2002). As a consequence, there are many who call for different systems of media regulation.[2] Along with many dynamic changes in the media field, the question arises of how to regulate the convergence. And, above all, how to regulate efficiently and at the same time offer high-quality media content? Accordingly, the organisational structure and the mission of television are going to change in the multichannel environment.

Television has been described as the first true 'mass' medium (McQuail, 2001). Consequently, it was granted a specific position in a situation which differed from print. There was an expectation to have its position preserved and it was 'granted' the mission of public good. The special position of the medium was transferred into the special position of the institution – public service broadcaster (PSB).

In new circumstances, there have been some modifications to the defining characteristics of a public service broadcaster, which had formerly been very defined along very strict non-commercial lines (Freeman, 2008). There is currently no clear public service model which can be regarded as a model for very single European PSB (Basic Hrvatin 2002). A prime example of this is Channel 4 in the UK which embodies the hybrid model of broadcasting, combining the characteristics of public service broadcasting with the characteristics of commercial broadcasting. It is a single broadcaster which acts simultaneously both a public and a commercial broadcaster. It has to fulfil special remits as a public service broadcaster – to satisfy the public good. However, it has to be widely accepted and confirm its success in the market every day to compete for revenue with commercial broadcasters.

In the terrestrial broadcasting market in the UK, there are two broadcasting models, the BBC, a public service broadcaster, and commercial broadcasters (for example, ITV and Channel 5). The BBC functions as a typical public broadcaster – and is sometimes regarded as a model of its kind in Europe. The BBC has a secure source of financing, the licence fee, which permits it a certain monopoly in the market. There are also, in the UK media market, many commercial terrestrial channels which are established as commercial broadcasters. The commercial competitors have clear supply–demand logic and they have fewer obligations to underprivileged niche markets, which Channel 4 is also taking care of when following strong public service remit.

In the early 1980s, Channel 4 was launched as a public commercial broadcaster in order to solve problems encountered by pure public or commercial broadcasters. Channel 4 offered alternative programmes to ITV and the BBC. Therefore, Channel 4 was established as a hybrid model which has tight public service remits, but it has to fulfil them in a way that would be accepted in the market.

Many broadcasters in Europe are in receipt of mixed funding streams, but they are in effect treated as PSBs. They can follow the supply and demand logic of the market only because at least a proportion of their financing is constant (consisting of state grants or licence fees). In addition, the commercial broadcasters have a clear commercial rationale, and they do not need to follow a mainly public interest, as is the case with Channel 4. Channel 4 is a public corporation that has no secure financing and it has no shareholders anticipating dividends. Any profits that do accrue are ploughed back into program and infrastructure development.

Obviously, Channel 4 is a unique model that has survived a certain period of media development, but why and how has it survived? How does it perform in today's multichannel era? Is this hybrid model a future model for European broadcasting? Can it simultaneously fulfil the aims of the commercial broadcasters (profit) and public broadcasters (the public good) and what are the possible approaches required to fulfil both aims? The hybrid model of broadcasting is a unique model of broadcasting in Europe which enables us to answer the question: are two different philosophies compatible in one broadcasting institution? Two broadcasting models, public and commercial, are combined into one, hybrid, model which has the characteristics of both, usually very diverse models. In fact, the thesis that there is a fundamental incompatibility between social responsibility in broadcasting and profit seeking needs to be examined.

4.2 Channel 4 – the hybrid model of broadcasting

4.2.1 Channel 4: general features

In 2001, the *Times* described Channel 4 as 'a British experiment in broadcasting, envied and admired throughout the world'.[3] It works because, as a corporation with no shareholders, it can take greater creative risks with its programmes which attract viewers sought after by advertisers. They recycle the profits directly back into programmes and new services. It is seen as a major cultural asset for a culturally diverse Britain, commercially financed without public funding. As a television company Channel 4 has several unique features.

The research focused on the activities of a broadcaster that acts as a hybrid model of broadcasting. Special circumstances for establishing the fourth channel, its programme, and financial strategy have also been analyzed. The success of Channel 4 is related to unique economic, political and cultural circumstances in the UK. Channel 4 was established as a 'fourth channel' and (more precisely) as a third national Broadcasting Corporation in the UK. This was a political decision with the intention of offering a new public broadcaster that would compete with ITV and the BBC. In addition, economic circumstances and the size of the market enabled the survival of new agents in the media market. The government supported the abolition of the 'funding formula' but insisted that the additional funds were to be invested in new technologies.

The Conservative government in the UK stressed the need for a greater proportion of British production in broadcasting (Blanchard and Morley 1982). Through a policy of commissioning programmes from a large number of independent producers, Channel 4 would support British companies. Additionally, media regulators in the UK pressed for particular genres of programmes to be offered by Channel 4 (Lambert 1982; Harvey, 2001). These were educational and innovative programmes for minorities, as stated in Channel 4's licence (Isaacs, 1989). The high level of self-regulation, media plurality and a long history of democracy in British society have contributed to the unique media environment of Channel 4 and light-touch regulation of broadcasters.

Channel 4 is organised as a publisher unlike other 'traditional' broadcasters. The 'publisher' structure is very rational and efficient and supports independent production in the British environment. Channel 4 was forced to adopt a unique model because its role was to offer something different to society, establishing it as a complement to both the BBC and ITV.

4.2.2 Performance measures of Channel 4

The criteria of traditional and economic measures were used as performance measures for Channel 4 because it is simultaneously a commercial and a public broadcaster (Zilic Fiser, 2007). Such an approach enables the discussion of the overall success of Channel 4 in the UK and in the European market. The findings will allow us to establish whether or not the public service remit and the economic interest can be successfully fulfilled at the same time. Our research concentrates on Channel 4 from its establishment onward; however, particular attention will be given to the data for the very dynamic period between 1997 and 2002. There are several reasons for choosing this period:

- In 1998 the funding formula was abolished and Channel 4 began to sell its own advertising time (therefore we can compare the 'success' of activities before and after the funding formula).
- In 1997 the terrestrial channel – Channel 5 – was launched (the first commercial broadcaster after 1982, after the launch of Channel 4).
- Channel 4 began some new services during this period (Film Four, E4).
- There was a first variation of Channel 4's licence in 1997.
- In 1998 ITC revised Channel 4's licence with additional provisions.
- In 1997 a new chief executive was appointed.

The period 1997–2002 was an extremely dynamic period for Channel 4 because it began to compete in the market on its own, the new commercial channel was launched and the multichannel era started. The year 2001 witnessed a serious setback for the advertising market and the beginning of a scramble for revenues. Furthermore, all of the broadcasters were confronted with new technologies – all of these factors speak in favour of the changing role of public service broadcasting. The selected period will be analyzed with traditional and economic performance measures.

4.2.2.1 Channel 4 according to traditional programme measures

Public service broadcasting realised its public role through responsible and quality programming that could be evaluated through the use of traditional programme measures. These programme measures are based on the requirements of the regulator. In the case of Channel 4, these are the measures that were controlled by the Independent Television Commission (today, it is OFCOM that regulates the media in the UK). The majority of these requirements were about the diversity of programme genres, arts and current affairs programmes, and news, factual, educational and multicultural programmes.

The report commissioned by the ITC (2002) indicates that there has been a narrowing in diversity across all UK terrestrial channels taken as a whole, and that some public service broadcasting programme genres were becoming rarer in peak viewing hours. As a result of the removal of programmes with a minority appeal from the prime time schedules, there has been a contraction in the range of programmes available to viewers.

Arts and current affairs programmes were the main casualties, with reductions of around 40 and 50 per cent, respectively. By contrast, the levels of factual material, including educational programmes, have been maintained, while there has been an increase in the amount of news coverage on Channel 4 (as well as the other two commercial channels). Peak-time religious programming has reappeared on Channel 4.

As expected, entertainment has increased as a percentage of peak time programming for all broadcasters. Drama has decreased by similar amounts across all broadcasters – with the exception of soaps, which increased by 2 per cent on Channel 4. An interesting feature of the main UK public service broadcasting channels is a very high proportion of original material – both produced from in-house resources and commissioned from independent producers – and particularly the amounts delivered in peak viewing hours. This is illustrated by the low levels of acquired programmes within the drama genre (including feature films and television movies) where the proportions have fallen on all channels over the past few years. On Channel 4 the hours fell from 14 per cent in 1997 to 10 per cent in 2001.

Channel 4 continued to deliver significant diversity beyond its simple genre mix (ITC, 2002). The strength and breadth of its factual output was marked, including investigative current affairs, special reports on race, drugs, the war against terrorism, and authored pieces both topical and historical.

With regard to news programmes, Channel 4 has continued its 55-minute format at 7 p.m. on weekdays, with further half-hour editions on Saturdays and Sundays. Channel 4 offers its viewers a contrasting approach, being more 'in depth', and in particular 'extending our international coverage to events and stories under covered by other channels' (ITC, 2001). Channel 4, as required explicitly by its remit, did perform more strongly in relation to international coverage.

In the genre of documentaries (where Channel 4 has a special remit) it is evident that the channel fulfilled its commitments to run in peak time and cover a range of demanding and social documentaries on both British and international subjects. Channel 4 increasingly sought to establish its reputation and identification with the audience through specialisation in particular sports, including racing and cricket.

In comparison with other broadcasters, Channel 4 had different genres in prime time. In the year 1997 it scheduled drama in prime time (1997: 30 per cent of drama in prime time, 2001: 22 per cent of drama in prime time) (ITC, 2001). There is evidence of a greater percentage of devotion to sport in prime time, while factual, educational and regional programmes decreased. Accordingly, it could be argued that in prime time Channel 4 offers a great diversity of programmes by genres (10 different genres). When it was introduced, the expectation was that Channel 4 would be a minority channel. It was intended that it would offer programmes that were not shown on any of the other three channels, and was sometimes even more 'cultural' and 'educational'. There are evident changes in the kinds of programmes offered by the channel in various periods. In the past few years it has begun to attract larger audiences and has become more of an 'entertainment' and 'sports' orientated channel.

There were a number of distinct changes in Channel 4's programme strategy. As the channel began to compete in the market it became more of a majority channel, particularly in prime time. The greatest changes can be recognised in its programming output. There was no change in the total number of broadcast hours; this stood at 167 hours in both 1997 and 2001. However, there has been an increase in the amount of factual programming. As expected, there has evidently been a smaller weekly output of documentaries (10 hours 31 minutes in 1997 and 6 hours 9 minutes in 2001). There has been a substantial increase in the hours of educational broadcasting (more than seven hours weekly in comparison to 1997), but this has been at the expense of children's programmes (which have fallen by around seven hours). There has been a smaller output of feature films and accordingly an almost one-third increase in entertainment programmes. Actually, one-quarter of the station's weekly output has been entertainment (39 hours 54 minutes). Furthermore, there have been more hours of sports broadcasting than in the 1990s (ITC, 2001; C4 Co, 2001).

Over the past few years most of the complaints about Channel 4 programmes referred to taste and decency, sexual portrayals, religious offences and language. In respect of meeting its core targets for 2002 the figures show that the average weekly requirements for news and current affairs, schools and multicultural programming were exceeded, while the broadcasting of an average of 11 hours for adult education was well above the stipulated minimum of seven hours (ITC, 2002). The comparatively low religious requirement of one hour per week was exceeded, but more than half of the transmissions were repeats. There were increases in sport and entertainment with decreases in feature films and arts. Overall, repeats were held at the level of 38 per cent (below the stipulated maximum of 40 per cent) and 18 per cent in peak time (against a maximum of 20 per cent). The programmes especially commissioned for Channel 4 comprised 66 per cent of the schedule (against a stipulated minimum of 60 per cent); in peak time they comprised 81 per cent (against a target of 70 per cent). Two-thirds of commissioned programmes went to independent producers (this could have been as low as 25 per cent). The expenditure on programmes commissioned from outside the London region rose to 29 per cent. Finally, the expenditure on training rose to 0.7 per cent of total revenue (against a target of 0.5 per cent).

According to the collected data it can be concluded that Channel 4 was able to fulfil its special remit and act as a flexible commercial channel. It followed the activities that were needed to remain economically competitive and invested heavily in technological advances. The development of new products and services as well as improvements in technologies and services played crucial roles in its success. Analysing in accordance with traditional measures, we could conjecture that Channel 4 has fulfilled its public remit even following the abolition of its funding formula. However, it is evident that the main channel has attracted a larger audience and not only minorities. It has tried to attract minorities through the provision of digital channels and other services. In addition, Channel 4 opened its schedule to new cultural practices, such as reality shows. The argument for the social responsibility of Channel 4 remained in the analysis of traditional measurements of its required public remit. Its social responsibility, through meeting suggested criteria, can be confirmed in the selected period. Additionally, we have tried to explain its new approaches to meeting targets. The shift from minority to majority channel and openness to new cultural practices were definitely the main steps. The fulfilment of the main social targets was accomplished more than was the case with other broadcasters in the UK market, and the first part of the thesis can be easily accepted. However, further economic criteria will show whether the channel was successful in the market as well.

4.2.2.2 Channel 4 according to market share measures

In the late 1980s the audience share did not seem to be the primary issue for those in charge of Channel 4. However, it should have been the most important issue for the channel in the late 1990s when the funding formula was abolished. The audience share of Channel 4 can be seen from two different perspectives. On the one hand, it had decreased during this period. On the other hand, it had stabilised in comparison with the 'bigger channels', such as BBC 1 and ITV.

Furthermore, what seems to be dangerous for Channel 4 is the increase of 'smaller channels' such as Channel 5. It can be stated that a stabilised audience is a great advantage for a channel but the multichannel dynamic market seems likely to undermine the stabilised share in the long run. Accordingly, audience and advertising shares are the primary concerns of a commercial public service broadcaster such as Channel 4 (Thompson, 2003).

It is evident from the data that Channel 4 Corporation plans to fulfil certain audience and programme gaps in the broadcasting environment and that thereafter it is aiming to secure a 'quality demography'. Viewing, which is one of the main indicators of market success, is stable in the most desirable category (ABC1). The viewing data showed that the overall viewing level for the main Channel 4 programme has experiences a slight decline. Accordingly, the main broadcasters, the BBC and ITV, have lost a far higher number of viewers than Channel 4. Channel 4 has increased viewing in the whole family of channels (including E4 and FF). In today's multichannel era, it is necessary to take into account the success of the corporation together with all digital channels. Accordingly, the results are very optimistic for Channel 4.

Today, Channel 4 is a general entertainment channel that specialises in programmes outside the peak time for an under-50s audience. It has the youngest audience of any of the UK's terrestrial channels and is the most upmarket in the commercial sector. The targeted audience are men aged 16–34 and upmarket adults. Since the early 1990s, Channel 4 has maintained its viewing share at over 10 per cent. In 1999, Channel 4 secured 10.3 per cent of all viewing and 19.0 per cent of advertising revenue. In 2000 it achieved a 10.5 per cent share of all viewing (ITC, 2001). It is important to stress that in multichannel homes viewing of Channel 4 had evidently increased (in comparison to the BBC and ITV) and the advertising share for Channel 4 had remained the same in all years, whereas in the case of ITV it had been decreasing throughout this period.

The answer to the question of its commercial success can be seen in its market share data, which explains Channel 4's market success. The measures of market share show that Channel 4 has increased its viewing in the whole family of channels and, moreover, that the audience share of Channel 4 stabilised in comparison with that of the 'bigger channels' (BBC1 and ITV). The part of the argument for its economic success can be confirmed through suggested criteria. Its economic success is to be more deeply explained by the other criteria (financial and managerial).

4.2.2.3 Channel 4 according to financial measures

From the figures extracted for the year 2001 (C4 Co, 2001), group turnover increased by 2 per cent to 731 million GBP (2000: 716 million). Channel 4's advertising and sponsorship revenue amounted to 85 per cent of group turnover in 2001 (2000: 91 per cent). The remaining 15 per cent (2000: 9 per cent) represented the increased contribution being made by 4 Ventures. With over 85 per cent of revenue derived from television advertising and sponsorship, the group remains highly sensitive to the economic health of the advertising sales market.

According to the figures, there is evidence of a reduction in profit for the year 2001. This is the result of a substantial investment in 4 Ventures and the losses incurred as a result of that investment. In 1997, it achieved a profit of 18.5 million GBP. Over the following period it recorded the following figures: 1998: 17.7 million GBP; in 1999 32.9 million GBP; in 2000 21.5 million GBP; finally, in 2001 it incurred a loss of 20.6 million GBP. However, Channel 4's share of terrestrial advertising has increased slightly to 23.5 per cent (2000: 22.0 per cent, 1999: 21.6 per cent, 1998: 21.7 per cent, and 1997: 21.5 per cent).

There are a number of important details that should be highlighted. The advertising share has been increasing, as expected, following the abolition of its funding formula in 1998. Channel 4's management probably anticipated greater revenues from advertising, but they did not expect the change in the global advertising market. From the perspective of remits for public service broadcasters, it is evident that they were able to fulfil the remits although they only received financing from the market. It should be emphasised that they did not use any other source of public funding such as state grants, subscriptions or licence fees. This shows that they were able to achieve sufficient audience figures to attract advertisers.

Undoubtedly, Channel 4 will present itself as an innovative, multichannel corporation which uses different platforms employing new technologies to augment its traditional services. It seems that they have been moving reasonably quickly towards technological development. However, these new technologies have caused a decline in profits. The numbers which show losses in the constituent parts of the 4 Ventures business are evident: 35.4 million GBP in 2000 and 65.0 million GBP in 2001.

It seemed that new platforms, with 4 Ventures, were a necessary driver for the development of Channel 4; however, they caused some financial damage to the channel. Consequently this raises a question: should new platforms be part of public service broadcasting? Building as many platforms as possible is probably the only way to attract the largest possible audience in the market.

The financial measures explained the economic success of Channel 4. There are two aspects of the financial results. The advertising share increased slightly in comparison to other channels in the UK market. The main reason for its successful share remains in the quality of its audience, which does not yield high ratings, but does secure a respectable market share. The channel's audience is demanding public which incorporates a number of focus groups for the main advertisers. The other aspect of the financial results explains the decline in profit as a result of the large investments the channel made in new digital platforms. We can expect that the positive result of new investments will be seen in the long run. It can be claimed that, judged according to their financial measures, Channel 4 has achieved significant success.

4.2.2.4 Channel 4 according to managerial measures

Today Channel 4 is still promoted as a creative, cultural and innovative channel, but in the 1990s it was also being promoted as a minority channel that stood out from the crowd. In recent times its commitments to innovations on the technological side have changed. Accordingly, Channel 4 places itself among the group of UK media companies that take advantage of new media platforms. They are building new cross-platform brands to better serve the demands of the audience. Furthermore, the commitment to innovation is a justification for exploring the potential of new platforms in a more effective and imaginative way than can be found among its competitors (for example, *Big Brother*).

Therefore, those aspects of the channel that had been promoted as innovative and creative during its earliest years (the development of genres such as minority programming, the arts, documentaries and marginal topics) can be contrasted with the present-day exploration of technological developments and the use of synergy with traditional and new media. Channel 4 is aiming to achieve the largest possible audience. At the launch of the channel in 1982, ratings were not an important consideration, but now and for the foreseeable future, Channel 4 is being forced to take them into account.

From a relatively small organisation, by the 1990s Channel 4 had grown into a large corporation. It is evident that it does not have a clear public service organisational structure but has more in common with commercial broadcasters such as Channel 5 and ITV. From its early years 'outside resources' (independent producers) played an important role for Channel 4. As it became established as a publisher, the organisation has been rational and effective in acquiring and appraising what is of particular value for the programme. Thus, the additional costs of research and creative talents have been evaluated according to the effect they have on the programme and their final results. Independent producers are in a better position to manage the creative talents and offer their projects to the broadcaster (publisher). Therefore, being a publisher rather than a broadcaster seems to have a greater effect on a successful schedule. The independent production companies assumed responsibility for the quality of the programmes and consequently have to manage their own budgets. The publishing company commissions those projects (final products) that it considers to be suitable for its programme schedule. The publishing company, Channel 4, must have a clear idea about what kinds of programme it wants to have in the schedule and how much it is prepared to pay. It calculates and decides on the expected ratings and the value of the programme.

In comparison with traditional broadcasting, the publisher-broadcaster has no burden of expense for the creative industry (talents) until the programme is broadcast and the purchase of technical and production equipment is excluded from the publisher's budget. The publisher-broadcaster is concerned with only two factors: innovative content and a managed schedule. This includes determining which programme is to be broadcast at what time, which is directly related to the preferences of the targeted audience. Accordingly, the establishment of a general programme strategy is a high priority for the channel. All of the departments have to follow this strategy and be financially responsible for their budget. They have their own responsibilities but are still accountable to the board. Every department has its own financial budget, personnel and programme obligations. A hierarchic, bureaucratic institutional structure would not be effective in the creative broadcasting environment. A modern flat structure is effective for the public-commercial publisher Channel 4, which helps to support British independent production and works efficiently in the market.

The managerial measures explain the importance of a vertically integrated model of organisation and flexibility with respect to market and public demands. Furthermore, the relationship between the producer and publisher is discussed as a new way of developing an efficient organisational structure. The modern flat structure is the precondition for being able to react quickly to complex social and economic demands. The establishment of the publisher, rather than a producer, brought many advantages seen in the better management of talent and content resources. In terms of these management approaches, Channel 4 is unique in the UK and even in the European market.

4.3 Conclusion

The case study of Channel 4 discussed in this chapter offers an outline of a broadcasting organisation which simultaneously fulfils both the economic and the public interest. Firstly, we introduced the performance measures needed for an examination of the overall success of broadcasters (McQuail, 1992). The criteria represent the idea of combination of economic and public interest in the measures for success. The traditional programme criteria explain the fulfilment of the public remit when market share measures, financial measures and managerial measures explain the fulfilment of economic success. The presented performance measures are applied to the broadcasters which act in the European market. The use of a unique hybrid model of broadcasting in Europe was a relevant research method and enables us to address our main question: is it possible to combine two different philosophies in one broadcasting institution? According to our analysis, it can be asserted that both the public and the economic interest can be fulfilled in special circumstances. Furthermore, modern managerial approaches are needed to fulfil the goals of a public-commercial institution.

According to the proposed criteria in the case study (economic and traditional programme measures) it can be established that Channel 4 is able to realise its special role. However, it could be argued that Channel 4 is fulfilling a public service role by complementing the programme and services provided by the other terrestrial channels. Additionally, it is evident that there were some changes in programme and management strategies following the abolition of the funding formula. Channel 4 began to attract a broader range of viewers with its programmes while still catering to minorities with new digital services. Accordingly, Channel 4 is the broadcaster which has started to break the gender stereotypes through social roles with the prime time shows (Lauzen, Dozier, Horan, 2008).

Channel 4 is financed through advertising revenues, but the broadcaster was set up on a 'not-for profit' basis. It was expected to pursue a public service remit that involved complementing the services provided by the other three channels. The special public role of Channel 4 can be seen in the support of independent production across the UK. The advantages of the suggested approach of being a publisher, rather than a typical broadcaster, can be seen in the fact that the organisation is managed more efficiently, the creative talents give better results, and it also supports the development of national independent production. Obviously, Channel 4 was able to satisfy the public interest while the commercial incentive was also very clear in the management of the corporation. In addition, satisfying the needs of a demanding public fulfils the special public interest and the selected groups also play an important role in the advertising industry. Therefore, there are not only high ratings that give good results, but the particular demography of its audience is very important both for the public remit and for furthering commercial interests (Zilic Fiser, 2007). This research on a selected period of the development of Channel 4 development shows considerable success in fulfilling both their public and their commercial missions.

The main aims of the media environment, which are to realise the public good and to be successful in the market, are seen clearly in the Channel 4 broadcasting model. Since it has special public service remits and acts in the market, it can be examined as a new model of a PSB in Europe.

While it appears at first sight that commercial networks and PSBs offer two diametrically opposed models, similar principles in terms of their functioning narrow the gap between them. There are many current changes in the role and position of television as an institution in society. Commercialisation is the most common trend in all PSBs in Europe (Costera Meijer, 2005; Steemers, 1999). Public and commercial broadcasters are each striving to achieve the same aims. It is no longer realistic to treat PSB as a narrowly elitist cultural institution. An overview of the media environment in different countries shows that the main source of media funding will be commercial funding and direct payment for programmes. It is also predicted that the content will be dispersed across a number of different media platforms. PSB should not become a 'ghetto' for content that is commercially unattractive. It must endeavour to attract as many viewers and listeners as possible. The audience must be a warrant that the special position of a PSB will be protected in future (Tracey 1998, Spencer, Straubhaar, 2006).

Accordingly, the idea of PSB is going to change as there is an increased blurring of the boundaries between public service broadcasting and commercial broadcasting. Some authors (for instance, Gunn, 2008) suggest that PSBs should be characterised by a higher level of public participation. The changes in the media environment will significantly change the status of PSB and commercial broadcasters. One possible solution can be seen in the creation of a hybrid model of PSB. Undoubtedly, the model of Channel 4 cannot be copied completely by other societies; however, some lessons can be learned from the existing hybrid model. The example of Channel 4 proves that a media institution can succeed in simultaneously satisfying the cultural and economic dimensions of a society.

Notes

1. Suzana Zilic Fiser is an Assistant Professor at the Faculty of Electrical Engineering and Computer Science, Institute of Media Communications, University of Maribor, Slovenia.
2. The biggest issue which provoked a new Communication Bill in the United Kingdom was the awareness that technology, content and media economy should not be regulated separately.
3. *The Times*, February 2001.

References

Albarran, A. 2002. *Management of Electronic Media*, 2nd edn, Belmont, CA: Wadsworth Thomson Learning.

Basic Hrvatin, S. 2002. *Drzavni ali javni servis: perspektive javne radiotelevizije v Sloveniji*, Ljubljana: Mediawatch, Mirovni institut.

Blanchard, S., and Morley, D. 1982. *What's This Channel Four?*, London: Comedia.

Channel 4 Television Company (C4 Co), 1983, 1984, 1985, 1986, 1987, 1988, 1989, 1990, 1991, 1992, 1993, 1994, 1995, 1996, 1997, 1998, 1999, 2000, 2001, 2002. *Report and Financial Statements*, London: Channel 4.

Costera Meijer, I. 2005. Impact or content? Ratings vs quality in public broadcasting, *European Journal of Communication*, 20(1), 27–53.

Dyson, K. and Humpreys, P. 1988 *The Context of New Media Politics in Western Europe: Broadcasting and New Media Policies in Western Europe*, London: Routledge.

Freeman, M. 2008. *The Changing Media Landscape: an Industry Perspective: Challenges for Media Content Producers*, Jönköping: Media Management and Transformation Centre.
Goodwin, P. 1998. *Television under the Tories: Broadcasting Policy 1979–1997*, London: British Film Institute.
Gunn, S.E. 2008. Redefining public service broadcasting, *International Journal of Research into New Media Technologies*, 14(1), 105–20.
Harvey, S. 2001. *Channel 4 Television: From Annan to Grade*, Oxford: Clarendon Press.
Isaacs, J. 1989. *Storm over Four: A Personal Account*, London: Weidenfeld and Nicolson.
Independent Television Commission (ITC). 1983, 1984, 1985, 1986, 1987, 1988, 1989, 1990, 1991, 1992, 1993, 1994, 1995, 1996, 1997, 1998, 1999, 2000, 2001. *Annual Report and Accounts*, London: ITC.
Lambert, S. 1982. *Channel Four: Television with a Difference*, London: BFI Publishing.
Lauzen, M., Dozier, D., and Horan, N. 2008. Constructing gender stereotypes through social roles in prime-time television, *Journal of Broadcasting and Electronic Media*, 52(2), 200–14.
McKinsey & Company. 1999. *Public Service Broadcasters around the World: A McKinsey Report for the BBC*, London: McKinsey & Company.
McQuail, D. 1992. *Media Performance*, London: Sage Publications.
McQuail, D. 2001. *Mass Communication Theory*, London: Sage Publications.
Negrine, R. 1992. *Television, Audience and Cultural Studies*, London: Routledge and Kegan Paul.
Ostergard, B.S. 1997. *The Media in Western Europe*, London: Sage.
Picard, R. 1998. *Evolving Media Markets: Effects of Economic and Policy Change*, Turku: Turku School of Economics.
Rozanova, J. 2007. Public television in the context of established and emerging democracies: Quo Vadis?, *International Communication Gazette*, 69(2), 129–47.
Spencer, D.R. and Straubhaar, J.D. 2006. Broadcast research in the Americas: revisiting the past and looking to the future, *Journal of Broadcasting & Electronic Media*, 50(3), 368–82.
Steemers, J. 1999. Between culture and commerce: the problem of redefining public service broadcasting for the digital age, *The International Journal of Research into New Media Technologies*, 5, 44–66.
Thompson, M. 2003. *Interviews with the General Director of Channel 4 Corporation (November, December 2003)*, Horse Ferry Road, London.
Tracey, M. 1998. *The Decline and Fall of Public Service Broadcasting*, Oxford: Oxford University Press.
Van Cuilenburg, J. and McQuail, D. 2003. Media policy paradigm shifts: towards a new communications policy paradigm, *European Journal of Communication*. 18(2), 181–207.
Zenith Media. 2001. *UK Television Forecasts to 2006*, London: Zenith Media.
Zilic Fiser, S. 2007. *Upravljanje televizije*, Ljubljana: FDV.

5
The Dynamics of Media Business Models: Innovation, Versioning and Blended Media

Patrick-Yves Badillo and Dominique Bourgeois[1]

5.1 Business models in the press: some elements

5.1.1 Main characteristics

'A business model involves the conception of how the business operates, its underlying foundations, and the exchange activities and financial flows upon which it can be successful' (Picard, 2002, p. 26).[2] Picard shows that historically the business model of US newspapers changed radically: during their first 100 to 150 years of publication, US newspapers served a relatively small audience, with very high prices and little advertising; in the last half of the nineteenth century US newspapers began to serve a larger audience, prices became very low and the level of advertising increased. Readership and advertising support continued to grow during the twentieth century until the appearance of television. Since the 1960s readership has declined steadily and Picard considers that newspaper readership will probably decline 'somewhere in the range of one-quarter to one-third of the population' (Picard, 2002, p. 31). It has to be noted that advertising has remained at a high level for the US newspapers: it provided about 80 per cent of the revenue of newspapers in the United States in the year 2000.

The business model of the French traditional press has certain distinct historical characteristics, including state subsidies. After the Second World War the principal choice was in favour of a general information and political press which was conceived as 'a quasi-public service conceded to private entrepreneurs' (*'un quasi-service public concédé à des entrepreneurs privés'*, Leprette and Pigeat, 2002, p. 93). This conception explains the importance and the complexity of the subsidy system which had the objective of guaranteeing diversity and pluralism. Thus profitability has not been a real goal for many

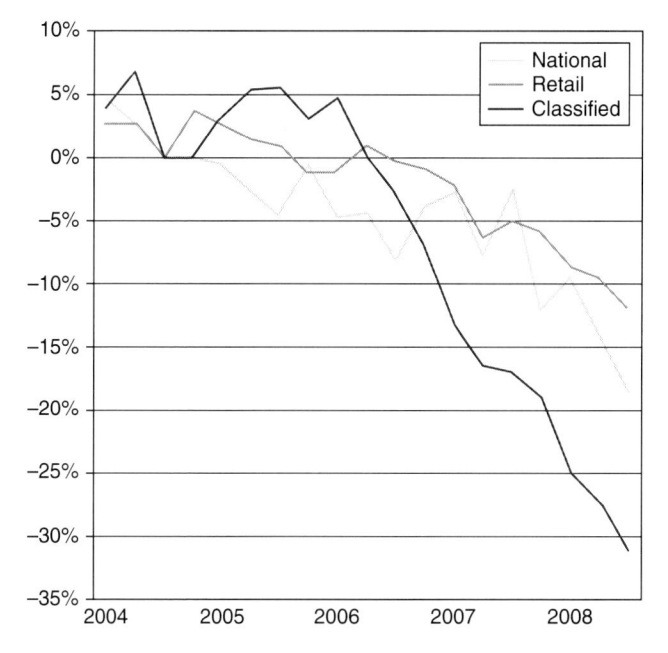

Figure 5.1 Newspaper advertising revenue in the United States, 2004–2008
Source: Newspaper Association of America.

years, at least in the general information press. Moreover, the level of advertising is quite low compared with the United States: if we consider only the general information press, in 2005–2006 advertising represented 87.7 per cent of the income in the United States and only 41.6 per cent in France (Albert, 2008, p. 43). Prices of French newspapers are relatively high compared with prices in the United States and distribution costs are also high (for more details see Leprette and Pigeat, 2002; Albert, 2008).

5.1.2 The emergence of the low-cost model

Although there are different business models for the traditional press, in many countries old media have been in decline for a long time although they have shown strong resistance. Since the beginning of the twenty-first century we observe the irruption of new media (like the Internet and the free press). Some interpretations suggest that these new media will replace old media, thanks to their new business models. These new business models are characterised in particular by advertising (that is to say, the second part of the two-sided model, advertising, is increasingly important) and the belief that everything could be free. Moreover, 'everybody is a journalist'[3] and Internet users can now write for a newspaper, so that the costs are declining and an online newspaper can be very cheap to produce. The 'low-cost' model of the press has emerged, linked to the rise of 'freeconomics'.

One of the promoters of this strategy in France is Alain Weill (the founder and chairman of NextRadioTV, which owns RMC (radio), BFM (radio), BFMTV, the first information TV channel in France, and Groupe Tests, a French press group that specialises in the exploitation of new technology). 'Alain Weill asserts a "low cost" model in the media, by externalising every administrative activity and never spending more than necessary. *"I do not know if we are 'low cost' or our competitors are 'high cost"*, he notices. It remains to see whether the recipes which made his success in the radio will be effective for television' (*Les Echos*, no. 19546, 23rd November 2005, p. 9; our translation).

Different studies seem to have confirmed both the trend towards the substitution of old media by new media and the importance of advertising in new media business models.

Concerning substitution, for example, Gentzkow (2007) studied competition between print and online newspapers thanks to a model applied to the Washington DC area, on the basis of a survey conducted between March 2000 and February 2003. He founds that 'print and online papers are clearly substitutes. (…) The magnitude of the crowding out of print readership is non-negligible. It is also small, however, relative to some earlier predictions. (…) Second, the welfare benefits of the online newspaper appear to outweigh its costs.' Other studies indicate that consumers are very sensitive to prices (see Findahl, 2008), which is obviously an argument in favour of the free press. The main empirical argument in favour of substitution is constituted by recent readership statistics: 'While the percentage of Americans who read online news went from 18% to 25% between 2006 and 2008, the percentage who read newspapers daily has decreased from 40% to 34% during that same time period' (Pew Research Center, 2008).

Concerning the importance of advertising in media business models, in a study on the United States, Mensing (2007) showed that 'despite aggressive competition for advertising revenue, newspapers as a whole have not altered their online strategies significantly from 1996 to 2005. (…) The primary revenue strategy for nearly all online newspapers is clear: advertising has proven to be the most successful source of revenue.' And, of course, the income of every online or offline free newspaper is equal to advertising. It should also be noted that the growth of advertising investments on the Internet is superior to the growth of all advertising investments at the global level,[4] which is a general indicator in favour of online media.

Nevertheless, there are also arguments which counterbalance the above approach. First, it is not certain that new media will replace old media. For example, Cao and Li (2006) found that the growth of Internet daily newspaper readership had a limited effect on the circulation of US daily print newspapers in the period 1995–2000. The declining trend in the print newspaper circulation was far from remarkable; consumers did not abandon print newspapers. According to them, 'the growth of new media may not be at the expense of the older media' (Cao and Li, 2006). Over the five-year period 2003–2007, newspaper circulation was down 8 per cent in the USA; but, first, this decline does not mean that print newspapers will necessarily disappear in the USA, and, secondly, at the global level the circulation of paid newspapers is rising, buoyed by demand in Asia and South America.[5]

Moreover, there may be complementarity between the two categories of media. For instance, during the Iraq War, large numbers of Americans were turning to the Internet as a source of supplementary information about the war. A survey completed between 14th May and 17th June 2004 shows that 24 per cent of American Internet users said they had gone online at one time or another for news that was not covered by the mainstream press (news stories, photographs or videos that other media outlets had decided not to publish or broadcast) (Fallows and Rainie, 2004). By contrast, many people choose to watch TV and not the Internet for 'special' events[6] and they often read the print newspaper on the following day.

Secondly, although advertising is a very important component of online media revenues, for the moment in the United States 'no simple model has been found to assure profitability for the online newspaper industry' (Greer and Mensing, 2006). In fact online advertisements did not yield the revenues that American newspaper publishers had hoped for. In the USA, there is a slowdown in online advertisements, and the effectiveness of these advertisements is discussed.

Moreover, 'all traditional media organizations, including public broadcasters, are re-examining the way their work reaches its audience and the impact of these new pathways on their business models. Not one of the traditional media industries has confidently identified its future revenue model' (Miel and Faris, 2008, p. 5).

Of course, the case of the United States must not be extended to other countries without analysis. For example, Findahl shows that

> traditional mass media, radio, television and newspapers, are still the main sources of information, news and entertainment in Sweden. There are no major changes during the last seven years [2000–07]. But among the young people, the importance of Internet has slowly increased, and today for them Internet is the most important source of information even if television still is the most important source of entertainment. (Findahl, 2008, p. 217)

In addition we must keep in mind that it is very difficult to make predictions about the future of the press industry in general, taking into account both the general economic framework with the financial and economic recession in the developed countries and the specific situation of the media industry.

5.2 The dynamics of media business models: first lessons from innovation theory

5.2.1 The life cycle model

Now we propose to explain the changes in the media no more by focusing on the short term but by a model of the dynamics on the long period.

Let us apply some elements of the economics of innovation to our subject, in particular the theory of product or technology life cycles. The diffusion of a product or the performance of a technology has a recognised pattern over time. It follows an S-curve: when the rate of adoption of a product or a technology performance parameter (y axis) is plotted against time (x axis), the result resembles an s-shaped diagram (sigmoid, eg logistic curve), called the S-curve (see Rogers, 1995; Khalil, 2000). Generally it is admitted that the life cycle includes three main stages:

1. The first period is characterised by the introduction of the innovation, which may be a new product, a new production process ... ; this innovation offers some economic advantage over prevailing products or methods, and there are few firms which are the producers and sellers; in this first period the rate of growth of the new product or new method or new technology ... is low.
2. The second period is characterised by rapid and sustained growth: information about the innovation is spreading among potential adopters and many firms are entering the market.

3. In the third period, the product or the technology is mature and progress in diffusion or in performance slows down. The market reaches a limit (a technology reaches its natural limit): the product or the technology is vulnerable to substitution or/and obsolescence.

We propose to apply this theory of the life cycle to the media industry but by considering that the diffusion process is dynamic and may be more complex than suggested by the S-curve. As shown for example by J. S. Metcalfe (1981), the standard diffusion model is static in nature and has largely ignored the supply side, that is to say the relationship between profitability and the pace of diffusion. So we consider that the S-curve is a simplified description of a model of innovation diffusion; for example, there may be many different successive incremental changes in a technology which lead to an envelope of successive diffusion curves, instead of a single diffusion curve. We consider also that it is necessary to relates innovation both to product and process evolution: in the case of the media, there have been new technological supports, in particular computers and the Internet, which have induced new production and diffusion processes; there have been new information products since information and communication technology has permitted to produce contents which meet the needs of users. The development of the free press relies on both new production processes and new products.

Following the work of Utterback and Abernathy (1975), we assume also that 'there will be a strong mutual relationship between a firm's choice of a strategy and its environment and given its strategy, between the types of product and process innovations that a firm undertakes and the way its productive resources will be deployed, particularly the state of development achieved in its production processes' (Utterback and Abernathy, 1975, p. 425). If we apply this approach to the media, we can understand, for example, why some traditional media firms have strategies which include the Internet and some others have difficulties to integrate online contents.

Finally, let us note that the second period of the life cycle could be broken up into two periods, corresponding respectively to a 'frenzy' phase (fast diffusion with new technologies) and a 'synergy' phase (coherent growth). When such a model is applied to a technological revolution, as shown by Perez (2002), between these two phases there appears a turning point, usually in the recession that follows the collapse of a financial bubble. Applied in a more restricted way to the media industries, this model helps to understand that the frenzy phase for the new media has developed with tensions (in particular, the profitability issue) that should lead to changes in business models. In the case of the French media system issues about regulatory changes are a main element of the turning point.

Figure 5.2 illustrates the life cycles of old media and new media. Old media, such as print paid newspapers, have declined for many years in many countries and new media, such as free print newspapers or online newspapers, are growing. We are in the second period characterised by a growing level of competition between the two types of media. The two curves will meet and the issues are: what will become of the old media? Will they disappear during the third period? Until when will new media continue to rise at such a high rate of growth?

Some data confirm our approach. In the United States the Internet has now surpassed the newspapers, but not television, as an outlet for national and international news (see Figure 5.3).

5.2.2 An illustration: changes in the French press

Let us analyse the case of the French press. Does the low-cost model explain the success of the free press in France? Does the media life cycle model, as illustrated by Figure 5.2, apply in the case of the French press?

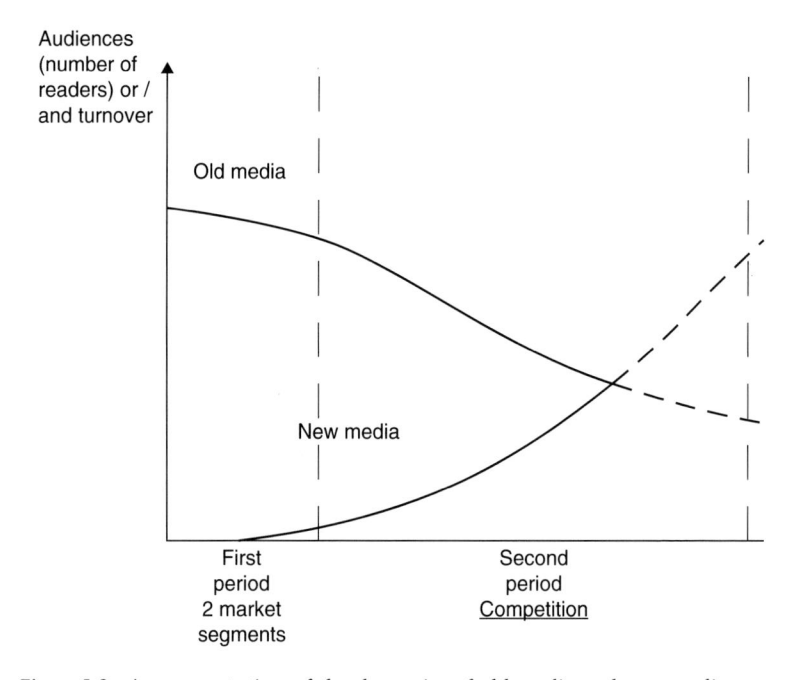

Figure 5.2 A representation of the dynamics of old media and new media

Where Do You Get Most of Your National and International News?

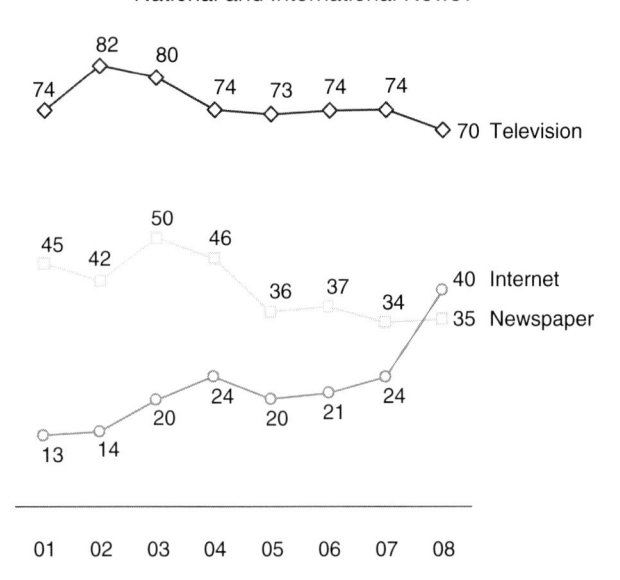

Figure 5.3 Surveys about the sources of news in the United States
Source: The Pew Research Center, 2008.

In recent years one of the key elements concerning the French press has been the new trend. As we have established,[7] there is a strong rupture of trend since the year 2000. This rupture is so strong that we can note a very strong decline of every segment of the French press, with the exception of the free press (see Figures 5.4 and 5.5; in Figure 5.4 the forecasts for 2008–16 are calculated on the basis of the 2000–07 data, which correspond to the new trend).

The development of the free press during recent years, and simultaneously the difficulties of the traditional press, in France, may be explained by the life cycle theory.

First it is clear that the French traditional written press has declined for a long time but has long resisted thanks to barriers to entry (high investment, social and legal protection, importance of the role of unions). This trend corresponds to the third period in the life cycle of this media. Since the beginning of the twenty-first century the emergence of new media, the Internet and the free press, has created new markets with lower barriers to entry. The French free press (the free written press and Internet newspapers) is indeed increasing strongly. As noted by Eveno,

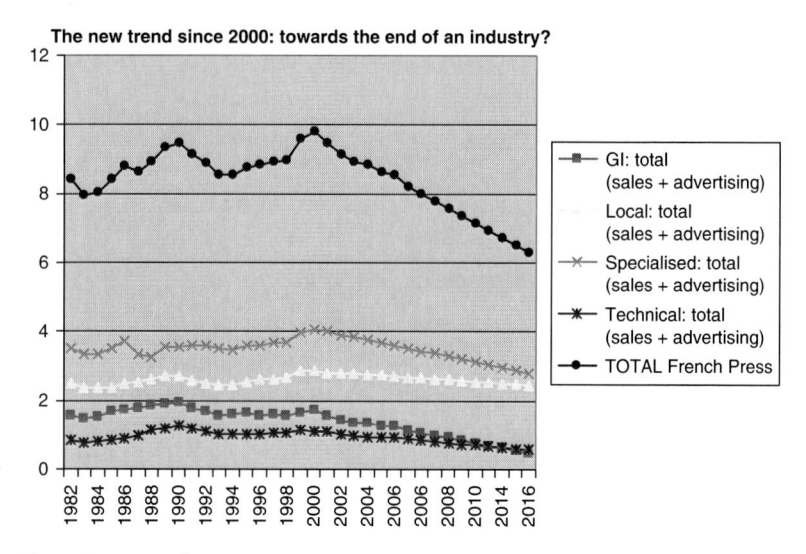

The new trend since 2000: towards the end of an industry?

Figure 5.4 French press resources (in constant euro) (GI = General Information Press)

'The absence of a popular newspaper in France has favoured the appearance and the rise of the free daily newspapers' (Eveno, 2003, p. 167; our translation). An inquiry into the audience for French daily newspapers (EPIQ – Etude de la Presse d'Information Quotidienne – July 2007–June 2008) highlights the recent popular success of free information dailies: with 2.4 million readers on average *20 Minutes* is now the most read daily newspaper in France just in front of *L'Equipe* (2.3 million readers), *Metro* (another free daily newspaper: 2.03 million readers), *Le Parisien/ Aujourd'hui en France* (2.01 million readers), *Le Monde* (1.89 million readers), *Le Figaro* (1.19 million readers) and *Libération* (806,000 readers).

Moreover, the new trend in the French press since 2000 has revealed a substantial decline in the advertising resources of the paid press (Badillo and Bourgeois, 2008). In general, advertising resources have declined since 2000 in France: in 2000 the global advertising market represented 2.1 per cent of GNP and in 2008 it represented only about 1.7 per cent of GNP (source: France Pub). But, if we observe the distribution of advertising resources in France, there are different trends: in particular, advertising in the free press and on the Internet has grown while that of the traditional press has declined. At the global level, the Internet is becoming the third channel for advertising, behind television and print but ahead of radio.[8]

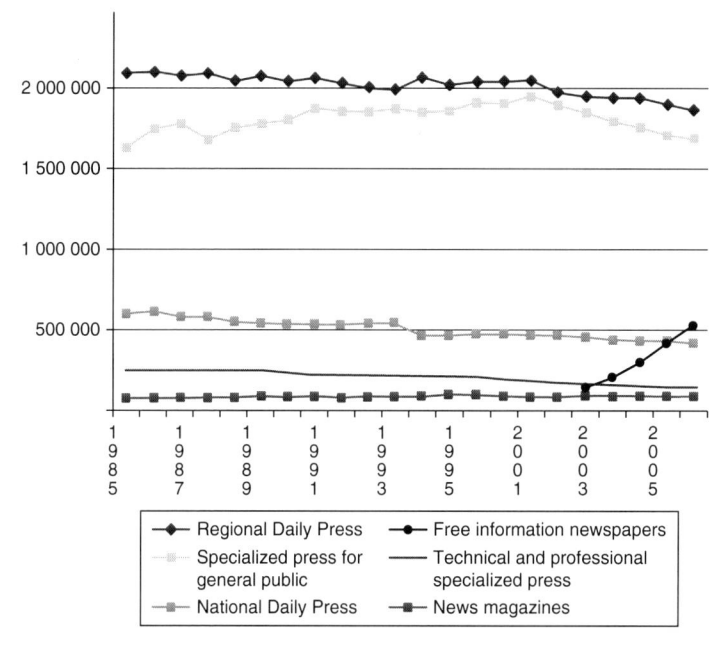

Figure 5.5 French press, total paid circulation (volume)
Source: Direction du Développement des Médias.

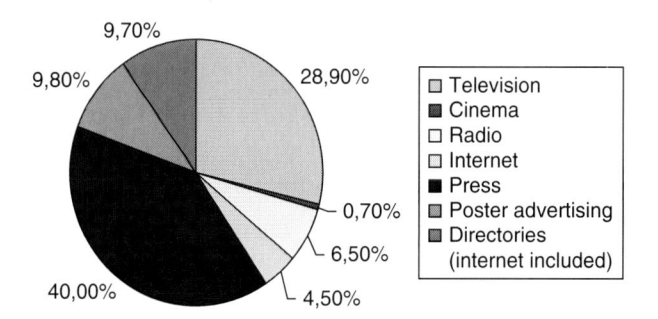

Figure 5.6 Advertising resources in France 2008
Source: IREP.

Let us consider specifically the free information written press in France. Of course, the free information press remains only a small part of the French press: about 3 per cent of the whole print press turnover in 2007 ('presse Editeur'). Moreover, compared to the advertising income of the national information press (about 583 million in 2007) or

Free information press in France: advertising
(in millions of current €)

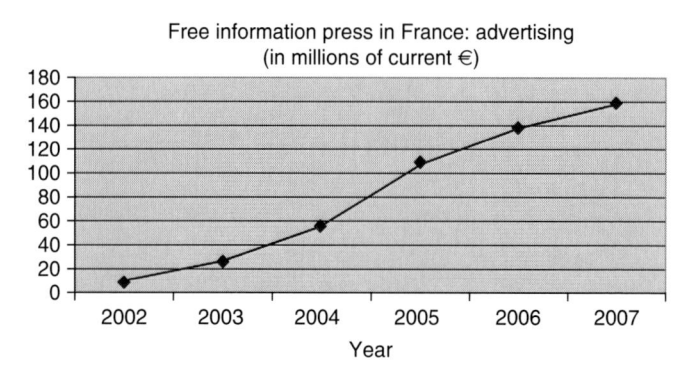

Figure 5.7 Turnover of free information newspapers in France

of the local information press (about 1,368 million in 2007), the turnover of the free written press (which is approximately equal to its advertising income) is still low. But since 2002 (the beginning of the official statistics on the free information press in France) the turnover of this press increased every year: +170 per cent, +100 per cent, +94 per cent, +27 per cent and +14 per cent (the increase in 2007 compared to 2006). The turnover amounted to 10 million current euros in 2002 and about 159 million in 2007. During the same period the advertising income of the national information press was quite stagnant and the advertising income of the local information press declined (in current euros). In 2007 the advertising income of the free written press represented 27.3 per cent of the advertising income of the national information press (only 1.6 per cent in 2002).

Our analysis shows that the low-cost model offers quite a good explanation of the success of the free press in France. However it should be noted that the issue concerning the replacement of old media by new media is not a straightforward one. A study (CNDI, 2008) considers that the competition from the Internet and the free press in the field of information is not a serious explanation for the erosion of circulation in written press titles in France. According to this study, there is no significant relationship between the recent evolution of the readership in the paid daily press and the rise in Internet use. Concerning the free written press, the study develops the argument that 'the effects of the free press compensate: on the one hand, it could divert fragile readers (who would have probably left in any case), but on the other hand it would give new readers the habit and taste to read a daily' (CNDI, 2008, p. 3; our translation). The dominant variable which would explain the evolution of the readership in the traditional press would be the judgement of the readers and non-readers concerning editorial contents. Such a conclusion, based on a serious study of the daily press in France, tends to indicate that there will be no straightforward substitution between the French old and new media in the future.

So we define the business models in the media as essentially dynamic. We have integrated the product life cycle approach as a factor of these dynamic business models. There is no pure model which will remain relevant in the long run. The dominant business model of the US press at the beginning of the nineteenth century was very different from the dominant business model of the twentieth century. Similarly, the dominant business model of the twentieth century has become exhausted for a few years while a new model appeared. In France, the declining trend of the traditional written press has accentuated during recent years while there has been a development of the free press.

However, in the same way, the low-cost model which has been the solution of the very early twenty-first century will perhaps no longer be the best solution in years to come.

5.3 Modelling the dynamics of the press: towards blended media

We propose now a simple model to describe the dynamics of the press. The first model (model A) includes only the traditional press. Then, in model B, we add the free press and the Internet (online news). We will show that the expansion of the Internet and of the free press has introduced complexity into the media system; segmentation and media market instability can be analysed by drawing some further lessons from innovation theory. Finally we will speculate about the emerging models which could be based on versioning and blended media.

5.3.1 Model A: only the traditional press (the paid press) is taken into account

We propose a first very simple model of the economy of the press. This model could be adapted without difficulty to all forms of media. The main characteristics of the press have largely been presented through the 'two-sided' model. The revenue of the paid-for press (noted below RP) is made up of advertising revenue (denoted RPP) and the revenue related to payments by readers (denoted RPL):

$$RP = RPP + RPL \qquad (5.1)$$

(revenue of the paid-for press = advertising revenue + revenue related to the readership)

However, equation (5.1) is not so simple since obviously the revenue from advertising is dependent upon the readership, and more precisely the readership of the paid-for press which will be denoted LP.

Equation (5.1) is thus written:

$$RP = RPP + RPL = f_1(LP) + h_2(h_1(LP)) \qquad (5.2)$$

(the revenue of the paid-for press is a direct function and an indirect function of the readership)

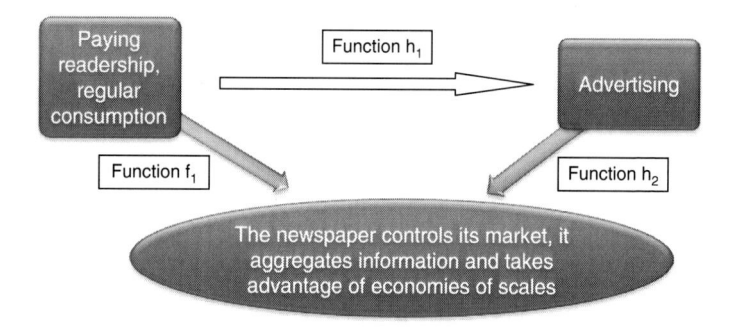

Figure 5.8 Diagram A: The traditional model of the press

5.3.2 Model B: the free press and Internet (online news) coexists with the paid press

Now let us introduce the emergence and the development of the free press into the model. Let us specify immediately that thereafter we will speak of free press, or more largely free information goods. It will be considered, without reconsidering this point, that the Internet, and thus online news, or more generally online information, belong to the free press. We also integrate into this category the free advertisement press (however, the latter remains very specific and has been available for a long time; we will not look further into this aspect). The revenue of the free press is primarily due to advertising:[9]

$$RG = g_2 \, (PUBG) \qquad (5.3)$$

(revenue of the free press = advertising revenue)

However, equation (5.3) is not so simple, since, obviously, the advertising-related revenue is dependent upon the level of readership, more precisely the readership of the free press which will be noted LG.

$$PUBG = g_1 (LG) \qquad (5.4)$$

Equation (5.2) thus becomes:

$$RG = g_2 (g_1 (LG)) \qquad (5.5)$$

(the revenue of the free press related to advertising is a function of the readership of this free press).

Those simple equations show that we are beyond the 'two-sided' model; we have a two-step model: advertising is not a completely independent market but constitutes an indirect market. The key to this market remains, of course, the readership. The total revenues of the press are written:

$$RT = RP + RG = f_1 (LP) + h_2 (h_1 (LP)) + g_2 (g_1 (LG)) \qquad (5.6)$$

This equation shows that the press has a single target but at least three different issues to be faced:

How to attract a paying readership?
How 'to sell' advertising thanks to this paying readership?
How to have readers of free news in order to sell advertising?

So, with the free press we are switching from a two-sided model to a three-sided model. But this 'three-sided model' is characterised by complex and indirect 'consumption' functions. Let us specify that, in this precise case, consumption is particular since it is the readership. For television, the former CEO of TF1, the first French television channel, Patrice Le Lay, started a controversy in 2004 by indicating that his company did nothing but sell available time of brain: 'There are many ways of speaking about television. But from the business point of view, let us be realistic: at the base, the trade of TF1, it is to help Coca-Cola for example, to sell its product. (…) What we sell to Coca-Cola, it is available time of human brain'[10] (our translation). In 2004, Le Lay's assertion was considered shocking. It actually only highlights the 'natural' objectives of large private media firms. In the context of the 'information society', Information and Communication Technologies (ICT) are changing the face of the media landscape; the rise of new media is done undoubtedly from the point of view of profit for the new players.

Admittedly, Le Lay's formula is a brutal one, although it merely corresponds to the reality of the market. Ultimately it is indeed the reader, the listener or the televiewer whom the media seek to attract.

78　*The Media Industries and their Markets*

Now, with the appearance of the free press and the Internet the diagram A is changed completely. Diagram B below illustrates the relations at stake.

The dark-grey and horizontal ellipse in the lower part of Figure 5.9 symbolises the 'low-cost model' which is able to conquer part of the free readership and part of advertising and the corresponding free press.

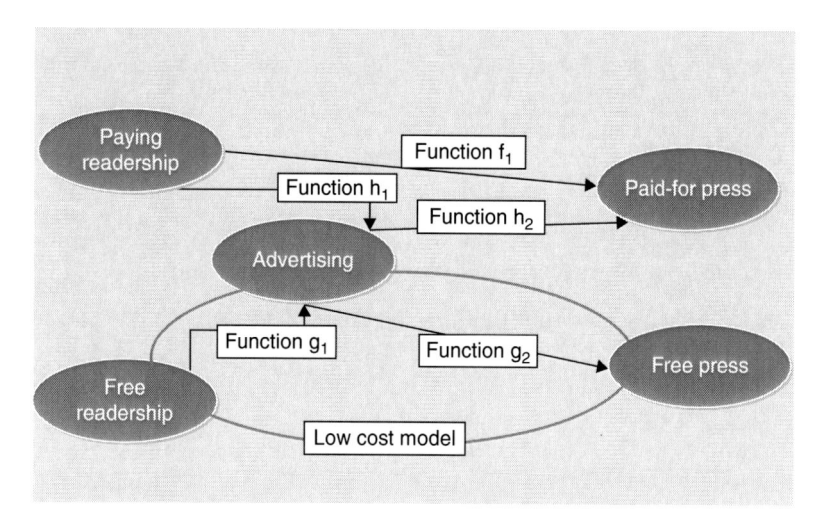

Figure 5.9　Diagram B: Coexistence of free press and paid-for press

5.3.3 Complexity, segmentation and media market instability: second lessons from the innovation theory

However, further thought needs to be given beyond the preceding diagram. The arrival of the Internet and the free press has introduced much complexity. This complexity is illustrated in Figure 5.10.

First the direct and indirect functions of the readership appear. It should be noted that the readership related to the emergence of the free press (including online free press) can partly be a new readership which so far has not been interested by the paid-for newspapers. We could consider that the total readership (LT) is the sum of the paid-for press readership (LP) and the free press readership (LG). However, obviously some readers simultaneously consume free newspapers and paid-for ones; they will be denoted (LG∩LP). The readers who consume only paid-for newspapers will be denoted LP and those who consume only free newspapers will be denoted LG. Hence:

$$LT = \underline{LP} + (LG \cap LP) + \underline{LG}$$

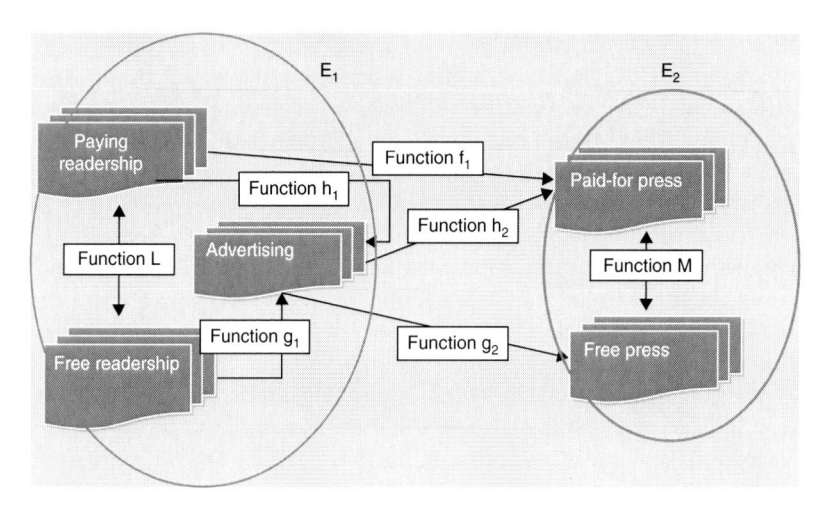

Figure 5.10 Diagram C: Complexity of the press system (with free and paid-for press)

The issue is to know up to what point the appearance of the free press widens the readership, and contributes (or not) to the reduction in the paid readership. In fact, it is the function L, symbolised in diagram C, which is affected. Which redistributions of readership and advertising revenues are caused by the development of the free readership? Obviously, there is an interrelationship between function L and function M which establishes the dividing lines between the paid-for press and the free press.

But a second element plays a part. The markets of the free and paid-for press, the readerships (paid or free), as well as advertising are measured on segmented, although strongly interdependent markets. There would be thus as many functions to write in order to carry out a complete modelling! Advertising concerning the segment i of the readership would be interdependent with all of the other advertising market segments. The market of the free press would be interdependent with all of the other markets of the free press and the paid-for press ...

In order to understand the rupture which is currently occurring in the media system following the arrival of the Internet, it appears useful to us to resort again to the innovation theories. The life cycle theory and, more particularly, the works of Abernathy and Utterback describe the first stages of an innovation in the following manner.

A market appears as the result of an innovation. When an innovation is established, generally only one innovator has the monopoly, as the result of his innovation, for a certain time. So, initially there is no competition, but a monopoly of the innovator and this company monopolises the profits. However, in particular when the patent no longer protects the innovator, many competitors appear and position themselves on this new and profitable market. Competition becomes increasingly intense up to a maximum point. A kind of normal curve illustrates this dynamics. Such a curve was revealed for many industries and it constitutes a kind of law concerning the evolution of competition in a given sector. In the first phase competition does not exist (there is a monopoly), in a second phase competition reaches a maximum with a large number of companies in the sector, then the product moves towards the end of its life cycle and the market remains controlled by a limited set of firms. An oligopolistic situation prevails in a relatively stable market.

In other words, innovation theory indicates that, when an innovation appears, initially it benefits a first innovator (and by extension a first group of innovators). It is the case of the free press, the Internet and the underlying low-cost model. There is an opportunity for the new entrant to control a new market.

But once past this first phase, on the one hand the level of competition on this market intensifies (the rise of free newspapers is an illustration) and on the other hand the market becomes destabilised. Then we enter a second phase and the market must concentrate in order to become more stable.

This idea can be better understood through a consideration of Figure 5.10: the market becomes extraordinarily unstable because of the multiplicity of interdependent markets controlled by distinct firms on segmented markets. With regard to this instability, it is advisable to organise new standards. These new standards will probably provoke an integration of the markets (see the ellipses E1 and E2), reinforced by a new and major characteristic of information: versioning.

5.3.4 The emerging models: versioning and blended media?

Shapiro and Varian (1999) have set down the bases of economics of information and in particular defined the idea of versioning:

> It means offering your information product in different versions for different market segments. (Shapiro and Varian, 1999, p. 54) ... In many ways, selling information on-line and off-line is like selling physical products through two separate channels of distribution [...] the key question to ask yourself is whether the on-line version is a complement or a substitute for the off-line version. If it is a substitute for the off-line version, then you'll want to charge for it, recovering costs through fees or advertising or version it so that

it doesn't directly compete with your off-line version. If it complements your off-line version, then you want to promote it as aggressively as possible, since it adds to the bottom line by encouraging sales of the off-line product. (Shapiro and Varian, 1999, p. 66)

The versioning strategy includes bundling: '*Bundling* is a special form of versioning in which two or more distinct products are offered as a package at a single price ... bundling makes sense if it reduces variation in willingness to pay' (Shapiro and Varian, 1999, p. 73).

We think also that a versioning strategy may be based on branding: 'Fundamentally, a brand is a name, term, sign, symbol, package design, or combination of these elements intended to identify and distinguish a product or a service from its competitors' (Chan-Olmsted, 2006, p. 58). For example, some old media, particularly in the general information press, have benefited for a long time from some brands which have represented both sociopolitical choices and editorial quality. If such brands are extended to new versions of products on new channels, the new versions should be associated with the images of trust and quality. Then consumers will identify easily the source of the news and this will help to gain a new market. But, of course, new versions of a product have to be adapted to new channels and perhaps new consumers.

Let us also note that customisation is another aspect of versioning.

With the Internet and the free press it is obvious that the business models of the media industries, and in particular that of the press, are substantially modified.

The old model of the press was characterised by strong economies of scale (as a result of the very high capital costs), with a situation of local monopoly where the law of proximity was fundamental, with a logic of quasi-fordist production. In France, this model was accompanied by the state for the general information press (subsidies).

On the contrary, the new model will be based on versioning, in a context where the economies of scope will be fundamental. Indeed an integration of the markets makes it possible to exploit at most the profitability of a production on various segments.

Figure 5.11 illustrates the situation. What is expensive is to produce information itself; but it can be reproduced on another support at a very low marginal cost: 'Information is costly to produce, but cheap to reproduce' (Shapiro and Varian, 1999, p. 3).

On the Internet the markets are unstable, even transient: between Eldorado and the flying Dutchman (the mirage of a market) the step is

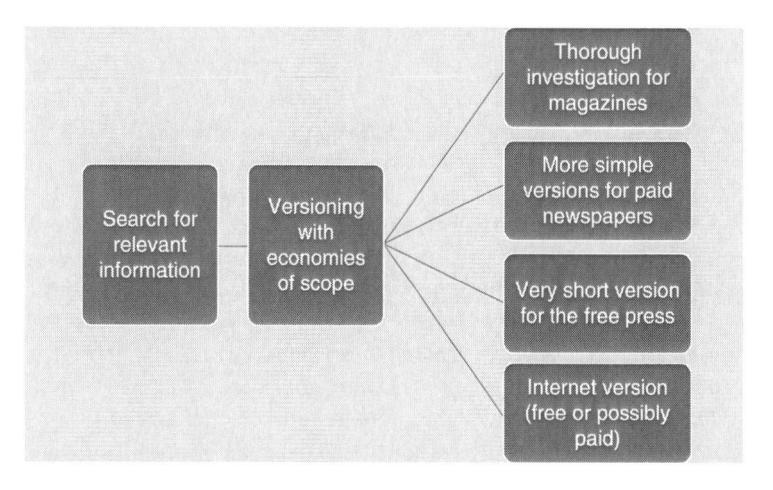

Figure 5.11 Versioning and media markets

quickly crossed. The new markets have presented a godsend, a windfall. But this windfall will become increasingly difficult to maintain. Exacerbated competition will reduce the shares of the new players. The new strategy will rest on versioning as indicated in Figure 5.11. It will consist of a multimedia strategy: one not only internal to the press but concerning various media (press, radio, television, television on IP, etc.).

Of course, the concrete strategies of media firms will be various according to different economic and social environments. Probably some firms will merge, some others will disappear, some will develop. And there will be different categories of blended media (we do not study here blended media models which include television, radio...).

We are moving from fordism in the press industry towards versioning which in fact supports the continuous occupation of a multiplicity of market niches. This is what we term 'blended' media. It should be noted that in these new markets the quality of the production of information but also the capacity to propose various versions on various channels will be decisive. That also implies a relevant management of digital information: memorising and stocking information and the accessibility of various versions will be strategic.

So the business media models are not only dynamic but tend to be blended. It is no longer old media versus new media models: now we are witnessing the emergence of blended media models. In the future the

Table 5.1 Number of visits to the internet sites of French media groups (20 largest numbers)

No	Groups	Total number of visits December 2008	Evolution over November 2008	Mean duration of visit
1	Skyrock	209 415 040	−6%	00:22:55
2	Pages Jaunes	67 377 430	−10%	00:05:28
3	Lagardère Active	62 347 544	−6%	00:14:25
4	EoRezo	51 693 076	+14%	00:14:05
5	L'Equipe	50 932 556	−10%	00:20:46
6	Dreamnex – Sexyavenue	44 063 161	+8%	00:09:52
7	Internext	35 968 942	+2%	00:07:15
8	Rentabiliweb	35 918 320	−1%	00:09:12
9	France télévisions	31 862 668	+5%	00:14:50
10	Le Figaro	30 210 250	−15%	00:16:14
11	AdThink Media	15 286 135	+12%	00:09:13
12	Index Multimedia	13 541 745	−3%	00:47:16
13	M6	13 486 130	−10%	00:08:12
14	United Champions France	11 901 436	−39%	00:06:23
15	Seloger.com	9 279 435	−18%	00:12:31
16	Radio France	7 530 398	−15%	00:06:28
17	PAP	5 089 102	−23%	00:09:05
18	Mondadori France Digital	4 016 676	−5%	00:04:07
19	Métaboli	2 971 256	+31%	00:05:11
20	Moniteur	2 452 052	−22%	00:06:35

Source: Médiamétrie-eStat. The data are limited to the companies which are customers of Médiamétrie-eStat. They do not include all the French Internet sites, but the main media groups.

dominant business models will be blended media: how to use, with appropriate economies of scope, different media (traditional press – with payment, free press, the Internet with not only text but also audiovisual contents, and possibly other supports like TV or radio). The blended media firm will take advantage of the economies of scope while traditional economies of scale are less and less important. The best dynamic business model will be able to take advantage of any new way to diffuse and to reach 'consumers'/users (for example, to take advantage of social networks and so on).

We can observe the introduction of such a strategy through the following statement from Alain Weill, the forerunner of the low-cost model in France:

> Nextradio does not want to miss the future market of television on mobile phones. The mobile terminals of the future, as genuine Swiss pocket knives, will mix voice, images and data. [according to Alain Weill, that corresponds to many components of the group], which includes radio channels, a television channel and Internet sites. *'Now, we think as an integrated group and we are condemned to grow on all the supports'*, summarises Alain Weill. (source: *Les Echos*[11]; our translation)

We can also see this mix of old and new media when we observe the companies which are the most present on the Internet in France. Indeed among the 20 first groups in this classification (see Table 5.1) about half of them are 'old' media companies which have defined a strong strategy on the Internet.

5.4 Conclusion

We have the main bases of a model which could be generalised to the whole press, even to all media industries. The model shows that the main issue is not the replacement of the old media by the new ones. The emergence of the Internet and the free press has disrupted the old business model. We are moving towards a new business model in which the media which will impose themselves will not inevitably be the new media, against the old media, but those media which are able best to define their strategy. A gaining strategy (strategies of niches will always exist) will be founded on economies of scope, versioning and blended media. The blended media model is defined by the capacity to exploit in a continuous way the same information according to a multimedia differentiation and the most powerful possible versioning.

Notes

1. Patrick Badillo is a Professor at Aix-Marseille University, France; formerly Director of the School of Journalism and Communication of Marseille; Director and Founder of the Research Institute on Information and Communication; Project Manager, French National Research Agency; Dominique Bourgeois is a Professor at the University of Fribourg, Switzerland, Chair of Communication and Media Sciences.
2. Of course, there are many definitions of a business model but they all insist on financial flows which can ensure business operations. See, for example, in the case of the media the following definition: 'According to Afuah and Tucci (2001), a business model is the method by which a firm builds and uses its resources to offer its customers better value than its competitors and to make money doing so. It describes how a firm makes money now and in the long term. A business model combines potential environmental factors and a firm's capability, and it combines the sustainable recipe to offer competitive products or services with a relevant revenue logic' (Sääksjärvi and Santonen, 2002, p. 3).
3. Bertrand Le Gendre, 'Tous journalistes!', *Le Monde*, 29 May 2004, p. 17. For another point of view, see P.-Y. Badillo, D. Bourgeois, J.-B. Lesourd and C. Peyron-Bonjan, Plus personne n'est journaliste, *Médiamorphoses*, 24, October 2008, pp. 79–85.
4. http://www.journaldunet.com/cc/06_publicite/epub_marche_mde.shtml.
5. http://www.usatoday.com/news/world/2008-06-02-newspaper_N.htm.
6. See, for example, the online article of BBC's technology correspondent, Rory Cellan-Jones on BBC News about Obama's inauguration: http://www.bbc.co.uk/blogs/technology/2009/01/inauguration_were_you_new_or_o.html.
7. Badillo and Bourgeois (2008).
8. Source: Carat, reported in: http://www.journaldunet.com/ebusiness/publicite/actualite/internet-va-devenir-le-troisieme-support-publicitaire-en-2008.shtml.
9. It should be noted that we do not study newspapers which rely on subsidies or donations.
10. In Collective of authors, preface by Ernest-Antoine Seillère, *Les dirigeants face au changement*, Paris: Éditions du Huitième Jour, 2004, pp. 92–3.
11. La presse écrite devient un média de luxe, *Les Echos*, no. 19546, November 23, 2005, p. 9.

References

Afuah, A. and Tucci, C.L. 2001. *Internet Business Models*, New York: McGraw Hill.
Albert, P. 2008. *La presse française*, Paris: La Documentation Française.
Badillo, P.-Y. and Bourgeois, D. 2008. *The French Press: Issues and Econometric Tendencies. Towards the End of an Industry?* Chapter 9 in Medina, M. and Faustino, P. (eds), *The Changing Media Business Environment*, Lisbon: Formalpress – Publicações e Marketing, pp. 204–23.
Cao, Z. and Li, X. 2006. Effect of growing Internet of US print newspapers, in X. Li (ed.), *Internet Newspapers. The Making of a mainstream Medium*, Mahwah, NJ and London: Lawrence Erlbaum Associates, pp. 121–37.

Chan-Olmsted, S.M. 2006. *Competitive Strategy for Media Firms*, Mahwah, NJ and London: Lawrence Erlbaum Associates, Inc.

CNDI (Centre National pour le Développement de l'Information). 2008. Crise et avenir de la presse: l'offre éditoriale face à l'évolution des publics, *Études de Presse – les notes du CDI*, 1(5), November.

Eveno, P. 2003. *L'argent de la presse française des années 1820 à nos jours*, Paris: Editions du CTHS (Comité des Travaux Historiques et Scientifiques).

Fallows, D. and Rainie, L. 2004. The Internet as a unique news source, Washington, DC: Pew Internet & American Life Project, http://www.pewtrusts.org/uploadedFiles/wwwpewtrustsorg/News/Press_Releases/Society_and_the_Internet/pew_internet_war_070805.pdf.

Findahl, O. 2008. The role of Internet in a changing mediascape: competitor or complement?, *Observatorio (OBS*) Journal*, 2(3), 209–21.

Gentzkow, M. 2007. Valuing new goods in a model with complementarity: online newspapers, *American Economic Review*, 97(3), 713–45.

Greer, J.D. and Mensing, D. 2006. The evolution of online newspapers: a longitudinal content analysis, 1997–2003, in X. Li (ed.), *Internet Newspapers: The Making of a mainstream Medium*, Mahwah, NJ and London: Lawrence Erlbaum Associates, pp. 13–32.

Khalil, T.M. 2000. *Management of Technology: the Key to Competitiveness and Wealth Creation*, Boston: McGraw-Hill.

Leprette, J. and Pigeat, H. 2002. *Tendances économiques de la presse quotidienne dans le monde*, Paris: Presses Universitaires de France.

Mensing, D. 2007. Online revenue business model has changed little since 1996, *Newspaper Research Journal*, 28(2), 22–37.

Metcalfe, J.S. 1981. Impulse and diffusion in the study of technical change, *Futures*, 13(5), 347–59.

Miel, P. and Faris, R. 2008. 'News and information as digital media come of age', *MEDIA RE:PUBLIC*, Berkman Center for Internet and Society at Harvard University, Cambridge, MA, December.

Perez, C. 2002. *Technological Revolutions and Financial Capital. The Dynamics of Bubbles and Golden Ages*, Cheltenham,UK: Edward Elgar.

Pew Research Center for People & the Press. 2008. Key news audiences now blend online and traditional sources, 17th August 2008. Available at http://people-press.org/report/444/news-media.

Picard, R.G. 2002. *The Economics and Financing of Media Companies*, New York: Fordham University Press.

Rogers, E.M. 1995. *Diffusion of Innovation*, 4th edn, New York: The Free Press.

Sääksjärvi, M. and Santonen, T. 2002. Evolution and success of online newspapers: an empirical investigation of goals, business models and success, *Virhe. Tyyliä ei ole määritetty*, http://project.hkkk.fi/vertigo/paperit/evolution_and_success_of_online_newspapers.pdf.

Shapiro, C. and Varian, H.R. 1999. *Information Rules: A Strategic Guide for the Network Economy*, Cambridge, MA: Harvard Business School Press.

Utterback, J.M. and Abernathy, W.J. 1975. A dynamic model of process and product innovation, *Omega*, 3(6), 639–56.

6
The Dynamics of Media Concentration: The American Experience

Eli M. Noam[1]

6.1 Introduction

For many years, observers have expressed concerns about the concentration of private power in the media. The deepest fear is of a media mogul with a political agenda: in America, a William Randolph Hearst who used his newspapers to help start a war and who promoted himself for mayor, governor, and president. Or in Italy, a Silvio Berlusconi, who leveraged his media holdings to gain political power. Or in Australia, where Rupert Murdoch affected national elections. Or in Brazil, Mexico, and Germany, where the Marinho, Azcarranga, Mohn, and Springer families exert influence. And today, with electronic media becoming smart, powerful, and pervasive, and with the regular announcement of media mergers, the same fear is expressed more acutely than ever before; in the end there will be only a handful of media companies remaining in the world, and running the world.

Recent years have witnessed the expansion of large media firms in the United States. This development has led to fears that the US communications media are increasingly controlled by an ever-shrinking number of firms, and that those firms are capable of affecting public opinion, democracy itself, the national agenda, and global culture. Other countries, too, are watching the debate closely, not only because of the global role of US communications firms, but also because US tendencies are often indicators of future developments elsewhere.

When it comes to concentration, views are strong, theories abound, but numbers are scarce. In America, to some commentators the sky has been falling for decades (Bagdikian 1983, 1987, 1990, 1992, 1997, 2004). Others, often from free-market Washington policy think tanks or from the libertarian Internet community, believe that market and technological forces are overcoming all barriers, that we are in the midst of a flowering of media and information (Thierer 2005), and that there is no problem apart from heavy-footed bureaucrats trampling on those flowers. There are only few attempts to enlist data analysis for enlightenment rather than for ammunition.[2]

Part of the reason for the heightened pitch of the debate is that for many critics, media concentration has been an ink blot onto which they project their hopes and fears. Deconcentrated media provide a greater *source diversity* of content. That, by itself, is essential to democracy. The argument for deconcentration could stop right here and be persuasive. But it does not, because many people earnestly believe that many other ills of society would be remedied by media deconcentration. Whether it is violence, gender stereotyping, racism, offensive policy, materialism, hedonism, escapism, low levels of political participation, lack of political debate, entrenched status quo, inequality, drug dependency, even obesity or bulimia – for all these and more, the media system is held partly responsible either as a contributing cause or as an absent remedy. The size and power of large media companies are seen as the cause of much that is wrong with media's negative impact on society. And since so many of society's ills are blamed on media, media reform becomes social reform.

What, then, are the facts about American media concentration trends? The answer to the empirical question is not as obvious as many sincerely believe. First, although numerous mergers have taken place and have led to huge and internationally far-flung companies, the mass media and information sector have also grown rapidly, despite widespread price declines.

Second, in the past, different information industries were clearly separated from each other by law and technology. With digital convergence a much discussed tendency, firms have been crossing the lines that once divided the mass media, telecommunications, and computer industries.

Third, the internationalisation of economies and services means that well-established media firms from other countries have gained a foothold in the United States.

Fourth, recent years have seen the emergence of new media; most notably the Internet, creating new distribution channels for new content providers.

Who is right? Are media increasingly becoming controlled by the few? Despite much conventional wisdom and anecdotes, the answer to the question is not an obvious 'yes'. And despite the hand-waving of the free marketeers, the answer is not an obvious 'no' either. To resolve this empirical question is the task of this chapter.

6.2 The conceptual model

The overall trend of media concentration is the composite of three separate dynamics that overlay each other. These three forces are:

1. The growth in *economies of scale* in information sector operations.
2. The lowering of *entry barriers*.
3. *Digital convergence*.

Together, these forces result in certain concentration patterns. The first two lead to an oscillation of concentration, with an upward trend. The third factor leads the concentration trend mass media to converge to that of the overall information sector.

We begin with *economies of scale*. There is a relation between the equilibrium market structure (that is, of market concentration) and the economies of scale of an industry. Where the latter are high, an industry is likely to consist of only a few firms. One example is the automobile industry. By contrast, where economies of scale are low, there will be many providers, as in the case of auto repair shops. Electronic technology has changed scale economies. Digital technology has shifted the ratio of fixed cost of investment and the variable costs of serving people. The incremental costs are very low in a digital environment, and the average costs therefore keep dropping. This translates into growing economies of scale. The incremental costs for operating a broadband network, of producing semiconductors or consumer electronic devices, of distributing software programs, video games, daily newspaper, or new recordings has also declined. On the Internet, incremental costs are typically minuscule.

A related kind of size benefits are, on the demand side, 'network effects'. Users of networks (and often of content) often benefit from the presence of other participants. They can reach more people and share common experiences with friends, colleagues and neighbours.

The second economic trend in many media and information industries is the tendency to *lower entry barriers*. Electronic technology, in particular, makes it easier to produce content – magazines, music recordings, film, and so forth. Wireless technology enables the entry of new networks and applications by smaller firms. Computers and IT hardware can be designed by small or smaller firms. The digital revolution has led to falls in hardware costs, exemplified by the exponential cost declines outlined in Moore's Law. Many products can be put together from off-the-shelf hardware and software components or they can be outsourced to specialists, thus making it unnecessary to develop many aspects of a product in-house.

One reason for lower barriers is the more rapid pace of innovation. This provides openings for new and nimble companies that can leapfrog the slower and longer-established firms. Another reason is the liberalisation of legal and governmental restrictions. Liberalisation policies have made it easier for new participants to enter than in the past, when monopoly franchises or limited spectrum allocations offered a degree of protection to incumbents. Similarly, there has been a lowering of trade barriers restricting international entry.

It is easy to confuse entry barriers with economies of scale. The two concepts are related but different. It may be easier than hitherto to enter the market in terms of up-front investment or legal restrictions, but that does not mean that there is an absence of efficiencies associated with larger operations in production. It is easier to start a phone company, a magazine, or an independent film company than it used to be, but it is not necessarily easier to compete with larger firms. The technology or innovation that makes entry easier is also usually available to all, including established firms, unless it is proprietary in nature.

This can be seen in Figure 6.1, which presents several states of an industry. The figure shows the cost unit of a product for each quantity produced. The barrier to entry is the distance on the vertical axis for the first unit of production. In State 1, this cost is A, whereas in State 2, this cost is lower, at B.

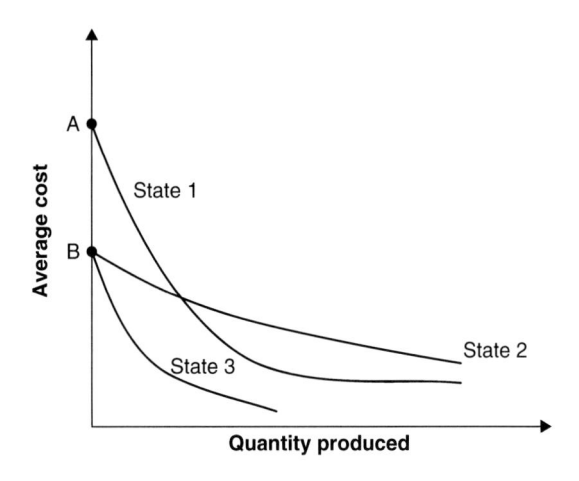

Figure 6.1 Economies of scale and entry barriers

Economies of scale, by contrast, are reflected by the *slope* of the cost lines. That slope depends on the incremental costs of production. If the incremental costs are low, the slope is steep, as it is in the case in State 1. In contrast, State 2 has relatively small-scale economies. (Of course, State 2 could also have low entry barriers as well as high economies of scale, resulting in State 3. The figure merely illustrates the difference of the two concepts.)

Applied to the debate over media concentration, one can characterise, perhaps somewhat simplistically, those who believe in wide-open media – the media-optimists – as focusing on the entry barriers and concluding that entry has become easy and plentiful. They are correct. In contrast, media pessimists are focused on the economies of scale, and they observe ever-growing media firms. They are correct, too.

It is necessary to consider both elements – entry barriers and scale economies. If one does so, a dynamic scenario unfolds. Scale economies and entry barriers can rise or decline. Where they move in the same direction, the impact on concentration is, if all other factors remain equal, generally unambiguous.

For example, if entry barriers drop while there is a decline in scale economies, there will be a larger number of firms contesting the market, while the optimal size of viable firms will shrink. Together, these two factors will lead to more surviving firms and to a lower market concentration. The opposite case occurs when both scale economies and entry barriers rise: in this case there will be fewer firms contesting and fewer firms surviving – that is, more concentration.[3] The ambiguous situations are those in which the two factors move in opposite directions. When entry barriers rise while there is a fall in scale economies, the result is an initial decrease of contestants (higher concentration) but an eventual survival of more (lower concentration), resulting in an inverted U-shaped concentration trend. And where entry barriers drop while scale economies rise, the opposite is the case: there will be initially more contestants (lower concentration) but eventually fewer survivors. The (higher concentration) trend is U-shaped. The trend of the two factors in recent decades has been just that – towards lower entry barriers and to higher scale economies. It is therefore unsurprising to observe the U-shaped concentration pattern through many industries of the information sector.

Let us assume that a stable industry, which has been based on certain economic characteristics, experiences a simultaneous change of lower entry barriers and higher scale economies. The adjustment to a new equilibrium takes several stages, which are depicted in Figure 6.2.

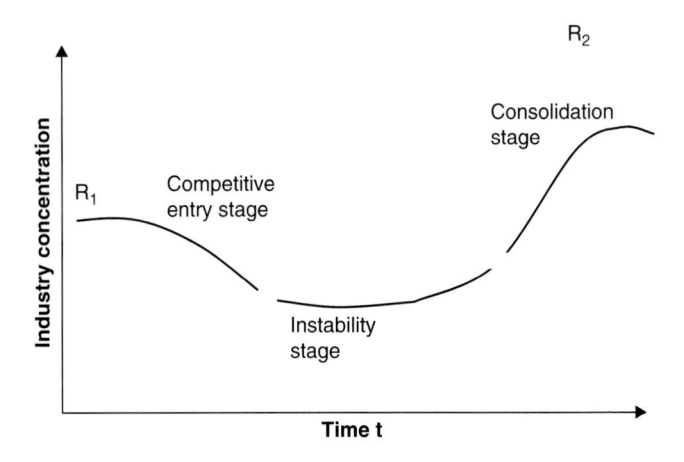

Figure 6.2 Cycles of concentration

Stage 1: *Competitive entry.* Lower entry barriers cause the entry of new participants; the lower early costs enable them to compete. The concentration of the industry drops.

Stage 2: *Instability.* In a competitive environment, companies contest with one another in terms of prices and features. In competition, prices tend to be set at marginal cost (long term). For information products and services, this marginal cost is near zero. But at that level, prices are too low to cover the early (fixed) costs. If such prices persist, companies fail, industries are in crisis, and new entry slows. There are many recent examples for this in the information sector.

Stage 3: *Consolidation.* Eventually, as some competitors fail, others consolidate and the industry reconcentrates. Prices rise again and profits return. This attracts new entrants, and a new cycle begins.

This would describe cyclical concentration. But even within the cycles there can be a trend based on the economies of scale. When these economies grow, they lead to relatively larger firms within an industry, that is, to a higher concentration level. Figure 6.3 shows the oscillations in concentration that one could expect in an environment in which entry barriers steadily decline while economies of scale rise steadily.

Let us begin with an initial Point A. Here entry barriers are fairly high, and scale economies are intermediate. This defines a highly concentrated industry. Now suppose that barriers drop while scale economies rise: the industry will go through the down–up trend described above, bottoming

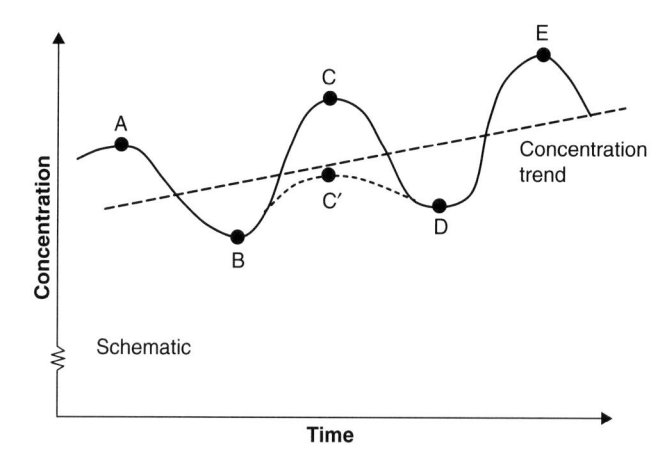

Figure 6.3 Concentration trends, with continuously rising scale economies and declining entry barriers

out at B, rising to C. In that range, competitive entry becomes viable again, and another cycle begins. Point C will be at a higher concentration if scale economies are rising. It could be at C^I (lower) if the impact of economies of scale is less than that of entry barriers, thus leading to an earlier competitive entry.

On the one hand, the trend of scale economies raises the trend of the peaks of the cycles and hence the overall trends of concentration around which fluctuations take place. On the other hand, the trend of lower entry barriers leads to more frequent challenges to any equilibrium and to greater instability. It affects the timing of swings of the instability (frequency) and the magnitude of oscillation (amplitude). Entry barriers affect the *frequency* and *amplitude* of the changes in concentration, whereas economies of scale determine the axis around which they oscillate.[4]

This results in a concentration trend that is fluctuating but rising. If the economies of scale were to shift, perhaps as a result of technology, the trend would reverse itself. This model can accommodate different combinations of scale economies and entry barriers.

This model can explain the trends within the media and information sector in recent years. But what about its subsector, the mass media industries such as print, music, TV, film, and so forth? Here, an additional factor comes into play: digital convergence. In the past, media were distinct from telecom networks, consumer electronics, and computer hardware and software. Their economic characteristics were

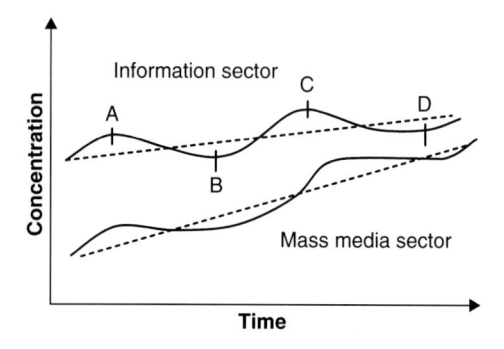

Figure 6.4 Convergence of concentration of overall information sector and mass media sector

different and hence so were their industry structures. This is no longer the case. In an increasingly electronic and digital environment, mass media assume many of the technical elements of networks and technology industries, and with them also fundamental economic characteristics of the information sector in general – low marginal costs, high fixed costs, and lower entry barriers. Hence, the concentration trends of mass media converge with that of the rest of the information sector. This can be shown schematically in Figure 6.4.

This convergence tendency suggests that the mass media sector, from a relatively lower level of concentration, will move to a higher level that is more similar to that of the overall information sector. This will create a steeper axis for the oscillations of this sector, thus underrating down-phases and strengthening the up-phases in the process of convergence.

6.3 Empirical analysis

6.3.1 Methodology

Having established a basic conceptual framework, we now proceed empirically. We look at the market concentration trends for 100 separate information industries in America. Examples of such industries are broadcast TV, cable TV, film distribution, daily newspapers, Internet service providers, TV set manufacturers, microcomputers, local phone services, and cellular mobile providers. For each of these industries, we tracked individual firms' revenues in the US market and calculated their US market shares. We used a wide variety of data sources, including Securities and Exchange Commission (SEC) filings, Federal Communications Commission (FCC) documents, Wall Street analysts' reports, news articles, consultants' studies, and so forth, for a period of 20 years. The effort was extensive, and the resultant database is unprecedented in its scope.

The simplest way to express market concentration is to measure the market share of the top company, presumably the one with the highest degree of market power. But this measure of concentration, known as the 'C1', ignores the respective size of the next firms. Are they few and huge, or many and fragmented? To capture the contribution of such firms to the measure of concentration, one traditional way is to combine the market share of the top four firms ('C4 ratio') for an industry. A C4 ratio is defined by the aggregate total of market share percentage of the four largest companies within an industry. It is given by:

$$C_{4j} = \sum_{i=1}^{4} S_{ij} < 1 \qquad (6.1)$$

Where: S_{ij} = firm's i market share of a given industry j and where firms are ordered by size of market share. Thus, if the market shares of the top 14 firms are 40 per cent, 30 per cent, 10 per cent, and 10 per cent, with 10 other firms holding 1 per cent each, respectively, the C4 index would be 90. However, the index has its limitations, because it cannot differentiate between markets heavily dominated by one firm and those in which four firms are of similar size. For this reason, the Antitrust Division of the US Department of Justice (DoJ) has been using a different index. The main index for concentration used by it, and mostly in this study, has been the Herfindahl–Hirschman Index. This widely used HHI concentration measure is equal to the sum of the squares of the market shares of all market participants.

$$HHI_j = \sum_{i=1}^{f} S_{ij}^2 \qquad (6.2)$$

where

f = number of firms participating in an industry,
S_{ij} = each firm's i market share in the industry j

The US Department of Justice defines an industry as 'highly concentrated' if its HHI is above 1800. An industry with an HHI below 1000 is considered 'unconcentrated'. And in the intermediate range of 1,000–1,800 the industry is defined as 'moderately concentrated'.

96 *The Media Industries and their Markets*

Having determined the concentration measures for a specific industry for the period 1984–2005, we then calculate average concentration trends for the entire information sector, as well as for subsectors such as mass media or telecommunications. The averaging takes into account industry sizes, weighting their concentration figures by their relative size. These numbers, for various years, can then be mapped into time lines. While it would be readily possible to run regressions, the graphic display is actually more instructive.

6.3.2 Concentration of the information sector

Figure 6.5 shows several findings for the overall information sector, covering 100 industries of the mass media, telecom, IT, and Internet subsectors.

1. The average concentration for an industry in the information sector declined in terms of the weighted average HHI for the 100 industries. This weighted average concentration fell from 2,108 in 1984 to 1,631 in 2005. But it showed considerable variation over that period. Before 1984, there was a high level of overall concentration. The weighted average for 1983 was HHI = 3,660, much of it as a result of AT&T's dominance of the telecom market segment, which was reduced following the antitrust divestiture of the company in 1984. Then, between 1984 and 1992, aggregate concentration declined fairly sharply, with new entry

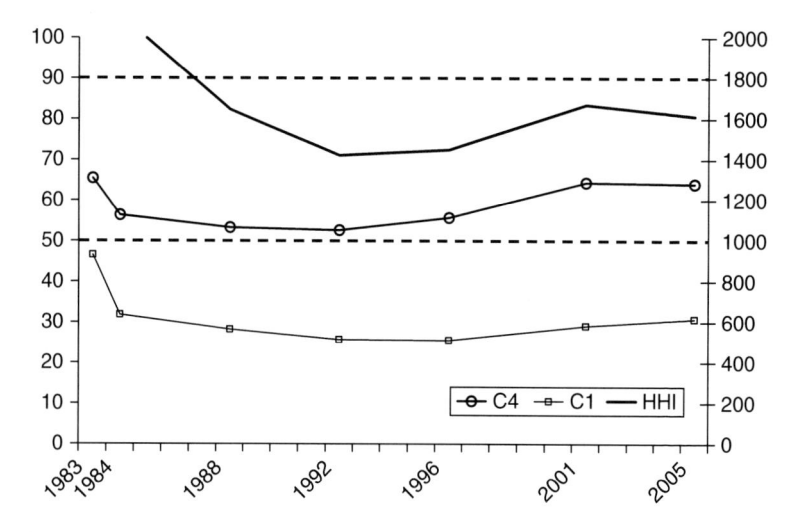

Figure 6.5 Information industry total, 1983–2005

due to lower legal, technological, and economic entry barriers. After 1996, the level of concentration rose pronouncedly when companies aggressively sought to achieve competitive advantage through increasing market share, that is, through scale economies and network effects. After 2001, concentration declined somewhat as there was a stabilisation of industries.

Thus, the average weighted HHI, our primary measure of sectoral concentration, was considerably lower in 2005 than it had been in 1984 (from 2,108 down to 1,613). But it was higher in 2005 than it had been between 1992 and 1996, when it was about 1,400. Soon after 1984, the information sector as a whole moved into the range of concentration defined by the US Justice Department as 'moderately concentrated' and remained there, with zigs and zags. Thus, did concentration rise in recent years? *No*, if the baseline year for comparison is 1984 or earlier. *Yes*, if the baseline year is 1992.

2. The C1 line in Figure 6.5 shows the average market share of the top company in an industry. It, too, exhibits a slight U-shape, although it is on the whole stable at about 30 per cent. In other words, the market share of the top firm tends to be almost one third of an industry.

6.3.3 Concentration of the four subsectors of the information sector

We now proceed to disaggregate the overall concentration measure into submeasures for the weighted averages for each of the four major subsectors of the information sector: mass media, telecommunications, IT, and the Internet (Figure 6.6).

1. The Internet, telecommunications, and IT sectors show a U-shaped trend line. For telecom and IT, it is at quite a high level, around 1,900. For the Internet sector, it is in the intermediate range, around 1,500. In stark contrast, the mass media sector followed a rising S-shaped pattern, steadily increasing the levels of concentration after 1988 – and in particular in the period from 1996 to 2001. However, it remained lower in concentration than the other three sectors, and moderately concentrated by the standards of the US government's Antitrust Merger Guidelines, at an HHI of 1,165.

2. In the case of mass media, the concentration trend is not U-shaped but S-shaped. The average (weighted) HHI concentration of mass media as a whole was fairly flat in the 1980s, having first even declined a bit. It rose after 1993, and slowed after 2001. Whereas the top four firms accounted in 1984 for one-third of an average mass media industry, that share rose to about one half by 2005. Yet the average industry concentration,

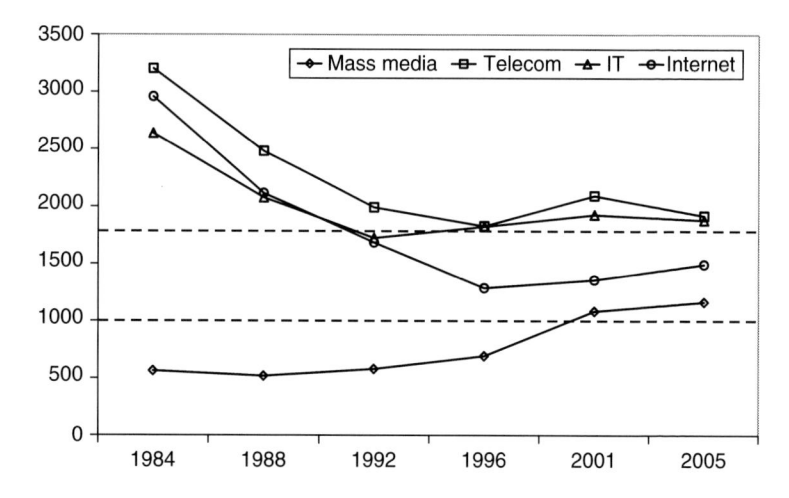

Figure 6.6 Concentration trends by subsectors (HHI)

even after the steady rise subsequent to 1988, is well in the lower end of the range defined by the US Department of Justice as 'moderately concentrated'. The weighted average HHI in 2004 stood at 1,160. But in 1988, it had stood at 520, well inside the 'unconcentrated' range.

3. The level of concentration in the mass media industries has edged steadily closer to the concentration levels prevailing in the rest of the information sector. Whereas in 1984 mass media HHI concentration was only around one quarter (27 per cent) of that of the overall information sector, it was 71 per cent in 2005.

4. The average share of the leading company in a mass media industry rose from about 12 per cent to 23 per cent. Together with the requirement that all shares must add to 100 per cent, the average media industry C1, C4, and HHI describe a typical market structure within a fairly well-defined band. It would be, approximately,

Top firm: 23 per cent
Next three firms, each 10 per cent
Next nine firms, each 5 per cent
Small firms totalling 2 per cent

These firms need not be the same for different media industries, although some of them extend their activities widely (see below).

Thus, in the average mass media industry, a dozen firms control most of what we read, watch, or buy, and four firms account for about one-half.

Even so, in most non-media industries, these numbers would not be considered high enough levels of concentration to lead to the triggering of US governmental antitrust action. Thus, if one seeks a systematic deconcentration of media below the one prevailing in 2005, the general antitrust process is not likely to work. Media would have to be treated in a different fashion.

6.3.4 Concentration of mass media industries

We now proceed to further unbundling. Within the overall mass media sector we can look at the several media subsectors. Figure 6.7 shows the national concentration trends for several categories of media: print, film, broadcasting, multichannel TV, and the Internet.

Figure 6.7 shows that, roughly, the newer and the more electronic and 'digital' a media subsector is, the more highly it seems to be concentrated. Thus, print media are relatively unconcentrated, with its HHI rising only slowly. Film and broadcasting, the next entrants, are more concentrated, in the order of their age. Multichannel TV national concentration is still higher. Internet media initially decline, stabilise during the Internet boom years, and concentrate towards 2005. Within the Internet, broadband, the newest of media, shows high concentration and increases after 1996.

The inference is that as media become more electronic and then more 'digital', they become subject to the more general economic dynamics of the information sector. These include increasing scale

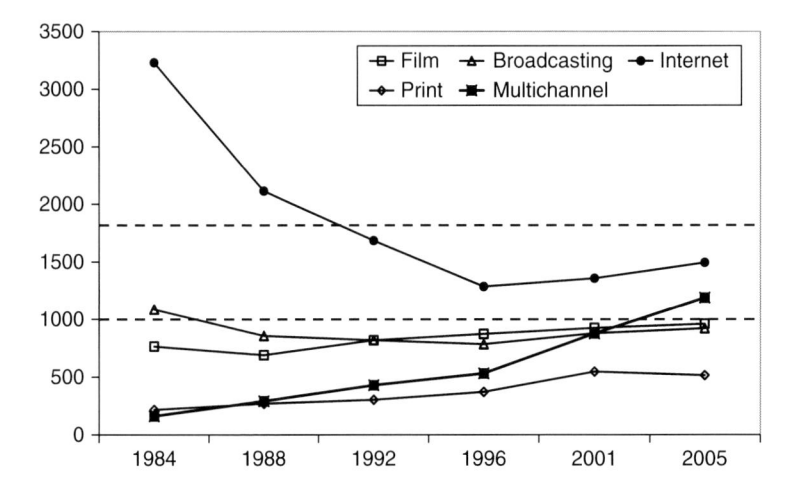

Figure 6.7 Concentration trends of various mass media industries

economies and the lowering of entry barriers, leading to more concentrated industries and to a periodic instability that leads to still further concentration. Print media have lower fixed costs than either film or the Internet. They have higher marginal costs than these media. Hence, the scale economies are lower, and the level of industry concentration is higher. Film is somewhere in between. Broadcasting has very low marginal costs. DBS has high fixed and low marginal costs. Cable also has high fixed/low marginal costs on a per channel/per user basis, and thus it has high scale economies. The ordering of industries by their fixed cost/marginal cost corresponds roughly to the industries' concentration levels.

6.3.5 The Internet

In the debate over media concentration, the openness of the Internet has been a major argument for relaxing controls over traditional media. However, strong economies of scale, network effects, distance-insensitivity, and the complexity of providing advanced service have led to a consolidation for the core of the Internet as well as for many major applications.

The aggregate concentration trend for the Internet industries has also been U-shaped, as shown in Figures 6.6 and 6.7. The trends existed for almost all of its major subindustries. Furthermore, most Internet industries were fairly concentrated in absolute terms, with the aggregate HHI at almost 1,500 in 2005, well above the level of the mass media. After 1996, there was a considerable increase in the levels of concentration.

5. This pours some cold water over the hope that the Internet will solve the media concentration problem. The basic industries of this sector exhibits the same dynamics leading to concentration. If anything, their greater dynamism drives them there faster. And the more advanced platforms for the Internet – broadband and fibre-based ultrabroadband – will strengthen that trend. (However, this sector experiences periodic bursts of innovation and entrepreneurship, however, and it has the potential to erupt again.)

6.3.6 The composition of top companies

1. We rarely found market shares to be in the monopoly range. Table 6.1 shows the entire set of firms which in 2005 held a market share of over 60 percent in a market, in all 100 industries.

For the other industries under investigation, no such single-firm dominance exists. American information and media industries are not monopolies – they are more like oligopolies. The average information sector industry has an HHI of 1,631, a C4 of 64 per cent, and a C1 of 31 per cent, results that correspond numerically to top firms with 31 per cent, another six firms with about 11 per cent each, and a few small players.

6.3.7 Vertical concentration and conglomerates

So far, the majority of this discussion centred on national concentration measures. But many of the problems in mass media concentration are vertical and conglomerate. A purely horizontal concentration measure cannot take account of the growth of firms that are active across several industries, a characteristic of media conglomerates. This is what we find:

1. Diversification. The 50 largest firms of the overall information sector participated, on average, in 7.4 information industries, 2.1 more than in 1984. The largest 25 mass media firms participated, on average, in 4.5 industries, 1.7 more than they had twenty years earlier. And the top five mass media firms participated in 8.4 industries in 2005, whereas it was 4.6 in 1984. This participation had peaked at 9.4 in 2001.

2. Cross-sectoral convergence. We do not find much direct expansion by firms active in one of the three traditional subsectors of the information sector – mass media, telecom, and IT (the fourth being the Internet) – into the other two subsectors. Of the 50 largest firms, none had a presence in all four sectors. Only Microsoft, Sony, AT&T, Verizon, and Time Warner had a presence in three sectors. However, Sony largely left telecom,

Table 6.1 Top company shares (over 60 per cent)

Industry	Dominant firm	Share (%)	Rival
Microcomputer Operating Software	Microsoft	95	Linux (growing)
Mainframe Hardware and Software	IBM	92	Networked small computers (growing)
Cable Music Channels	Viacom	84	No direct rival, but MP3 downloads are growing
CISC Microprocessors	Intel	80	AMD (growing)
MP3 Players	Apple	74	CE industry
Search Engines	Google	51	Yahoo, Microsoft (61 in 2008)

except for mobile handsets as the junior partner in a joint alliance with Ericsson. The old AT&T first entered and then left computers and cable TV. The new AT&T and Verizon sought a role in TV distribution. Time Warner's role in IT was minor; its broadband and voice-over telephony grew substantially, but were also spun off in 2009. The exception to the absence of much cross-sectoral convergence has been the Internet, which drew many of the largest information firms from all sectors. It seems the ground on which other firms from the more traditional sectors meet, test, and contest.

3. The combined share of the top 50 firms in the overall information sector did not increase, but declined from 68 per cent to 58 per cent. The average top-50 information sector firm in 1984 had 1.4 per cent of the overall information market. Almost 20 years and countless mergers later, the average top 50 firms had a *lower* share – 1.1 per cent in 2005.

4. More telling is the trend line of the top 10 companies (see Figure 6.8). This shows a substantial *decrease*, from 48 per cent to 27 per cent, in the aggregate share of the biggest ten companies until 1996, when it started to fluctuate at a level of around 30 per cent. But those companies ranked in the positions 11–50 show the opposite trend. Thus, the relative market share of the large firms became progressively more symmetric during this period. The smaller of the large firms increased their shares, whereas the largest firms saw their shares reduced.

5. For the top mass media firms, trends were, again, quite different. The numbers show a steady upward trend in the overall sectoral share held by the top firms. Together the top five mass media firms accounted for about 13.4 per cent of the overall mass media sector in 1984. By 2005, their share had doubled to 26.2 per cent. The increase was largest for the top five firms, which each gained, on average, a 2.5 per cent share for a total of 5.2 per cent since 1984 (Figure 6.8).

Figure 6.8 shows a continuous and pronounced upward trend of the top five firms between 1988 and 2004. Even so, their aggregate share, at 26.2 per cent of the overall mass media sector, was much lower than that prevailing in the telecom and IT sectors, where the top five companies held in 2005 an aggregate share of 61.2 per cent and 43.0 per cent, respectively.

6. If we look solely at the electronic mass media, the top five firms' share was 42 per cent, again double that of 1984 (21.6 per cent).

7. For the combined electronic video mass media market (TV and cable networks, TV stations, DBS, cable MSOs – the part of the mass media most likely to be under the regulatory supervision of the FCC) – the

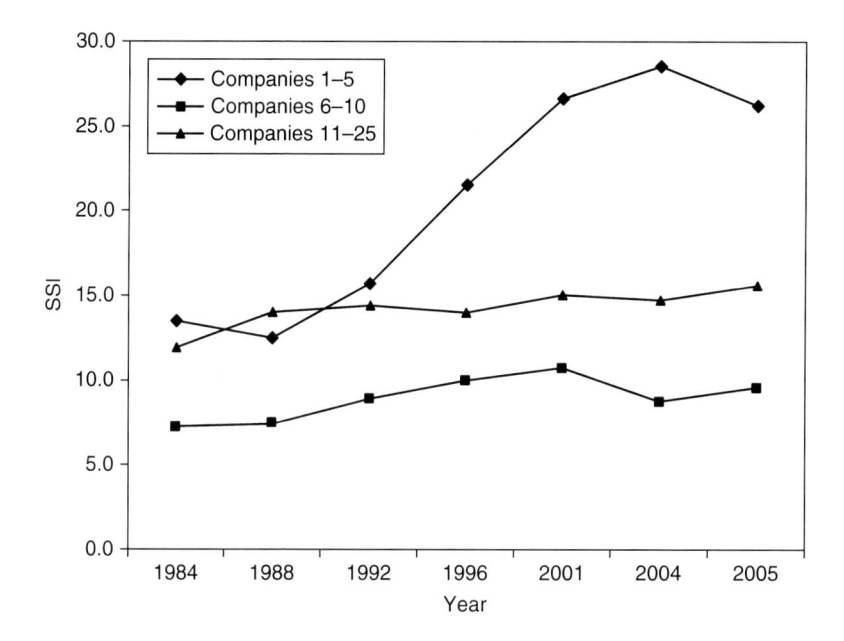

Figure 6.8 Total share for companies ranked 1–5, 6–10, and 11–25 in the mass media sector (1984–2005)

market share of the top five firms declined slightly to 18.1 per cent in 1992, before rising markedly, to 40.3 per cent in 2001 and 42 per cent in 2005.

8. For the combined telecom services market, the share of the top four firms dropped from 66 per cent in 1984 to 52 per cent in 1992 and 1996, before rising again to 88 per cent by 2005.

To conclude: in the overall information sector, vertical integration has increased in terms of participation but has declined in terms of overall share. It has increased by both measures for the mass media sector.

6.3.8 Ownership

Of the largest 30 American individual fortunes in 2005, half originated in the information sector. This sector shows some of the gold rush aspects of railroads in the nineteenth century. A substantial part of the world's top wealth holders earned their wealth in the media, information, and communications fields.

1. But this wealth does not mean that ownership is in the hands of those billionaires. If anything, the opposite has been the case. The ownership by 'insiders' – that is, by managers, board members, or shareholders

with more than 5 per cent – declined significantly for most of the largest information sector firms. Even for mass media firms, where it is higher than in the rest of the information sector, it fell from 34.6 per cent to 19.6 per cent between 1988 and 2005. Technology and new media companies became stock market favourites, and inside ownership decreased as founders cashed out. For the combined IT/Telecom sectors it rose from 4.8 to 6.4 per cent, much lower than for mass media.

2. Similarly, within the individual top 50 firms, there was a decline in the ownership concentration of the major five shareholders. The same holds in general for the top mass media firms. Ownership became more fragmented among more shareholders, often without a dominant shareholder.

3. One major change has been the greatly increased ownership by large institutional investors in the information sector. Decades ago, media ownership was primarily in the hands of a small group of individuals and families. But by the late twentieth century, new technology and new media had created a massive need for capital, and this required many sources and hence a widespread ownership. This trend has been most evident in the computer and high-technology industries, where relatively young companies need to rely upon equity capital – initially by way of venture capital investment – to finance their future growth. A high degree of institutional ownership – whether public or private equity – is an inevitable consequence of burgeoning technology and new media. Institutional investors are attracted to high-technology stocks because of their significant growth potential.

Information sector companies became an attractive investment vehicle for the ever-growing mutual and pension funds. Mutual funds' ownership of top information sector firms almost quintupled between 1984 and 2004, from 5.5 per cent to 24.5 per cent. Institutional ownership rose from 39.6 per cent in 1984 to 57.2 per cent in 2005 for the mass media sector and from 49.0 per cent to 61.5 per cent for the IT and telecom sector. Most of this increase occurred after 1990. The largest firms in the mass media had the highest share of institutional investment during the same period: from 52.6 per cent in 1984 to 65.3 per cent in 2004.

4. However, some major mass media companies were reluctant to relinquish owner-family control. The print media industries, given the prevalence of family control, have generally received less institutional investment than technology companies.

5. Who then owns the media? In 2005 the funds with the most significant equity positions in the major media companies were State

Street Global Advisors ($68 billion), Barclays ($57 billion), Capital Research & Management ($47 billion), Fidelity Management & Research ($41 billion), Vanguard Group ($30 billion) and Wellington Management ($29 billion). The educators' pension funds, such as TIAA/CREF, had $19 billion invested in the media and information sector. Many of these institutional investors invest significant amounts in several of the largest information sector firms. Moreover, they are holding onto their shares for longer periods than in the past, thus establishing more of a stake in company management. They often also hold sizable chunks of media companies' debt in the form of long-term corporate bonds and short-term commercial paper.

6. However, even though the institutional owners hold (at most) only a few percent of any single company, they often have stakes in a large number of different firms. Just 14 large institutional investors hold 21.2 per cent of the average top 25 mass media firms and hold 26.0 per cent of IT and telecom companies. This is a remarkable share. In addition, they set the tone for the many smaller funds and can trigger market changes for the major funds. If they acted in concert they could exercise industry-wide power. But there is, so far, little evidence for such coordinated activity, especially for activity aimed directly at content.

Thus, the claim that convergence in the information industries has resulted in a small group of media moguls is not an accurate one. A better description is one of many institutions owning narrow slices of a big pie. Among them, a dozen or so set the tone and have the highest stakes across virtually all media firms. Collectively, they let media managers run their businesses in a micro-sense but in a macro-sense they put performance pressure on them through their 'buy-and-sell' decisions. However, such pressure arises from the existence of private media firms in a profit-oriented market economy rather than from concentrated ownership. Indeed, strong owners with substantial ownership control who run a media company have been the most problematic to many critics – owners such as Rupert Murdoch or Silvio Berlusconi.

6.4 Conclusions

We find that throughout the decade of the 1990s the American media sector has grown in concentration. We conclude that the economic and technological dynamics at work for media are increasingly the same as those affecting the information sector in general, and that this leads to an upward concentration trend for media that converges with that of the information sector. The information sector's concentration level is fluctuating, but in a trendline to a higher level. And the dynamics of digital convergence lead the mass media industries to assume the market structure characteristics of the rest of the information sector.

This situation leads to concentration levels that might be economically efficient but are not usually favoured from a societal perspective. But it will be quite difficult for any set of policies to contain the fundamental economic and technological forces that are at play here, even if one ignores the political dimensions. It is also clear that any policy to enhance a content or ownership diversity that is not provided for in an open media market needs to be supported by real resources – money, spectrum, and so on – beyond structural and access policies. Diversity is valuable, and it cannot be achieved on the cheap.

This conclusion is part media-pessimist – concentration is increasing and will continue to do so. It is part media-optimist – concentration is lower than often feared, and lowered entry barriers lead to periodic deconcentration. But it is, mostly, media-realistic – the structure of media are being transformed by broad forces, and concentration is their symptom, not cause.

Are the American findings specific to one country, or are they symptomatic for media trends around the world? This is an important question for future research.[5]

Acknowledgements

The author wishes to thank the editors, Patrick-Yves Badillo and Jean-Baptiste Lesourd, for encouraging this work, and Joost van Dreunen for his assistance in the data research. A more complete version of this research is Eli Noam, *Media Ownership and Concentration in America* (Oxford and New York, 2009).

Notes

1. Eli M. Noam is a Professor, Columbia University Business School, Columbia University, New York, and Director of the University's Columbia Institute for Tele-Information (CITI).
2. For a data-oriented analysis, see Compaine and Gomery (2000).
3. Would the increased scale economies lead to a greater dominance of the top firm? More likely is that they will help a small group of firms that are large enough to benefit from the scale.
4. Amplitude will depend on the change in entry barriers; frequency on the rate of change.

5. An international project on this question is in progress, led by Koichiro Hayashi and Kiyoshi Nakamura in Japan; Patrick-Yves Badillo, Dominique Bourgeois and Jean-Baptiste Lesourd in France; and Eli Noam and Joost Van Druenen in the United States.

References

Bagdikian, B. 1983, 1987, 1990, 1992, 1997. *The Media Monopoly.* Boston, MA: Beacon.

Bagdikian, B. 2004. *The New Media Monopoly*, Boston, MA: Beacon.

Compaine, B., and Gomery, D. 2000. *Who Owns the Media?: Competition and Concentration in the Mass Media Industry*, 3rd edn, Mahwah, NJ: Lawrence Erlbaum Associates, Inc.

Noam, E.M. 2009. *Media Ownership and Concentration in America*, Oxford and New York: Oxford University Press.

Thierer, A.D. 2005. *Media Myths: Making Sense of the Debate Over Media Ownership.* Washington, DC: The Progress & Freedom Foundation.

7
Measuring Media Concentration for the Purposes of Ensuring Pluralism and Diversity

Petros Iosifidis[1]

7.1 Introduction

The subject of this chapter is the exploration and analysis of the different methodologies for measuring media concentration. The appropriate measure depends on the objective of the measurement which might be on the one hand the examination of economic power, or on the other an assessment of whether market structure might restrict diversity in the media industry. Media academics frequently borrow measures that have been developed by economists. Regarding the examination of economic power, economists have used companies' market share, shares of assets, value-added, sales, advertising revenue or even the number of employees in forming an opinion of their weight in the economy. These measures are more appropriate for examining industrial structure and the manufacturing sector. In the media, because of their nature and their significant role in culture, society and politics measures examining the media firms' economic power alone seem to be inadequate. The particular social significance attached to the media's role in disseminating information requires an investigation of whether a concentrated media market restricts the free flow of information.

To overcome this limitation of economic-based measures media analysts have proposed a number of media concentration measures which take into account their importance to the public. The view that emerged in the 1990s from the debate on media concentration at both European (initiated by the EU 1992 Green Paper *Pluralism and Media Concentration in the Internal Market* – CEC, 1992) and national (Arthur Andersen's 1994 study *UK Media Concentration* – Shew, 1994) levels, is that it is possible to measure the 'influence' exerted by the media by applying audience-based criteria. It has been suggested that while financial units are close to the traditional systems of concentration measurement which permit the assessment of media market concentration or even the existence of a dominant position (the concentration of resources), audience-based methods are coherent with the cultural/political standpoint and can be held to be most effective for the measurement of pluralism and influence in the marketplace for ideas. Nevertheless, influence over the audience cannot be assessed by using audience-based criteria, whether that is readership, audience reach, viewing or listenership share, and so on. *Audience exposure* to mass media is certainly not the same as *influence over the audience*. What end-user methods measure is market power and not 'influence' which is notoriously hard to establish.

This chapter examines the problems associated with both types of concentration measures and assesses their appropriateness in the broad context of media concentration's impact on pluralism and diversity. It starts by providing a background on the concentration of media ownership and then moves on to explore the methodologies for measuring media market concentration, as well as the debate relating to the assessment of shares in the political and cultural market. It is argued that both financial and audience-based units apply, since economic power and diversity (especially in terms of the range of material on offer) are closely linked.

7.2 Background

The concentration of media ownership is a phenomenon of increasing importance in Europe and beyond. At a time when the media are becoming major actors in world businesses, and cable, satellite and the digital revolution are increasingly providing the conditions for a global media market questions are raised about the possible effects of media concentration on the traditional role of broadcasting and the press in democratic societies. Although the media concentration phenomenon is not a new one – for instance, Charles Havas' and Reuters news agencies dominated the international flow of information from the second half of the nineteenth century (Tunstall and Palmer, 1991) and the phonographic and cinematographic industries have experienced the phenomenon of oligopolistic competition from the beginning of the twentieth century – nevertheless concentration of control over mass media has intensified recently in both the USA and Europe (see Bagdikian, 2004) as a result of technology (convergence) and regulation relaxation. Concentration therefore has been both a market reality and a public concern.

7.2.1 Concentration as market reality

In the USA in 2005 the ten largest TV station group owners controlled 300 stations – up from a figure of 104 stations in 1995. Group owners can also now purchase TV stations with a maximum service area cap of 39 per cent, up from the previous limit of 35 per cent (the reader should be reminded that the limit was just 25 per cent in 1985). Further, with rules relaxed on cable ownership 90 per cent of the top 50 cable companies are owned by the same parent companies that own broadcast networks. Similar deregulatory trends are evident in Europe, though different rules are in force in different countries. Of course, EU media firms are smaller than those in the USA in terms of market capitalisation and sales, and mergers and acquisitions are to a reduced scale compared with those in the USA. Most EU firms function in one national market, with the notable exception of the large German multinational company Bertelsmann and Vivendi Universal (now General Electric-owned NBC Universal). However, an analysis of some past competition decisions in the media sector reveals that the EC has become sympathetic to the formation of large European corporations in order to enable them to expand on a global basis (Iosifidis, 2005).

This can also be viewed as a lever to promote market liberalisation that would nurture European champions. After all the predominantly pro-liberal and pro-competition provisions of the European Treaties reflect what Van Cuilenburg and McQuail (2003) have dubbed as a 'new paradigm' of media policy prioritising economic goals over social and political welfare. Meanwhile, in the broader context of restructuring of the European audiovisual scene merger cases have become more complex and entail increased competition concerns, resembling the 1990s merger boom in the USA when the major TV networks were acquired by industrial interests. The complexity of mergers in both sides of the Atlantic is a result of a shift in the nature of industry concentration, from one based on horizontal mergers to those involving vertical integration, as operators sought out alliances which would enable them to acquire the broad set of skills needed to address new markets (Iosifidis, 2005).

7.2.2 Concentration as public concern

Excessive media concentration can endanger media pluralism (the presence of a number of different and independent voices) and also diversity in the media (different political opinions and representations of culture within the media). Therefore a pluralistic, competitive media system is a prerequisite for media diversity. Although the terms pluralism and diversity are used interchangeably in this chapter it is worth going through some definitions of the concepts to establish why the lack of these ideals in a highly concentrated media market might be an issue of public concern. A broad definition of media diversity has been provided by Hoffmann-Riem (1987) who, referring to the broadcasting scene a couple of decades ago, distinguished four dimensions of diversity. For him there must be *diversity of formats and issues,* meaning that all the various fields and topics – entertainment, information, education and culture – have to be taken into account. Secondly, this should be complemented by a *diversity or plurality of contents.* This means that programmes should provide comprehensive and factual coverage of the different opinions expressed in a society. Thirdly, *person and group diversity* must exist. Programmes have to cater for the interests of all parts of the community. The main point here is access, but also representation. Finally, Hoffmann-Riem pointed out that broadcasters should include local, regional, national and supranational content. To sum up, a programme has to ensure that *issue, content, person* and *geographical diversity* is provided.

A similar identification of the dimensions of diversity has been provided by McQuail (1992, pp. 144–5) who argued that the media can contribute to diversity, firstly by *reflecting* differences in society, secondly by giving *access* to different points of view, and thirdly by offering a wide range of *choice*. Diversity as reflection means that pluralistic mass media are expected to represent or reflect the prevailing differences of culture, opinion and social conditions of the population. Diversity as access refers to the channels through which the separate 'voices', groups and interests which make up the society can speak to the wider society, and also express and keep alive their own cultural identity. McQuail mentioned the most essential conditions for effective access, namely the freedom to speak out, any effective opportunity to speak (a prerequisite is the existence of many and different channels) and autonomy or adequate self-control over media access opportunities. Finally, diversity as more channels and choice for the audience represents a great deal of variety or range of products or services available to consumers, thereby giving them greater freedom.

In order to assess diversity in relation to media market structures and media concentrations in more particular one also needs to distinguish between *external* and *internal* diversity. The former, according to McQuail (1992, pp. 145–7), refers to media structure because it is related to the idea of access. It relates to the degree of variation between separate media sources in a given sector, according to dimensions such as politics, religion, social class, and so on. In a given society, there are many separate and autonomous media channels, each having a high degree of homogeneity of content, expressing a particular point of view, and catering only for its own 'followers'. The latter, McQuail adds, refers to the media content and connects with the idea of representation or reflection mentioned above. It relates to the condition where a wide range of social, political and cultural values, opinions, information and interests find expression within one media organisation, which usually aims to reach a large and heterogeneous audience. A particular channel might be assessed according to the degree of attention given to alternative positions on topics such as politics, ethnicity and language and so on.

More recently and with regard to simplifying the complex issue of pluralism and diversity and putting the results of the research into operation, the Independent Study on Indicators for Media Pluralism in the Member States – Towards a Risk-Based Approach (2009)[2] split the concept of pluralism into three normative dimensions – political, cultural, and demographic pluralism – as well as three operational dimensions – pluralism of media ownership/control, pluralism of media types, and genres. It is clearly mentioned in the study that the main threat to the pluralism of media ownership/control is represented by a high concentration of ownership with media which can have a direct impact on editorial independence, create bottlenecks at the distribution level, and lead to further interoperable problems. This affects pluralism from the point of view not only of supply but also of distribution and, in particular, accessibility (p. 75). The main threats to the pluralism of media types include:

- A lack of sufficient market resources to support the range of media, which causes a lack of/underrepresentation of/dominance of media types (p. 75).
- Threats to media genres and functions include lack of/underrepresentation of/dominance of some functions, or genres are missing (p. 76).
- Threats to the political pluralism dimension are the unilateral influence of media by one political grouping, an insufficient representation of certain political/ideological groups or minorities with a political interest in society (p. 77).
- Threats to the cultural pluralism dimension include the insufficient representation of certain cultural, religious, linguistic and ethnic groups in society, and a threat to national cultural identity (p. 77).
- Finally, threats to the geographical pluralism dimension are the lack or underrepresentation of various national geographical areas and/or local communities (p. 79).

To sum up, this study, which forms part of the European Commission's three-step approach for advancing the debate on media pluralism within the EU, is a prototype for a *European Media Pluralism Monitor* – a risk-based, holistic, user-friendly and evolving monitoring tool that includes indicators of a legal, economic and socio-demographic nature. These indicators relate to various risk domains, including media ownership and/or control (the very subject of this chapter), media types and genres, political, cultural and demographic pluralism. The study makes it clear that while it urges the application of the same analytical framework in all Member States to ensure comparability of results obtained, it is not a call for the harmonisation of policies in this area. As in previous relevant EU documents and Treaties (see for example CEC, 1992; EU, 2007) it is repeated in this study that the sensitive matter of how to protect media pluralism is ultimately left to the discretion of Member States (p. viii). Paradoxically, even though the EU has substantially influenced market developments, principally on the basis of competition rules, where it enjoys direct powers, it nevertheless has no specific competence in cultural matters such as pluralism and broadcasting. By commissioning these studies, however, the EU has come to explicitly recognise the importance of socio-cultural policy objectives, citizen's rights and pluralism and diversity. This is a welcome development, although clearly the EU's substantive policy output remains centered on economic and competition considerations.

7.3 Methodologies of measuring media market concentration

Surprisingly, there is little real research, academic review or agreed measurements on concentration (and diversity) and no universal measuring methodologies have been developed. The purpose of this chapter is therefore to contribute to this discussion by going through the pros and cons of the different methodologies that have been adopted to date that would enable the development of a satisfactory universal methodology for measuring market power, concentration and pluralism/diversity. But before exploring the various existing methodologies, it is worth noting that in media and communications policy there has always been a conflict between economic and cultural goals and it has been proved difficult to reconcile economic ideals (for example, the promotion of fair and open competition, and the prevention of the formation of dominant positions) with cultural values (such as media pluralism and cultural diversity). This value conflict in media and communications policy – the need to cater simultaneously for economic and non-economic goals – also helps to explain differences between traditional media policies based on normative ideals and those recent policy reforms which seek sound empirical proof. As Just (2009) informs us, the most recent such approaches are the Diversity Index (DI) in the USA (2003), the public interest or plurality test in the UK (2003), the Integrated Communications Market (SIC) in Italy (2004), and a new approach to weighting the influence of various media by the German regulator KEK (2006). The task of developing a robust methodological approach which could result in a concentration measure equally catering for competition and pluralistic issues is further complicated by commercial and technological change and especially media convergence which has blurred the boundaries between different communication sectors. Responding to this convergence trend companies have expanded their activities into various sectors, thereby making it even more difficult for regulators to develop an effective tool that could capture economic and political/cultural power.

As mentioned above, the appropriate measure depends on the *objective* of the measurement – in other words, one has to clarify the *purpose* of the measurement: is it the examination of *economic power* or rather an assessment of whether market structure restricts *diversity* in the media industry? Although there are no universal measuring methodologies it appears that the following four methods (and in particular the first three) are frequently called upon when the objective is the assessment of economic power.

7.3.1 Concentration ratios (CRs)

These compare the *revenues* of the top four or eight firms to the total revenues of the industry in which they operate. Put simply, if the revenues of the top four are higher than 50 per cent or the revenues of the top eight higher than 75 per cent of total revenues then the market is classified as being characterised by high concentration. Although the CR4 and CR8 concentration ratios have been used to measure concentration within media industries (Owen, Beebe and Manning, 1974; Picard, 1988), they can also apply to cross-media ownership, that is, to measure concentration levels across industries (Albarran and Dimmick, 1996).

7.3.2 Herfindahl–Hirschman Index (HHI)

Since the 1980s the HHI has been used regularly by the US antitrust division of the Department of Justice. It is basically a way of placing concentration on a continuum from 0 to 10,000, the latter representing a monopoly. The index is determined by summing the squared value of the market shares of all of the firms in a market. But at what point is the market considered to be concentrated? Stigler (1983), one of the supporters of using the HHI for concentration measurement purposes, argued that one can roughly identify markets with HHI > 1,500 as tight oligopolies and those with HHI < 1,000 as loose oligopolies. If the index falls well below 1,000 then the market is un-concentrated and when it falls above 1,800 then the market is highly concentrated. The index is more definite than CRs, but it has been criticised for being a very simplistic and 'pure' number, or that it can be tedious in a multiple company market in that each firm's revenue needs to be accounted for and added together in order to arrive at the total market revenue (Albarran and Mierzejewska, 2004). Further, and as was discussed by Noam (2004), while the HHI is a pretty good litmus test for market power, it is not an appropriate measure for media as it does not make any allowance for pluralism. It appears that the antitrust HHI only works effectively in the analysis of media when it is applied to proposed industrial alliances such as mergers and acquisitions.

7.3.3 Lorenz Curve

Another method to measure concentration is the Lorenz Curve, which assumes each player of a market has a theoretically equal share of the market and then graphs out the actual share compared to the theoretical model (see Albarran, 2002; Albarran and Mierzejewska, 2004). The curve though, similarly to HHI, is more challenging to use in a multi-company market.

7.3.4 Diversity Index (DI)

The DI has been introduced by the Federal Communications Commission as an indication of a risk to pluralism in local markets because it counts each media outlet as a 'voice'. It involves a weighting process which assigns grades to media based on audience use of various media within a local market. However, the DI – as well as several alternative means of assessing concentration and pluralism like the Noam Index (Noam, 2004) and a suggestion by Hill (2006) – has been proved highly controversial and therefore is not widely accepted.

7.4 Concentration and free flow

The above measures are more appropriate for both the industrial structure and the manufacturing sector. In the media, because of their nature and the significant role they play in culture, society and politics measures that examine the media firms' economic power alone appear to be inadequate. The special social significance attached to the media's role in disseminating information requires an investigation of whether or not a concentrated media market restricts the free flow of information. As Karstens (2008) argues, 'measuring pluralism by economy-based criteria runs the risk of falling short of what is desirable from the perspective of political culture, art and science, minority opinions, and cultural identity'. And he continues 'paying only lip service to these values and assuming that free competition will take care of them anyway may not do justice to Europe's cultural tradition and, indeed, competitive advantage'.

To overcome this limitation of economic-based measures a number of media analysts have proposed a number of media concentration measures which take into account their importance to the public. The view that has emerged from the past debate on media concentration in Europe (initiated by the EU 1992 Green Paper) is that it is possible to measure the *'influence'* exerted by the media by applying *audience-based criteria*. This approach has now been abandoned both because it has been proved difficult to design an audience-based methodology on a Europe-wide scale that would accurately calculate shares across sectors and construct weightings for each sector based on their relative influence or marker power, and because of differences of opinions within the European Commission and between different European bodies (see Iosifidis, 1997; Doyle, 2002).

Likewise in the UK, the May 1995 Green Paper on Media Ownership attempted to determine the thresholds of ownership in terms of the *'total share of voice'* for markets beyond which acquisitions would have to be referred to the media regulator (UK, 1995). The Green Paper's approach was derived largely from a submission by the British Media Industry Group (BMIG, 1994) which advocated using consumer usage of media (newspaper circulation, TV/radio ratings) to calculate the total share of voice of any proprietor. Where ownership of a media outlet was shared between firms of proprietors the share of voice would be allotted in proportion to the percentage of ownership. But in mid-December 1995 the UK government published its Broadcasting Bill which did not contain any such proposals. The then National Heritage Secretary conceded that there was little agreement on the share of voice concept.

However, the audience-share model has now been used in Germany for more than a decade in order to determine concentration levels in the national television market – in 2008 a broadcaster could own an unlimited number of TV services provided s/he did not achieve a dominant position in the cultural and political market (that is, a more than 30 per cent audience share). In the course of its review of the proposed merger between ProSiebenSAT.1 Media AG and Alex Springer Media AG, the German regulator responsible for ensuring media diversity (Commission on Media Concentration – KEK) developed a new weighting approach on diversity of opinions that considers potential influences of different media. According to Just (2009), this weighting approach has provoked criticism on manageability and validity grounds, alongside issues relating to KEK's competence to intervene in broadcasting issues at a national level, given that Germany is a federal state but broadcasting issues are dealt with at a *Laender* (state) level.

In contrast, in the UK the Communications Act 2003 introduced a new approach to determine media diversity, the so-called 'public interest test' or 'plurality test', which applies to major players who wish to increase their interests in other areas of media, by buying newspapers, radio or television assets. The test examines whether such a deal would damage the plurality of media voices and owners. Office of Communications (Ofcom), the new super-regulator, makes an initial assessment and if concerns arise it passes the case to the Competition Commission or Office of Fair Trading for an in-depth examination. However, the only media merger that was scrutinised on public interest grounds concerned satellite operator BSkyB's acquisition of 17.9 per cent of ITN shares in November 2006. In January 2008 the acquisition was allowed as the Competition Commission concluded that the resulting company is not expected to operate against the public interest.

Another recent attempt to define the total media market share (including radio, TV, cinema, the press, advertising and the Internet, but excluding telecommunications) was the 'sistema integrato delle comunicazioni' (Integrated System of Communication – SIC) in Italy. With this schema Italy entered the line of countries seeking to depart from commonly pursued market definitions in media and communications and instead to begin to consider the media market in its entirety. SIC's market definition is too broad, thus making it unlikely that a firm will have a dominant position under this schema. But as Just (2009) argues, this newly introduced communication policy verifies the trend (noticeable on both sides of the Atlantic) towards reduced ownership regulation and the promotion of competition in the digitally converged communications market.

7.5 Measuring shares in the political and cultural market: an assessment

Large companies' sales and turnover may be the best indicator of their economic power and reveal their ability to gain market advantages compared to the rest. In other words, very powerful firms can influence economic conduct, performance and pricing behaviours and have an impact on barriers to entry and limitation of output. Therefore, when the purpose is the traditional examination of market power then a high revenue company share may provide a useful guide. When it comes to the media, however, the concern is not only over the impact of concentration on economic aspects but also the question of the social performance of the market (pluralism and diversity). Are measures tailored to measure economic concentration good enough to capture concentration levels in the political and cultural market, the so-called 'marketplace for ideas'?

A follow-up question can be put: there is certainly a broad consensus in democratic societies that pluralism and diversity are important, but is there a practical or legal way to officially define and measure the vigour of a marketplace for ideas? It has been argued that it is possible to identify a sort of relevant 'market for ideas', which does not coincide with the economic definition of the relevant market; and that de facto restrictions of pluralism and diversity are the results of an abuse of power in such a market (abuse of political and cultural power). There are three problems associated with such an approach. Firstly, there are substantial difficulties in defining a suitable notion of relevant market in the political and cultural sense. As the relevant product tends to extend across different media, the cultural/political notion of the relevant market may be significantly broader than the economic one. The problem is bound to be exacerbated as multimedia conglomerates expand their activities further, and the ownership of complex transnational media chains becomes widespread. To illustrate, how does one assess the effective combined share of, say, News International in the broader market for information, culture and political opinion, comprising newspapers, TV outlets and Internet portals in several countries? Secondly, the exact nature of the potential abuse is not clear and explicable and cannot be specified in the same way as abuses of economic market may be specified. What then counts as an abuse of power in the political/cultural market? Beyond the general assumption that all media exercise some form of political and cultural influence on the public, there have emerged no satisfactory criteria so far for the definition of a broad political and cultural market in which spheres of influence by a single controller could be assessed.

The most serious reservation concerning this approach, however, relates to the selection of the criteria for measuring diversity in the marketplace for ideas. It has been suggested that while financial units are close to the traditional systems of concentration measurement which permit an assessment of media market concentration, audience-based methods are coherent with the cultural/political standpoint and can be held to be most effective for the measurement of pluralism and influence in the marketplace for ideas. Nevertheless, influence over the audience cannot be assessed through the use of audience-based criteria, whether that be readership, audience reach, viewing or listenership share, or some other measure. Audience exposure to mass media is certainly not the same as influence over the audience. In the end, these end-user measures are nothing but refinements of measurements of market power. They measure market power, albeit in a more sophisticated manner. They are a form of market share measurement, which is a classic economic measure. Audience-based units are the equivalent of, say, measuring sales, that is, market share, which is a classic economic measure of market power.

7.6 Economic power and diversity: a symbiotic relationship

In any case, political/cultural diversity and economic power are closely linked. It might be worth at this point spelling out the arguments about the relationship between economic power and the range of material on offer. There is a clear relationship between economic measures of media power and influence/pluralism because economic power determines the control over choices offered. In fact, in terms of the public interest and debates about regulation and concentration of media ownership, there are two widespread arguments. On the one hand, there is the argument saying that a highly concentrated market structure in the media sector is of concern not only for the possibility that it may lead to abuses of economic market power, but also for the potential effects on pluralism. A large media player who controls a substantial portion of at least one media sector (for example, daily press, TV or the Internet) has the potential for forcing his/her views across a range of products (political/cultural bias), and thus for restricting the choice of products available to the public in political and cultural terms. In this sense, a competition policy decision aimed at curbing an abuse of economic market power (for example, excessive pricing or the creation of barriers to entry) may also increase pluralism, at least in the sense of reducing bias.

On the other hand, there is the argument that states that increase competition may produce a lower level of pluralism in the market. Increasing the number of firms in an industry does not necessarily imply greater diversity in the quality and variety of products on offer – especially where the level of price competition is weak. If firms compete on price, product differentiation provides a device for softening the intensity of competition: in a simplified world with only two companies, they will have an incentive to locate themselves as far as possible from each other on the product line (that is, to offer as diverse a product as possible in terms of both variety and quality). Proximity of location would mean that prices are gradually eroded as the companies compete for each other's business. However, if there is no explicit interaction in the firms' pricing decisions, the opposite result obtains: the firms will locate as close as possible to one another, as the 'market share effect' (the incentive to be where the demand is, or to increase one's market share given the market structure) prevails over the 'strategic effect'(the interdependence of the two firms' pricing decisions). Thus the incentive to differentiate products is weaker when companies are able to operate in the near-absence of price competition. The tendency to converge on tried-and-tested formulae poses a potential danger to welfare in terms of the variety of products offered by the market. Hotelling (1929, p. 41), who provided the original discussion of this effect, talked of 'an undue tendency for competitors to imitate each other'. Therefore, a more fragmented industry structure in the media sector may not necessarily deliver the socially desirable level of product differentiation because it may be more profitable for the companies to locate 'where demand is' (stick to the middle ground in order to catch the widest audience).

A further important question relates to the possibility that too much competition might display a bias in favour of certain types of products and neglect others. The particular bundle of commodities that are actually produced in the media market (the type of programmes/titles available) might be suboptimal from a social welfare point of view. When demand for products in a particular category is generally inelastic, the products which are being actually offered may end up being positioned too close to each other (suboptimal product diversity); and those products for which the elasticity is comparatively lower may not be produced at all. The implication could be that some segments of tastes and preferences might not be catered for in any form, even in the presence of a large number of different media products (Dixit and Stiglitz, 1977). So, strictly from the point of view of pluralism, there might be no automatic advantage to be gained from a more diverse media structure.

On the other hand, so the argument runs, a very concentrated industry structure might lead to great diversity, if the dominant firm(s) seeks to prevent entry in the market by filling all gaps in product space.

7.7 'Best' criterion: an illusion?

Having provided, to some extent, an argument that economic power affects the range of material on offer, and having spelled out the arguments as to whether concentration or a fragmented industry can deliver best the desired diversity, we now turn to the question of which criterion is 'best' for measuring concentration levels for the purposes of media pluralism. The close relationship between economic power and pluralism/diversity indicates that criteria that are being used for the measurement of market power can also be used, at least in principle, for the measurement of media influence and vice versa. Financial criteria, for instance, a long-established method for measuring market power, could also be adopted for measuring 'influence' (audience exposure to the mass media); and audience- figures, supposed to be more efficient for measuring diversity in the marketplace for ideas, could also be a measure of economic power, especially as they are sold to advertisers.

The two different sets of methods illustrated above (audience- and revenue-based) are said to correspond to two levels of measurement of concentration in the information market: the political/cultural or pluralism and the economic or concentration of resources. It has been put forth that revenue-based methods are close to the traditional systems of concentration measurement which permit the assessment of the existence of a dominant position (concentration of resources), whereas audience-based methods are coherent with the cultural/political standpoint and can be held to be most effective for measurement of pluralism. However, as a result of the close relationship between economic power and pluralism, audience figures could also measure market power. In fact, audience-based measures are a form of market share measurement, which is a classic economic measurement. 'Audience' is the equivalent of measuring sales (that is, market share), which is a classic economic measure of power. Therefore, the distinction between economic measures and cultural/political measures is irrelevant. Both sets of media market measurement assess market power. In the absence of a direct way of establishing 'impact', crude measures based on market power (criteria about market structure) are used instead. And what the audience- and revenue-based methods are doing is in fact simply that – they are evaluating market power.

The conclusion is that one should not be forced to choose between economic-based measures (measures of market power) and measures of pluralism/diversity, but could incorporate both. In the absence of a direct measure of influence, this chapter argues that it is necessary to develop an approach combining the various sets of methods to establish impact. The propositions include a combined test involving advertising and/or subscription revenues and audience shares, the setting of a percentage of market share in terms of revenue/expenditure as a threshold for the further examination of the position, and an approach combining more measures such as numerical criteria, revenue share, audience share and audience time spent consuming a medium. What all these suggestions have in common is that they attempt to mix different measures and develop an approach that is applicable to all information services with different characteristics. This is because it is impossible to establish a method of measuring multimedia concentration for the purposes of ensuring pluralism and diversity on the basis of a single unit. Combining different types of measurement is more likely to provide a valid method. The use of a combination of measures is essential since no single measure captures both the quantity and the quality of consumption which will tend to determine the degree of influence exerted and the extent of access and of content diversity offered. In the final analysis, it is the duty of regulators to use the measurement approaches they deem necessary to build up a complete picture of the market and the actions required to ensure the outcomes the regulation aims to achieve. But the more information a regulator has about the market position of media firms has the less disputed there will be about his/her judgement. Just as the Chancellor of the Exchequer receives a wide range of information to decide whether inflationary pressures are sufficient to justify a rise in interest rates, so any media regulator will need a great deal of information extracted from a wide range of indicators to help him/her decide whether the influence of a particular company is a cause of concern.

Notes

1. Dr Petros Iosifidis is a Reader in Media and Communications Department of Sociology at the School of Social Sciences, City University of London, Northampton Square, London, United Kingdom.
2. The objective of the study was to develop a monitoring tool for assessing the level of media pluralism in the EU Member States and identifying threats to such pluralism based on a set of indicators, covering pertinent legal,

economic and socio-cultural considerations (p. vii), (see http://ec.europa.eu/information_society/media_taskforce/doc/pluralism/pfr_report.pdf, accessed 8 June 2008).

References

Albarran, A.B. and Dimmick, J. 1996. Economics of multiformity and concentration in the communication industries, *Journal of Media Economics*, 9, 41–9.
Albarran, A.B. 2002. *Media Economics: Understanding Markets, Industries and Concepts*, 2nd edn, Ames, IA: Iowa State Press.
Albarran, A.B. and Mierzejewska B.I. 2004. *Media Concentration in the U.S. and European Union: A Comparative Analysis*. Paper, 6th World Media Economics Conference. HEC Montreal, Canada, 12–15 May.
Bagdikian, B.H. 2004. *The New Media Monopoly*, Boston, MA: Beacon Press.
British Media Industry Group (BMIG). 1994. *The Future of the British Media Industry*, February.
Commission of the European Communities (CEC). 1992. *Pluralism and Media Concentration in the Internal Market: An Assessment of the Need for Community Action*, Commission Green Paper, COM(92) 480 final, Brussels, 23 December.
Dixit, A. and Stiglitz, J. 1977. Monopolistic competition and optimum product diversity, *American Economic Review*, 67, 297–308.
Doyle, G. 2002. *Media Ownership: The Economics and Politics of Convergence and Concentration in the U.K. and European Media*, London: Sage.
EU (European Union). 2007. Treaty of Lisbon, *Official Journal* C306, 17 December.
Hill, B.C. 2006. Measuring media market diversity: concentration, importance and pluralism, *Federal Communications Law Journal*, 58(1), 169–94, http://www.law.indiana.edu/fclj/pubs/v58/no1/HillPDF.pdf.
Hoffmann-Riem, W. 1987. National identity and cultural values: broadcasting safeguards, *Journal of Broadcasting*, 31(1), 57–72.
Hotelling, H. (1929) Stability in competition, *The Economic Journal*, March, 41–57.
Independent Study on Indicators for Media Pluralism in the Member States – Towards a Risk-Based Approach. 2009. Prepared for the European Commission DG Information Society and Media by K.U. Leuven – ICRI, Jönköping International Business School – MMTC and Ernst & Youn Consultancy Belgium, Preliminary Final Report, Leuven, April.
Iosifidis, P. 1997. Methods of measuring media concentration, *Media, Culture & Society*, 19(3), 643–63.
Iosifidis, P. 2005. The application of EC competition policy to the media industry, *International Journal of Media Management*, 7(3–4), 103–11.
Just, N. 2009. Measuring media concentration and diversity: new approaches and instruments in Europe and the United States, *Media, Culture and Society*, 31(1), 97–117.
Karstens, E. 2008. Risk management in media policy: balancing stakeholders, European Journalism Centre, 29 January: http://www.ejc.net/magazine/article/risk_management_in_media_policy_balancing_stakeholders (accessed 8 June 2009).
McQuail, D. 1992. *Media Performance: Mass Communication and the Public Interest*, London: Sage.

Noam, E. 2004. How to measure media concentration, *Financial Times*, 30 August: http://www.ft.com/cms/s/da30bf5e-fa9d-11d8-9a71-00000e2511c8.html (accessed 8 June 2009).

Owen, B.M., Beebe, J.H. and Manning, W.G. 1974. *Television Economics*, Lexington: Lexington Books.

Picard, R. 1988. Measuring concentration in the daily newspaper industry, *The Journal of Media Economics*, 1(2), 61–74.

Shew, W. 1994. *UK Media Concentration* (Arthur Andersen Economic Consultancy), London: News International plc.

Stigler, G. 1983. *The Organisation of Industry*, Chicago: University of Chicago Press.

Tunstall, G. and Palmer, M. 1991. *Media Moguls*, London: Routledge.

UK. 1995. *Media Ownership – Government Proposals*, Green Paper, May.

Van Cuilenburg, J. and D. McQuail. 2003. Media policy paradigm shifts: towards a new communications policy paradigm, *European Journal of Communication*, 18(2), 181–207.

8
Concentration in the French Press Industry: Quantitative Analysis

Patrick-Yves Badillo and Jean-Baptiste Lesourd[1]

8.1 Introduction

The recent evolution of the media industry is related to the dynamics of the so-called *'knowledge-information society'*,[2] and this modifies radically the situation of this industry worldwide. This concerns both the written press (dailies and magazines) and the broadcast media (radio and television), together with the new web-based media. In a work related to this problem, Downe (2000) refers to a *'new media economy'*. Clearly, we are dealing with evolutions that can be rather different in various developed economies, emerging economies, and developing economies. However, a number of common features can be observed worldwide, as this evolution is *global*. This global evolution is, firstly, a technology-based evolution, and, secondly, an evolution of the regulatory environment. This is because the new information and communication technologies have been submitted to an increasingly fast evolution during the past twenty years. The media industry has also been submitted, during these years, to a deregulation movement which is quite similar to the deregulation movement observed in other industries (such as the electricity industry). While this deregulation movement can differ in various countries, according to national traditions and to the various political and cultural environments, one can identify a global deregulation trend. This global trend concerns geographical areas such as Europe. It also became an object of international negotiations, whether global negotiations such as the ongoing WTO international trade discussions, or bilateral or multilateral negotiations between various countries. The consequences of this evolution are well known, and can be summed up as follows:

- Technological innovations, technological convergence, and economic globalisation lead to the emergence of a mega-industry of

communication (in a broad sense), in a number of countries and worldwide, and this mega-industry is subject to an ongoing ebullience;
- The regulatory evolution concerning this market triggers economic changes in this mega-industry, which are faster and faster: regulation has considerably changed during the last 20 years, first in, the telecommunication industry, and later in the media industry; in the United States, the deregulation process has maintained at a strong momentum since 1996, and, more recently, an even stronger momentum since June 2003.

Here, the technological environment is crucial: the boundaries which formerly existed between hitherto distinct industries such as the computer industry, the broadcasting industry, the media in general, or the telecommunication industries have almost completely vanished. Telephone operators, computer and software companies, publishers, movie studios and television networks, among many other industries, all use the same information and communication technologies, and they converge towards one and the same industry. In the case of the United States, Noam (2003) uses the expression '*industry meltdown*', referring, in other terms, to the merging of industries which used to be distinct industries. Today, signals related to telephone, television, and to various services related to information processing and transfer are all converted into digital signals which are very similar from a technical point of view. The digitalisation of information is thus one of the major innovations in the field of the information and communication technologies. However, digitalisation is only one among many technological changes that go along with the emergence of a mega-industry of communication. Besides the changeover from analogical to digitalised transmission, one can observe, for instance, the shift from traditional semiconductors towards microprocessors. The tremendous increase in microprocessor speed (Moore's law) leads not only to an accelerated reduction in costs but also to the development of new applications in computers and in multimedia systems. Increased possibilities in file compression and decompression, encoding and decoding, transmission and storage, also lead to fast changes in the merging telecommunication, computer and broadcasting industries. In the particular case of media, and, more precisely, of the written press, which is of interest to us, these technological advances certainly can facilitate the entrance in the press industry of actors with strong capacities in the information and communication technologies. In France, the examples of Lagardère controlling Hachette, and of Dassault controlling Le Figaro are quite significant. In addition, concentration in the media industry in France fuels a vivid debate, similar to debates in several other countries, such as the United States (Kiyindou and Mathien, 2007). Some authors contend that such a concentration threatens press freedom (in the case of the French media, cf. for instance Diard and Goguey, 2005, and Ramonet et al., 2005); for some others, on the contrary, it reflects the lack of dynamism of the French press groups (Eveno, 2005). A media company, just as any other company, however, cannot escape some kind of economic and financial logic (on the specific characteristics of media economics, see, for example, Mathien, 2004, and Sonnac and Le Floch, 2005). However, if one is interested in the phenomenon of concentration in the media industry, one should note that various authors distinguish between economic concentration as such, and concentration on what one might call the market for ideas, referring, more generally, to press and media diversity. The idea developed by several authors, including Noam (2003, 2004) is that the well-known Herfindahl–Hirschman Index (HHI) of concentration measures economic concentration and market power, but that a concentration index reflecting the diversity of press titles and of ideas is another matter. Noam (2003, 2004) therefore proposes another diversity-oriented concentration index for the press and media industries that will be discussed later.

This work aims at studying the concentration of the French press industry, using as quantitative benchmarks several concentration indexes, such as the Herfindahl–Hirschman Index, and the diversity index adapted to the media sector recently introduced by Noam (2003). This Noam index has, so far, not been used extensively, at least to our knowledge.

Our chapter is organised as follows. The second part begins with a media industry-oriented discussion various statistical indexes of concentration, and proposes an application of these various indexes to the case of the French written press. A discussion of the results follows. Finally, the main conclusions of our research are developed.

8.2 The case of the French press

As has already been discussed in the two previous chapters, there are several market concentration indexes available, which are more or less adapted to a quantitative description of the intensity of market power (or, for very concentrated markets, monopoly or oligopoly power), and are therefore indicators of the intensity of competition on a given market. As discussed above, most of these concentration indexes are related to market shares, as measured, for instance, by shares in global sales. A concentration index which is often used is the concentration ratio, defined as the sum of market shares for a small number n < N of firms, with usually n = 4 or 8, N being much larger than n. These concentration ratios lead to some problems. It does not describe the whole sample of enterprises, the sum of market shares being truncated at n < N. This means that if n = N, our ratio would trivially be equal to 1. A more representative index is the well-known Herfindahl–Hirschman concentration index (HHI), defined as the sum of the squares of market shares. If market shares are in %, as often practiced, HHI = 10,000 for n = 1 (monopoly), while HHI = 0 in the limiting case of infinite n and zero market shares (perfect competition). In other terms, HHI obeys some pertinent hypotheses regarding the degree of market concentration. American anti-trust law authorities such as the US Federal Trade Commission consider that HHI < 1,000 corresponds to low concentration on a market, that $1,000 \leq HHI \leq 1,800$ corresponds to moderate concentration, and that, finally, HCC > 1,800 corresponds to high concentration. The US Federal Trade Commission also introduced a so-called diversity index (DI) which aims at taking into account the number of distinct media outlets, or 'voices' whether they are under one and the same ownership or not. DI is thus defined as formally identical to HHI, but with the audience shares of the various outlets 1,2,----, i,----, m, if one assumes that there are m outlets corresponding to n enterprises in the media industry under study ($m \geq n$). This DI index enables one to distinguish between the diversity of titles, and of radio and TV stations under the control of given owners, and market power, as reflected by a HHI index which takes into account total market shares of all independent media firms. The idea underlying this other NI index is that media groups can own several independent media, competing with each other on a 'market for ideas' which is not identical to the market as such. However, as shown by several authors, including Noam (2003, 2004) and Hill (2006), have criticised DI as a pertinent diversity index. In particular, Noam proposes a media-specific diversity index, the Noam index (NI). Let m be the total number of independent media outlets. Some of these outlets with too small audiences (below a given threshold, for example 1 per cent) are not taken into account. Under these conditions, the Noam index (NI) is defined as the ratio of HHI to the square root of m:

$$NI = \frac{HHI}{\sqrt{m}} \qquad (8.1)$$

Obviously, NI ≤ HHI, and NI = HHI = 10,000 if, and only if, there is only one firm operating only one media outlet. In all other cases, NI < HHI.

After this preliminary discussion, let us present the situation of the French press, and the recent concentration phenomena to which it has been submitted, as an interesting case. Historically,[3] the nineteenth century, and the beginning of the twentieth century can be considered as a golden age for the French press, which, since the end of the First World War, has entered into a period of relative decline. In 1914, there were 322 dailies in France; this number fell successively to 179 in 1945, and only 66 in 2000. The number of national daily newspapers, which stood at 26 in 1945, was only about ten in 2000. However, in addition to this fall in the number of titles, a dramatic decrease in circulation also took place. In 1914, one of the main national newspapers, *Le Petit Parisien*, had a daily circulation of about three million copies. In comparison, the two main national dailies, *Le Monde* and *Le Figaro*, have together a daily circulation of about 600,000 copies – a fall of some 80 per cent. If the French national daily press experiences financial problems, however, other press products, which are apparently more profitable, are growing steadily in the French environment. This is the case for magazines, and for the specialised general public press, which grew from 754 titles in 1985 to 1,595 titles in 2001. The professional specialised technical press is another strongly growing segment of the market, up from 1,109 titles to 1,504 titles during the same period.

Over the past few years, there has been an ongoing concentration movement in the French press. One recent example can illustrate this: the takeover of the Socpresse group by the Dassault group, following the sale of the L'Express-l'Expansion group to a Belgian media company. In March 2004, the Dassault aerospace group took control of Socpresse, the largest French press group. Socpresse, which was an offshoot of the Robert Hersant family group, accounts for about 30 per cent of the French press, with a circulation in millions of copies of national and regional weekly magazines and dailies. In particular, Socpresse owned 70 publications, including the dailies *Le Figaro*, *Paris-Turf*, a number of provincial dailies, and the weeklies *L'Express*, *L'Expansion*, and *La Maison Française*... By January 2002, Dassault had already secured a 30 per cent stake in Socpresse's capital. In 2004, after reaching an agreement with most of the inheritors of Robert Hersant and his wife, the stake of the Dassault group rose to 82 per cent of Socpresse's capital. Securing the initial stake in Socpressein January 2002 implied for Dassault an investment of about €450 million. In addition, in September 2002, Socpresse bought the L'Express–L'Expansion magazine group to Vivendi thanks to a short-term loan of €230 million from Dassault. It was agreed that this loan would be converted into Socpresse shares if it could not be redeemed in cash. Socpresse being unable to redeem its loan, Dassault converted it into Socpresse shares. Recently (2005–06), however, Dassault sold the Express–Expansion group to Roularta, a Belgian media group, and its media activities now mostly include Le Figaro group with sales of €630 million. Another example is the example of the media segment of the Lagardère group (also an aerospace group), which is the largest French media group, with sales in its media activities accounting for €8.032 billion. Thus, there is, in France as elsewhere, an ongoing trend of takeovers of media companies, often undergoing financial problems, by industrial companies which are, on the contrary, highly profitable.

The weekly magazine *Le Point* is controlled by the Pinault luxury and department stores group. One can also, finally, refer to the recent purchase of 60 per cent of the Editis publishing group by Wendel Investissement for 660 million € from the Lagardère group. Editis owned a number of French publishers, including Le Robert, Bordas, Nathan, Plon-Perrin, Robert Laffont, Julliard, Nil, Omnibus, La Découverte, Presses de la Cité, Belfond, Pocket 10/18 ... B. d'Armagnac (2005) explains how various industries and various family investors control the French press, and attempts at explaining the difficulties of the daily press:

> The 1945 liberation gave rise to a number of newspapers which were founded by individuals or families, under a social agreement with the union of press workers, the syndicat du Livre CGT, on printing and distribution activities, under the control of the French state. This system had for a long time remained at standstill in its after-war configuration. But the general picture of the French press is now on the move and it has not reached its final shape.

It is also worthwhile mentioning that the average size of French press groups is much smaller than that of the larger American and European press groups. For instance, the turnover of the newspaper group Le Monde is smaller than €700 million; the turnover of the Dassault group in the media industry is €1 billion, while the corresponding figures for Pearson and Bertelsmann are, respectively, €7 billion and €20 billion; moreover, the turnover of the press subsidiary of Bertelsmann, Gruner und Jahr, is €3 billion). The Lagardère media group is the only French multimedia group of an international dimension with a media turnover of €8 billion (including €3.8 billion in publishing and press activities), and subsidiaries worldwide. One can wonder, therefore, whether the

French press, after a intense period of takeover and merger activities from French investors, is not going to be submitted to a further period of in-depth reshaping as the result of takeovers from transnational groups.

In the case of the financial press, one of the two French financial dailies, *Les Echos*, used to belong to the Pearson group, a major international actor in the financial information industry, the owner of the *Financial Times*. Similarly, *La Tribune*, the other French financial daily, used to belong to the large LVMH luxury group. However, the Pearson group recently (in 2007) sold *Les Echos* to LVMH, while LVMH sold *La Tribune* to News Participation, a group owned by Alain Weill, an independent French investor. One can see again that a large French international group, not related to the media industry, is involved in the sector of specialised press.

In order to develop our analysis of the market of the written press in France, we have listed about 20 groups which are involved in the written press and in publishing (Table 8.1). This table offers a summary of the main press firms operating in France, with details on their characteristics and on their owners. It is possible to classify the ownerships of these firms into three broad categories:

- First of all, we find firms that belong to large national or international companies, often quoted public international groups with activities in the media industry and in other industries (G category). These are clearly the largest actors.
- Secondly, we find smaller firms under family ownership, often private, family-owned companies, or private companies owned by independent investors such as not-for-profit foundations and religious communities (FI category). These would be very difficult to takeover, at least whenever they are profitable. This is, for instance, the case of *Ouest-France*, one of the largest provincial newspapers in France: the Ouest-France group is exclusively owned by a foundation.
- Thirdly, we distinguished two actors previously under independent ownership, which underwent significant financial problems, and that are now at least partially owned by large companies, and are recovering in financial terms (category R).

We have here press groups which are still more or less independent, but which are still difficult to manage in financial terms, so that their ownership might change again in the future.

Clearly, larger groups, whether national, international, or global (G), are today very important and even dominant in the French press as they

Table 8.1 The main titles and groups of the French press

Groups	Owners	Titles (dailies and magazines)	Press Sales[4]	Categories	Market shares
Lagardère media segment (Lagardère Active, Lagardère Publishing, Lagardère Services)	Lagardère Group (Aerospatial industry)	*La Provence, Nice-Matin, Paris-Match, Elle*	1848	G	18.80%
GHM Hersant Media	Hersant Family (Press)	*France-Antilles, Paris-Normandie, L'Est Eclair*	1060	G	10.21%
Ouest-France	Independent	*Ouest-France*	1000	FI	9.63%
Roularta France	Roularta (Belgium)	*L'Express, L'Expansion*	760	G	8.32%
Amaury – Le Parisien – L'Equipe	Amaury Family (75%) (Press)	*Le Parisien, l'Equipe*	650	G	6.26%
La Vie – Le Monde	PRISA (Espagne), Lagardère group	*La Vie – Le Monde, Diplomatique*	650	R	6.26%
Le Figaro	Dassault (Aerospatial industry)	*Le Figaro, Paris-Turf, Le Progrès, Le Dauphiné Libéré, Le Maine Libre, Presse Océan, Le Bien Public, Le Journal de Saône-et-Loire*	630	G	6.07%
Prisma	Bertelsmann (Allemagne)	*Capital, Management, Femme Actuelle, Prima, GEO, Télé Loisirs, Télé 2 Semaines*	584	G	5.63%
Mondadori France	Mondadori (Italy)	*Télé poche, Télé star, Auto plus, Auto journal...*	437	G	4.21%
Bayard Presse – Milan Presse	Assomptionnist religious community (100%)	*La Croix, Côté Femme, Notre Temps, Pomme d'Api, Okapi*	433	FI	4.17%

L'Est Républicain DNA	Lignac Family	L'Est Républicain	353	FI	3.40%
Groupe Sud-Ouest	Lemoine Family (80%)	Sud-Ouest, La Charente Libre	325.4	FI	3.13%
La Voix du Nord	Rossel (Belgium)	La Voix du Nord, Nord-Eclair	198	FI	1.91%
DI Groupe – La Tribune	News Partcipation (Alain Weill)	La Tribune, Investir	168	G	1.62%
Centre France – La Montagne	Independent	La Montagne	162.7	FI	1.57%
Marie Claire	Prouvost Family	Marie-Claire	150	FI	1.44%
Le Nouvel Observateur – Perdriel	Independent (including Claude Perdriel)	Le Nouvel Observateur, Challenges	150	FI	1.44%
La Dépêche du Midi	Baylet Family (67%)	La Dépêche du Midi	146	FI	1.41%
Les Echos	LVMH – Moët Hennessy (Luxe)	Les Echos	126.2	G	1.22%
Le Télégramme	Independent	Le Télégramme de Brest	108	FI	1.04%
La Nouvelle République du Centre-Ouest	Independent	La Nouvelle République, La République du Centre	100	FI	0.96%
Le Républicain Lorrain	Crédit Mutuel	Le Républicain Lorrain	90.6	FI	0.87%
Sud Communication – Valmonde	Pierre Fabre	L'Eveil de la Haute Loire, Valeurs Actuelles	63	G	0.61%
L'Alsace-Le Pays	Crédit Mutuel (80%)	L'Alsace, Le Pays	63	G	0.61%
Le Point-Artemis	Pinault	Le Point	62	G	0.6%
Libération	E. de Rothschild (38,87%), Pathé (10%)	Libération	34	R	0.33%
L'Humanité	Independent : 80%	L'Humanité	29	FI	0.28%

Source: Research Centre of Ecole Supérieure de journalisme, Lille, France, and personal research.

Table 8.2 CR4 and HHI concentration indexes for the French press industry

CR₄ (All firms of Table 8.1)	HHI (All firms of Table 8.1)
45.0%	791.4

represent more than half of the sales listed in Table 8.1 (62.1 per cent). However, independent groups, some of which are comparatively large, and smaller family-owned firms (FI) still account for a sizable share of the sales (31.3 per cent). Groups in a situation of financial recovery account for 6.6 per cent of our sales.

Finally, we calculated several concentration indexes on the firms listed in Table 8.1, including the market shares of the largest four, and of the largest ten groups, and the Herfindahl–Hirschman Index for all of them (Table 8.2).

Although, because of the heterogeneous character of the firms in our sample, and of the approximations in our evaluations of sales, the figures given are only rough orders of magnitude, the discussion of these indicators leads us to some pertinent conclusions. One can see that the largest four press firms account for 45 per cent of sales; the HHI of 791.4 leads to the conclusion that the level of concentration in the French press industry is still low, knowing that, as mentioned above, a high concentration starts at a HHI index of 1,800. These estimates can be compared to the C4 and HHI estimated by Noam (2009) for all American printing and publishing media enterprises, which were, respectively, of 38.2 per cent and of 463 for 2006, significantly smaller than in the French case according to our calculations.

The number of titles in the French press, currently around 4,000, leads us to the conclusion that the Noam diversity index (NI) would be even smaller. With the figures in Table 8.1, and a total of 4,000 titles, an estimate (again a quite approximate) of NI is 12.5, reflecting the diversity of the French press, rather than market concentration. However, one should stress again that this estimate is approximate, and corresponds to the aggregation of heterogeneous press products that are not comparable to each other (national dailies, regional dailies, professional and general public journals and magazines...).

An analysis in the case of the French national daily press, which is much more concentrated, perhaps leads to more accurate estimates based on average circulation data, which are comparable to each other and concern a more homogeneous segment of the market. We have therefore restricted ourselves to the French daily national press, with 11 titles (excluding the *New York Herald Tribune*, which is published in

Table 8.3 Evaluations of HHI and of NI on the French national daily press (2008 figures)

Titles	Ownerships	Mean daily circulation (2008)
Le Figaro		319996
France-Soir	Socpresse	23934
Paris Turf		68930
Aujourd'hui – Le Parisien	Amaury	512539
L'Equipe		311443
Le Monde	La Vie – Le Monde	300522
Libération	Libération	123327
Les Echos	LVMH	137448
La Croix	Bayard	94963
La Tribune	Alain Weill	75480
L'Humanité	L'Humanité	49061
Total		2017643
H4 %		82.33
Herfindahl–Hirschman Index in %		2434.2
Diversity Index in %		1495.9
Noam Index in %		733.9

Source: OJD.

France, but mainly for an international audience); Table 8.3 gives comparable mean daily circulation figures for 2008.

The Herfindahl–Hirschman Index is found to be equal to 2,434.2 in 2008, quite a high figure, reflecting a strong concentration of French press groups on the segment of national dailies. However, with 11 titles, the Noam diversity index is at a much lower value of 733.9. In the case of France, these figures reflect the financial problems of the French national general information dailies.[5] However, our estimate is only an assessment of the situation in 2008, and it is interesting to see whether there has been a significant evolution over the past decade. The results of such an estimate for various concentration and diversity indexes (HHI, DI and NI) are given in Table 8.4 for the period 1997–2008.

These figures can be analysed in the terms of evolution over time of all three indicators. We carried out simple linear econometric regressions over time of the form $Y = A + B*TIME$, where Y is the dependent variable, A is a constant intercept and B is a variation coefficient. As far as HHI is concerned, we find that HHI does not vary significantly over time and can therefore be assumed as being equal to a constant which statistically is the mean value of HHI over the period (2,365.4). On the

Table 8.4 Various concentration and diversity indexes for the French daily press in 1997, 2000, 2004, 2006 and 2008

Years	1997	2000	2004	2006	2008
HHI	2421.8	2283.4	2443.7	2345.8	2434.2
DI	1218.7	1366.6	1439.0	1441.4	1495.9
NI	730.2	688.5	736.8	707.3	733.9

Source: Our calculation from OJD data.

contrary, both diversity indexes calculated here are found to increase significantly over the period of study. This means that while concentration in terms of ownership has not changed significantly, diversity has significantly decreased, and indeed the circulation of some of the titles decreased strongly between 1997 and 2008. This reflects the difficult situation of some titles, the circulation of which has strongly and probably irreversibly decreased during this time. For instance, the circulation of *France-Soir* decreased from 170,499 in 2007 to a very small figure of 23,934 in 2008; similarly, the circulation of *Libération* also fell sharply, from 173,090 in 1997 to 123,327 in 2008.

If we now discuss the case of the regional press, in most regions, there is just one daily newspaper. These monopoly situations are anticipated, since there are important economies of scale in the production of information. This situation can leads to weakening the smaller firms, so that, on small markets such as the local markets for regional dailies, lead to a monopoly situations.[6] These monopoly situations correspond to both HHI and NI indexes of 10,000. One can, however, calculate HHI and NI in two regions where there is more than one daily: Alsace, with two competing titles (*L'Alsace-Le Pays* and *Les Dernières Nouvelles d'Alsace*), et la Lorraine with three competing titles (*L'Est Républicain, Le Républicain Lorrain* and *Est Eclair*). Table 8.5 gives both HHI and NI for these two regions (2008).

This calculation leads to HHI estimates of 5,343.5 and 4,415.9 for, respectively, Alsace and Lorraine, which correspond as anticipated to very high concentrations and duopoly situations (two competitors). A similar conclusion can be drawn from the evaluations of the NI indexes, which are of 3,778.4 and 2,549.5 for, respectively, Alsace and Lorraine. These figures can be compared with the HHI of 7,621 calculated by Noam (2004) in the case of the US local press, for which the same phenomenon of a quasi-monopoly situation is observed in most states and cities.

Table 8.5 Evaluations of HHI and of NI in the case of the regional daily newspapers in two regions where there is more than one title (Alsace and Lorraine)

Regions	Titles	Circulation (2008)	HHI	NI
Alsace	L'Alsace-Le Pays	105,459	5,343.5	3,778.4
	Les Dernières Nouvelles d'Alsace	180,376		
Lorraine	L'Est Républicain	192,729	4,415.9	2,549.5
	Le Républicain Lorrain	142,129		
	Est Eclair	27,948		

Source: OJD.

8.3 Conclusion

Finally, it appears that the French press is involved in an ongoing evolution towards more concentration. Larger groups, whether or not they belong to the media industry, still have the possibilities of taking over some smaller groups, especially if these smaller groups undergo financial problems. A rough estimate of the Herfindahl–Hirschman Index (HHI) as calculated on the sales of the groups of the press industry, is 791.4, still a comparatively low figure. One can, in this situation, anticipate increased concentration in the future.

Large groups such as LVMH or Pinault, whose main activities lie outside the media industry, might, for instance, either sell their media assets to large French media groups that are already present, or can themselves increase their presence in the media industry, by taking over smaller titles that are experiencing financial difficulties. The same is true of a number of international media companies, such as Prisma, a subsidiary of the German company Bertelsmann. Nevertheless, in the sector of the French written press, the situation is still that of a competitive market. With a HHI index of 791.4 (even if this is a quite approximate estimate), one cannot really speak of high concentration on this market. This situation attracts competing international actors on the French market, among which one can mention Prisma (a subsidiary of the German Bertelsmann Group), the Belgian Roularta group, the Italian Mondadori group, and the Spanish PRISA group. Conversely, some large French press groups are developing internationally. This is the case, for instance, of the Lagardère group, with sales in the media sector of €8 billion, and subsidiaries in most European countries, in the United States, in Canada, in Australia, as well as in a number of Asian emerging economies (South Korea, Singapore, China).

As discussed previously, the situation of the French national daily press is quite different. The ongoing financial problems of this segment of the market, while they do not favour competition, lead to concentration effects, attracting a small number of large press groups. Accordingly, the HHI of the market was found to be 2,365.4 as a mean over the 1997–2008 period, and this corresponds to high concentration. However, diversity indexes were found to increase significantly over this period. This means that while concentration in terms of ownership has not significantly changed, diversity has significantly decreased over the period.

An examination of the French regional press (essentially a daily press) shows that is also highly concentrated, with titles in a monopoly situation in most regions, and a duopoly or quasi-duopoly in only a few regions. This concentration phenomenon is also observed in other countries, and, in particular, in the USA.

Our research leads to a number of developments. Further studies of the concentration phenomenon in the French press are, obviously, of some interest. A comparative study involving situations in other countries, including, for instance, European countries, would be quite interesting. In addition, a theoretical analysis of the underlying phenomena, leading to a discussion of existing concentration indexes adapted to the press industry, and, more generally, to the media industry, would also be interesting. Finally, an analysis of the dynamic evolution of the media sector, as related to technological changes in the new information and communication technologies, would be a fundamental and topical project.

Notes

1. Patrick Badillo is a Professor at Aix-Marseille University, France; formerly Director of the School of Journalism and Communication of Marseille; Director and Founder of the Research Institute on Information and Communication; Project Manager, French National Research Agency; Jean-Baptiste Lesourd is a Professor at Aix-Marseille University, France.
2. A number of analyses have been concerned with the knowledge-information society (Castells, 2000; Machlup, 1962; Porat, 1986; Webster, 2002, among others). The expression is used here between quotes, since it refers to a rather controversial concept.
3. For an historical analysis, from an economic point of view, since about 1820, see, for example, Eveno (2003); for a more recent historical analysis (since 1945) see also Charon (1991).
4. Sales figures are 2006 sales in € million, or latest available estimate in some cases.

5. The model of Sonnac, Laussel and Gabszewicz (2002) attempts at explaining this sort of financial problems in the case of the political press.
6. According to Sonnac, Gabszewicz and Laussel (2002), whenever two local newspapers compete in a given region, the dynamics of tha market is a tendency towards a monopoly situation.

References

Albert, P. 2004. *Economie des médias*, Paris: La Documentation Française.
D'Armagnac, B. 2005. Industriels et familles règnent sur la presse française, *Le Monde*, 22 January.
Bell, D. 1976. *The Coming of Post-Industrial Society*, New York: Basic Books.
Castells, M. 2000. *The Rise of the Network Society. The Information Age: Economy, Society and Culture*. Volume 1. Malden, MA: Blackwell.
Carluer, C. 2001. Le développement global des médias économiques et financiers et le caractère national de l'information. Le cas de Bloomberg Television. *Les Enjeux de l'Information et de la Communication*.
Charon, J.M. 1991. *La Presse en France de 1945 à nos jours*, Paris: Seuil.
Diard, M., and Goguey, A. 2005. L'information face à la communication, *Le Monde*, 29 March, p. 13.
Downe, D. 2000. The medium vanishes? The resurrection of the mass audience in the New Media Economy, *Media/Culture*, 3(1). Available at http://journal.media-culture.org.au/0003/mass.php.
Eveno, P. 2005. Vive la concentration dans les médias!, *Le Monde*, 29 March, p. 13.
Eveno, P. 2003. *L'argent de la presse française des années 1820 à nos jours*, Paris: CTHS.
Fitzpatrick, T. 2002. Critical theory, information society and surveillance technologies, *Information, Communication and Society*, 5(3), 357–78.
Hill, B.C. 2006. Measuring media market diversity: concentration, importance, and pluralism, *Federal Communications Law Journal*, 58, 169–94.
Kiyindou, A. and Mathien, M. 2007. *Evolution de l'économie libérale et liberté d'expression*, Brussels: Bruylant.
Machlup, F. 1962. *The Production and Distribution of Knowledge in the United States*. Princeton, NJ: Princeton University Press.
Mathien, M. 2004. *Economie Générale des Médias*, Paris: Ellipses.
Noam, E. 2003. The effect of deregulation on market concentration: an analysis of the Telecom Act of 1996 and the industry meltdown, *The Columbia Science and Technology Law Review*, 4, 1–12.
Noam, E. 2004. *Local Media Concentration in America*, Communication, 6th World Media Economics Conference, Montreal.
Noam, E. 2009. *Media Ownership and Concentration in America*, Oxford: Oxford University Press.
Ramonet, I., Brémond, J. and Malverde, F. 2005. *Sur la concentration dans les medias* (Préface d'Armand Mattelart), Paris: Liris.
OECD. 1986. *Trends in the Information Economy*, Paris: OECD.
Porat, M. 1977. *The Information Economy*, Washington, DC: US Department of Commerce.

Schiller, D. 2000. *Digital Capitalism*. Cambrige, MA: MIT Press.
Sonnac, N. and Le Floch, P. 2005. *Economie de la presse,* Paris: Editions La Découverte.
Sonnac, N., Laussel, D. and Gabszewicz, J.J. 2002. Advertising and the political differentiation of newspapers, *Journal of Public Economic Theory*, 4(3), 249–59.
Sonnac, N., Gabszewicz, J.J., and Laussel, D., 2002. Concentration in the Press Industry and the Theory of the Circulation Spiral. *CORE Discussion Paper 2002*.
Webster, F. 2002. *Theories of the Information Society*. London: Routledge.

9
The Effects of Competition on the Profitability of European Television Channels

Juan P. Artero, Cristina Etayo, Mónica Herrero, Mercedes Medina and Alfonso Sánchez-Tabernero[1]

9.1 Introduction and literature review

As history shows, until the 1970s, television in Europe had not yet benefited from the effects of competition. Television channels were owned by the state and their aim was to supply information, education and entertainment to all citizens. Television was, therefore, just a mere public function rather than an audience competition between different channels.

During that period, the literature considering television in Europe has focused in particular on topics such as the balance of information, the fulfillment of the public service obligation, the rights of minorities and the opportunity to educate good citizens. Television was far from being a marketplace. Given this situation, neither academics nor the people working in the field considered the economic aspects of the channel.

However, in the past three decades, the deregulation of the audiovisual sector – shaped by technological and legal factors (Brown and Picard, 2005) – has changed the landscape of television in Europe. Today, in each national market, very different channels coexist:

- Between two and three state-owned channels which reach a national audience.
- Between two and four private channels seeking to increase their market share.
- Multiple regional, local and some specialised channels which broadcast to audience that have common interests.

The field of media economics analyses the behaviour and structure of media markets. According to Picard (2003: 78), 'media economics is the study of how economic and financial pressures affect a variety of communications activities, systems, organisations and enterprises, including media and telecommunications'. Albarran also includes consumers in his definition. According to him, 'media economics is the study of how media industries use scarce resources to produce content that is distributed among society to satisfy various wants and needs' (2002: 5). On the other hand, Doyle points out that it 'combines the study of economies with the study of media. It is concerned with the changing economic forces that direct and constrain the choices of managers, practitioners and other decision-makers across the media' (2002: 2).

Since the 1980s, the majority of studies have focused on the privatisation of television companies and market liberalisation and their influence on television programmes and audiences. The diversity of approaches have cohered into three distinct schools of research.

Firstly, there is the critical school which advocates media protectionism to avoid excessive concentration and to guarantee pluralism. This literature argues that the communication sector is an industry which has a substantial impact on the development of society. According to them, media products must be protected because of their cultural nature, and that is how it is understood in distinctive circles and international institutions (Wright, 1994; Shaughnessy, 1990; Machet, 1998). Some of these theorists consider the position that media hold as hegemonic, in line with a type of research known as Critical Theory, which draws on Marxist approaches taken from sociology, cultural studies and the political economy of the media. All of the authors appear to share certain misgivings about the operation of the market, and so defend state control. In this sense, the work carried out by Mattelart (1979), Garnham (1990), Dyson and Humphreys (1990), Mosco (1996), Golding and Murdoch (1997), Compaine and Gomery (2000) and Bagdikian (2000), among others, seems relevant.

Secondly, the liberal school is committed to a free market of ideas that regulates itself and balances itself out. In contrast to the protectionism of the previously mentioned school of thought, this market analysis of the media is carried out based on an assumption of the advantages of the free market, in respect of both company management and media consumption. The market itself brings with it balance and pluralism in the news. In respect of cultural issues, the most significant are those of the competitive market in which the media operate. These authors introduce a tradition of applied research and the most liberal ones hold that the media should not be subjected to any state intervention.

For those authors who belong to the moderate third school, protectionism is simply not possible within the global context of communication. Nonetheless, neither is absolute liberalism, unless it is considered that the freedom of the agents is founded on the responsibility of achieving the common good. Among the proponents of this approach are Toussaint (1996), Picard (2002), Albarran (2002), Nieto and Iglesias (2000) and Doyle (2002). Some authors have studied the market with a more practical objective in mind – that is, with the aim of influencing regulation. Specifically, those that stand out are Noam (1985), with his study on the implications of the growth of competition, and Hendriks (1995) and Sánchez-Tabernero and Carvajal (2002), with their analysis of media concentration in Europe. With respect to international expansion and the creation of multinational media companies, it is worth mentioning the research conducted by Gershon (2000) and Hollifield (2001). Finally, there are those that have centred on the study of a specific market, Dunnett (1990), for example; or that of one country, for example Collins, Garnham and Locksley (1989).

Alongside the theoretical framework, in recent years academics have paid special attention to particular aspects of the television industry:

(i) Main problems related to the issue of cultural identity (Antcliff, 2005). This field includes the study related to the effects of the globalisation of television markets – in particular, in small and medium-sized countries – and also related to the interrelationship between television firms and political power.

(ii) Television management, which includes articles and monographs about corporate and business strategies. These have included studies about the different aspects related to the governance of the television firms which have focused on the following subjects:

- Studies about models and strategies of channel programmes (Adams, 1993; Litman et al, 1994; Park, 2005).
- A management advertising analysis, the search for an alternative to the conventional 'spot' and advertising price policies (Leahy, 1997).
- Answer to the growing intensity of the competition such as specialisation of subjects, the creation of distinctive brands and the identification of profitable market niches (Barrett, 1995; Mashi, 1999; Powers, 2001; McDonald and Lin, 2004; Gabszewicz, Laussel and Sonnac, 2004; Van der Wurff, 2005).

- Pay television channel strategies and theirs prices subscription policies (Anstine, 2004).
- New business models based mostly on technological innovations that affect the distribution and marketing of audiovisual products.

(iii) Television market analysis. In this area, some monographs and articles stand out because of their content which is essentially the phenomenon of deregulation and concentration and also the consumer's behaviour and the development of products and substitute services (Burnett, 1992; Chan Olmsted, 1996; Li, 1999; Young, 2000; Yan, 2002). Frequently, such studies identify the market's most relevant aspects and the ways in which channels compete with one another. Within this context researchers study aspects such as the diversity of companies, vertical or horizontal integration strategies, and in general models of the companies' growth (Brown and Picard, 2005).

(iv) Research which integrates economic and technological aspects such as the digitalisation of the channels, new content based on public participation and new ways of distribution such as the Internet or the mobile phone (Davis and Walker, 1990; Wu et al., 2004). From our point of view, considerable merit is to be found in those works that not only describe what technology can allows companies to achieve but that also outline business models that will favour the development of high-tech projects.

In the past few years there has also been an increase in the range of methodological approaches to the study of television economics. On the one hand, the descriptive model applied to successful television companies has been applied widely in academic writing. In the case of public television, the BBC has been studied from different perspectives as a model of a publicly funded organisation (Ojer, 2009), whereas the German public channels, ARD and ZDF, have been analyzed as offering examples of an intermediate model. On the other hand, and considering commercial television, there are very few studies about the international expansion of commercial television channels such as Fininvest or RTL. Finally, the activities of Canal Plus and BSkyB have established the principles for the development of pay television channels (Herrero, 2003).

Moreover, as a consequence of the uncertainty in the European audiovisual sector, comparative pan-European studies have played an important part in this research field (Sánchez-Tabernero and Carvajal, 2002; Medina, 2005). Recently, there has also been substantial development of the empirical method. The search for quantitative evidences that can validate the hypothesis is the main aim of this kind of research, in which intangible values play a substantial role. The results can be of benefit to both policy makers and media managers.

9.2 Methodology

9.2.1 Sample

In order to study those factors that influence the profitability of television networks, we have analyzed data from the period 1995–2004, which correspond to 11 television networks that operate in five European countries: Spain, France, the United Kingdom, Germany and Portugal. The size of the sample was determined by the difficulty of obtaining data for some of the variables that have been studied. Although it would have been desirable to have used information from a larger number of networks, the difficulties of securing accurate company information about the networks and, therefore, of ascertaining its financial status, has prevented us from drawing upon a wider range of observations. Nevertheless, it is necessary to emphasise that the sample includes networks that are very different in nature. For instance, there are public and private networks, as well as both recently created and longer established television companies.

9.2.2 Measurements

Dependent variables

We used data corresponding to three variables of different results in order to obtain an accurate picture of the economic behaviour of the television network in terms of results.

The first variable we considered is the margin or sales profitability, defined as the operating profit obtained in the economic exercise divided by the amount of sales of the period. This variable shows the profit obtained in that period, considering the income.

The second variable considered is the financial profitability of the company, ROE (return on equity), which is defined as the quotient of the net benefit of the exercise of their own funds.

Finally, we also studied economic profitability as a dependent variable, ROA (return on assess), defined as the quotient of the operating benefit by the company assets.

The use of these three variables allows us to clarify if there are current patterns of influence of the independent variables. In this way it is possible to obtain better information on the management mechanisms or managerial aspects that are influenced by the different exogenous variables under consideration.

The data regarding these three variables were obtained from the balance and results accounts of each one of the considered television networks.

Independent variables

In our analysis, we used information about four independent variables, which have been considered, from the theoretical point of view, to have a potentially high influence on the level of profitability enjoyed by television networks.

Audience. The variable audience reflects the audience share of each network in terms of a percentage of the total television audience in each country. Data on this variable have been obtained from the annual reports compiled by the European Audiovisual Observatory.

Channels per household. This variable attempts to gather information on the existing competition level in the television market of the country in which the network operates. For this purpose, we created this variable, which was defined as the number of channels/networks existing in each country divided by the number of households (in thousands). Higher values of this variable are indicative of vigorous competition in the television market, since a greater number of channels contend for the same number of homes. Lower rate values respond to a situation with a smaller degree of competition. The information on the number of households in each country was obtained from Informa Media Group, 2002.

Time. This variable indicates the average number of minutes per day that the inhabitants of each country devote to watching television. Higher values of the variable indicate that it is a country whose inhabitants dedicate a long time to watch television. The data on this variable were obtained from the European Audiovisual Observatory, 2005.

Seniority. This variable gathers the number of years that each channel/network has been in operation, that is to say, its seniority as a television broadcaster. Seniority data were obtained from the date of appearance of the channel/network.

9.2.3 Estimation method

In view of the structure of the sample, with data of a series of companies for a series of years, the estimation methods used are based fundamentally on techniques of panel data, since these allow the combination of the cross-section structure of data with temporary series.

Thus, we estimated three different models for each dependent variable. In the first place a model of minimum ordinary squares was considered, which does not take into account the existence of several observations for the same company. Later, we studied models of both fixed and random effects. The election, among the three of them, of the definitive model was made using LM and Hausman tests. The first of the tests has allowed the determination of the convenience or not of the panel data models against the model of ordinary least squares, whereas the second has allowed a choice to be made between the model of fixed effects and that of random effects (Greene, 2003).

9.3 Results

As previously mentioned, we considered three models for each of the dependent variables under consideration. The results obtained for the dependent variable margin appear in Table 9.1. The most suitable model, in agreement with the values obtained for the test LM (9.50, p value = 0.002487) and the test of Hausman (49.47, p value = 0.0000), is the model of fixed effects, whose results are commented on below.

According to the information provided in Table 9.1, the variables that are significant in the model of fixed effects are the audience rate, the number of channels per household and the age of the network. Both the audience share and the network seniority have a positive influence on profitability, that is to say, the higher both the audience share and the number of years of broadcasting in the country, the greater is the margin. On the other hand, the number of channels per household has

Table 9.1 Estimations of the explanatory models for margin (N = 77)

Variable	OLS Coefficient	S. e.	Fixed effects Coefficient	S. e.	Random effects Coefficient	S. e.
Audience	0.749***	0.202	2.935***	0.458	1.005***	0.292
Channels per household	−39.592***	3.187	−53.906***	14.334	−43.170***	4.702
Time	−0.539	0.090	−0.122	0.091	0.098	0.077
Seniority	−0.943***	0.145	1.693***	0.499	−0.665***	0.219
Constant	46.920**	19.591			7.927	16.529
R2	0.754		0.912			
Adjusted-R2	0.740		0.891			
F	55.21***		45.67***			

* $p < 0.10$, ** $p < 0.05$, *** $p < 0.01$.

a negative influence: the greater the competition within the country measured in terms of the number of existing channels divided by the population (the number of households), the lower is the profitability of the network. However, the time devoted to watching television in each country does not turn out to be a significant variable in explaining the profitability of the chains.

In addition, three models were considered, once again, for the variable of financial profitability, ROE. The tests LM = 5.19 (p value = 0.022744) and Hausman = 7.14 (p value = 0.128439) and for a significance level of 1 per cent, the most suitable model to explain ROE is the model of random effects. The results obtained are presented in Table 9.2.

As may be observed, the audience rating of the channel is not explanatory of the dependent variable in this case and the seniority of the network has a negative influence on its financial results. On the other hand, the variable number of channels per household is significant with a negative sign, which indicates a positive effect of company concentration on financial profitability. Time is not a variable that explains ROE, just as it happened in the case of the variable margin.

Finally, we estimated the explanatory model of the variable economic profitability, the ROA. The results of this estimation appear in Table 9.3. The tests LM (8.96, p value = 0.002758) and Hausman (10.69, p value = 0.030254), for a significance level of 1 per cent, indicate that the most suitable model to explain ROA is the model of random effects.

Table 9.2 Estimations of the explanatory models for ROE (N = 70)

Variable	OLS Coefficient	S. e.	Fixed effects Coefficient	S. e.	Random effects Coefficient	S. e.
Audience	1,002	0.434	3.814**	1.580	0.921	0.6040
Channels per household	−56.376***	12.090	−63.549	221.144	−52.282***	14.0448
Time	−0.349*	0.191	−0.305	0.265	−0.161	0.1986
Seniority	−2.025***	0.328	0.412	2.172	−1.901***	0.4662
Constant	145.421***	39.653			105.184**	41.63
R2	0.460		0.643			
Adjusted-R2	0.427		0.560			
F	13.85***		7.76***			

* $p < 0.10$, ** $p < 0.05$, *** $p < 0.01$.

Table 9.3 Estimations of the explanatory models for ROA (N = 38)

	OLS		Fixed effects		Random effects	
Variable	Coefficient	S. e.	Coefficient	S. e.	Coefficient	S. e.
Audience	0.930***	0.315	2.226	1.369	0.865**	0.441
Channels per household	–64.952**	29.172	–332.801***	97.909	–121.067***	44.735
Time	–0.376***	0.112	–0.337***	0.120	–0.329***	0.100
Seniority	–1.248***	0.260	–2.549**	1.085	–1.517***	0.365
Constant	135.767***	29.151			152.653***	34.060
R2	0.433		0.746			
Adjusted-R2	0.365		0.664			
F	6.32***		9.14***			

* $p < 0.10$, ** $p < 0.05$, *** $p < 0.01$.

As can be seen from Table 9.3, all of the variables included in the model are significant in the explanation of ROA. The coefficient of the variable number of channels per household has a negative sign, showing that competition in the sector reduces the level of economic profitability. The variable time, that is to say, the average number of minutes that the inhabitants devote to watching television in a given country, also has a negative sign. In other words, the greater this value, the lower the level of economic profitability of the network.

The variable audience has a positive influence on the economic results of the company, so that a greater audience means a higher level of channel profitability. Finally, the seniority of the network negatively influences its economic results, as had been the case in relation to financial results.

9.4 Conclusions and discussion

Results regarding return on sales (ROS) confirm the main research hypothesis, which is related to this independent variable. The critical factor on profitability is the ability of television networks to attract massive audiences in order to 'sell' them to advertisers, media buyers or advertising firms. Differences on gross profit margin among channels with a similar audience market share are explained in terms of both internal causes – that is, sales force efficiency or cost control pressures – and external ones – that is, aggregate advertising expenditure in each country, rules established by each regulatory institutions and the impact of substitutive advertising media on each national market, as it is the case of below-the-line commercial communication.

The correlation between seniority and profit margin arises from the ability to create valuable brands throughout experience in a particular market and stable habits of audience consumption. This phenomenon is especially pronounced in the case of European television markets, because the oldest private televisions broke the public monopolies and they appropriated the positive attribute of favouring the public's freedom and choice. The newest television networks tend to neutralise their competitive disadvantages through a variety of strategies: to develop a cost structure that is sustainable on audience shares of less than 10 per cent; to look for 'killer applications' in programming – such as the acquisition of sports rights – to attract viewers from other channels; to hire well-known professionals who are traditionally linked with the leading networks – these personalities play a role as 'sub-brands' providing prestige and credibility; to promote particularly creative marketing campaigns; and to establish a very aggressive commercial policy, with strong advertising discounts for advertisers. Nevertheless, in most cases, the leading networks in the late 1990s have been able to dominate the market continuously and to obtain higher levels of profitability than new entrants.

The negative impact of the number of channels on profitability is the logical effect of the intensification of competition in television markets. In part, the relatively slow development of digital television in Europe may be explained by the dominant operators' attempts to delay the implantation of a technology that will supposedly challenge the oligopoly situation that has prevailed in domestic television markets over the course of the past three decades.

The results of this piece of research do not confirm one of the hypotheses. Consumption time does not prove to be significant, in spite of the fact that wider television consumption would seem to imply an increased ability to attract advertising expenditure in competition with other available options for advertisers. The high level of television consumption seems to depend moreover on supply variety, on existing entertainment alternatives, on weather conditions and on economic and cultural development. It is probable that the greater time devoted to television consumption does not imply an increase in the average profitability of the industry, in as far as two generators of consumption – the large number of competitors on the market and a fall in the level of revenues – are unlikely to lead a higher gross profit margin.

However, on having measured the results related to other dependent variables such as return on equity (ROE) and return on assets (ROA), we can observe some differences that are opposite to the factors associated with the high profit margin.

With regard to ROE, firm's audience share and market experience stop having positive correlation. This is explained by the fact that the leading channels are also the oldest in the market and those which normally fund their operations through the accumulated reserves they have achieved in previous years. When the denominator of this ratio of financial profitability grows substantially, logically there is a diminution of the quotient. The variables of number of channels – or competition intensity – and of consumption time behave in a similar manner as seen in the analysis of gross profit margin. The first affects in a negative manner. The second does not demonstrate any correlation.

As far as ROA is concerned, the number of channels independent variable presents a negative correlation, as in both previous ratios and for analogous causes. In this instance the average viewing time also has a negative significance. Paradoxically, ROA is low on markets with higher levels of consumption. Probably the level of economic profitability is ballasted again by the fact that high consumption depends in turn on the extent of supply and on the relatively small average revenue per viewer. Market experience also impacts negatively, as in the case of ROE and for similar reasons. On the other hand, the audience recovers the positive correlation demonstrated in ROS, probably because the denominator of the quotient – in contrast to ROA – includes all of the company's assets, including the part financed with external resources. It seems to be reasonable to conclude that companies with higher audiences, having generated more cash flow, are less indebted.

The results of this research are entirely provisional, because the number of case studies is insufficient to draw definitive conclusions. Furthermore, this study could be useful in outlining new hypotheses for further and wider quantitative analysis. In order to achieve this aim it is desirable that television companies should be increasing their transparency, so that the analysis of their balance sheets and profit and loss accounts – often presented alongside other assets from the same group – give a fair and complete information of their economic and financial reality.

Note

1. Juan Pablo Artero is an Assistant Professor of Media Management and Structure of Media Industries at the School of Communication of the University of Navarra, Spain; Cristina Etayo is an Assistant Professor at the School of Communication of the University of Navarra, Spain, Department of Media Management; Mónica Herrero is an Assistant Professor of Media Management and Dean of the School of Communication, University of Navarra, Spain; Mercedes Medina is a Professor at the University of Navarra, Spain; Alfonso Sánchez-Tabernero is Vice-President of the University of Navarra, Spain, and Professor of Media Management in the university's School of Communication.

References

Adams, W.K. 1993. Program scheduling strategies and their relationship to new program renewal rates and rating changes, *Journal of Broadcasting and Electronic Media*, 3(7), 465–74.

Albarran, A. 2002. *Media Economics: Understanding Markets, Industries and Concepts*, Ames, IA: Iowa State Press.

Anstine, D.B. 2004. The impact of the regulation of the cable television industry: the effect on quality-adjusted cable television prices, *Applied Economics*, 36(8), 793–802.

Antcliff, V. 2005. Broadcasting in the 1990s: competition, choice and inequality?, *Media, Culture and Society*, 27(6), 841–59.

Bagdikian, B. 2000. *The Media Monopoly*, Boston, MA: Beacon Press.

Barrett, M. 1995. Direct competition in cable television delivery: A case study of Paragould, Arkansas, *Journal of Media Economics*, 8(3), 77–93.

Bielby, W.T. and Bielby, D. 2003. Controlling prime time: organizational concentration and network programming strategies, *Journal of Broadcasting and Electronic Media*, 47(4), 573–96.

Burnett, R. 1992. The implications of ownership changes on concentration and diversity in the phonogram industry, *Communication Research*, 19, 749–69.

Brown, A. and Picard, R.G. 2005. *Digital Terrestrial Television in Europe*, Mahwah, NJ: Lawrence Erlbaum Associates Publishers.

Brown, K. and Alexander, P.J. 2005. Market structure, viewer welfare, and advertising rates in local broadcast television markets, *Economic Letters*, 86(3), 332–7.

Chan-Olmsted, S.M. 1996. From Sesame Street to Wall Street: An analysis of market competition in commercial children's television, *Journal of Broadcasting and Electronic Media*, 40(1), 30–44.

Collins, R., Garnham, N. and Locksley, G. 1989. *The Economics of Television: The UK Case*, London: Sage.

Compaine, B. and Gomery, D. 2000. *Who Owns the Media: Competition and Concentration in the Mass Media Industry*, Mahwah, NJ: Lawrence Erlbaum.

Davis, D.M. and Walker, J.R. 1990. Countering the new media: the resurgence of share maintenance in primetime network television, *Journal of Broadcasting & Electronic Media*, 34, 487–93.

Doyle, G. 2002. *Media Ownership: Concentration, Convergence and Public Policy*, London: Sage.

Dunnett, P. 1990. *The World Television Industry: An Economic Analysis*, New York: Routledge.
Dyson, K. and Humphreys, P. (eds). 1990. *The Political Economy of Information: International and European Dimensions*, London: Routledge.
European Audiovisual Observatory, *Yearbook*, 1999, 2000, 2005. Strasbourg, France.
Gabszewicz, J.J., Laussel D. and Sonnac, N. 2004. Programming and advertising competition in the broadcasting industry, *Journal of Economics & Management Strategy*, 13(4), 657–69.
Garnham, N. 1990. *Capitalism and Communication: Global Culture and the Economics of Information*, London: Sage.
Gershon, R.A. 2000. *The Transnational Media Corporation: Global Messages and Free Market Competition*, Mahwah, NJ: Lawrence Erlbaum.
Golding, P. and Murdoch, G. (eds). 1997. *The Political Economy of the Media*, Lyme, NH: Edward Elgar Publishing.
Greene, W.H. 2003. *Econometric Analysis*, Englewood Hills, NJ: Prentice Hall.
Hendriks, P. 1995. Communications policy and industrial dynamics in media markets. *Journal of Media Economics*, 8(2), 61–76.
Herrero, M. 2003. *Programming and Direct Viewer Payment For Television*, Pamplona: Eunsa.
Hollifield, A. 2001. *Transnational Media Management*, Mahwah, NJ: Lawrence Erlbaum.
Informa Media Group. 2002. *European Television*, 6th edn, Rockville, MD: Informa Media Group.
Leahy, A.S. 1997. Advertising and concentration: a survey of the empirical evidence, *Quarterly Journal of Business and Economics*, 36(1), 35–50.
Leandros, N. and Tsourvakas, G. 2005. Intensive competition and company failures in subscription television: some European experiences, *The International Journal on Media Management*, 7(1–2), 24–38.
Li, S.S. 1999. Market competition and market performance: examining prime-time series in Taiwan, *Asian Journal of Communication*, 9(2), 1–16.
Litman, B., Hasegawa, K., Shirkhande, S. and Barbatsis, G. 1994. Measuring diversity in US television programming, *Studies in Broadcasting*, 30(3), 131–53.
McDonald, D.G. and Lin, S. 2004. The effect of New Networks on US television diversity, *Journal of Media Economics*, 17(2), 105–21.
Machet, E. 1998. *Television and Culture: Policies and Regulations in Europe*, Manchester: European Institute for the Media.
Mashi, R. 1999. An empirical analysis of the demand for commercial television advertising, *Applied Economics*, 31(2), 149–63.
Mattelart, A. 1979. *Multinational Corporations and the Control of Culture: the Ideological Apparatuses of Imperialism*, translated from the French by Michael Chanan, Brighton: Harvester Press.
Medina, M. 2005. *European Television Production: Pluralism and Concentration*, Pamplona: Eunsa.
Mosco, V. 1996. *The Political Economy of Communication: Rethinking and Renewal*, London: Sage.
Nieto, A. and Iglesias, F. 2000 *La Empresa Informativa*, Barcelona: Ariel.
Noam, E., 1985. *Video Media Competition: Regulation, Economics, and Technology*, New York: Columbia University Press.

Ojer, T. 2007. *La BBC como modelo de gobierno corporativo, financiación y calidad de los contenidos*, Doctoral thesis, Pamplona: Universidad de Navarra.

Park, S. 2005. Competition's effects on programming diversity of different program types, *The International Journal on Media Management*, 7(1–2), 24–38.

Picard, R. 2002. *The Economics and Financing of Media Companies*, New York: Fordham University Press.

Picard, R.. 2003. The study of media economics, in A. Arrese (ed.), *Empresa Informativa y Mercados de la Comunicación*, Pamplona: Eunsa, pp. 75–85.

Powers, A. 2001. Toward monopolistic competition in US local television news, *Journal of Media Economics*, 14(2), 77–86.

Sánchez-Tabernero, A. and Carvajal, M. 2002. *Media Concentration in the European Market: Trends and Challenges*, Pamplona: Media Market Monograph.

Shaughnessy, H. 1990. *The Cultural Obligations of Broadcasting: National and Transnational Legislation Concerning Cultural Duties of Television Broadcasters in Europe*, Manchester: European Institute for the Media.

Toussaint, N. 1996. *L´economie des medias*, Paris: Presses Universitaires de France.

Van der Wurff, R. 2005. Competition, concentration and diversity in European television markets, *Journal of Cultural Economics*, 29(4), 249–75.

Wright, P.L. 1994. Attacking global markets or defending cultural diversity, *Intermedia*, 22(3), 10–11.

Wu, I.M., Dey, R.A. and Duwadi, K. 2004. The impact of competition and technology on telecommunications regulation: call for further research on regulatory procedures and the convergence of wireless, wireline and cable, *Info*, 6(4), 225–33.

Yan, M.Z. 2002. Market structure and local signal carriage decisions in the cable television industry: results from count analysis, *Journal of Media Economics*, 15(3), 175–91.

Young, D.P.T. 2000. Modeling media markets: how important is market structure?, *Journal of Media Economics*, 13(1), 27–59.

10
Preference for Flat-Rate Media Access Fees: A Behavioural Economics Interpretation

Hitoshi Mitomo and Tokio Otsuka[1]

10.1 Introduction

This chapter examines the existence of users' preference for flat-rate media access fees and further identifies those factors that influence such preferences. Specifically, we explore consumer addiction to flat-rate pricing plans, defined as 'flat-rate preference', and examine such concepts from the perspective of behavioural economics.

A selective tariff system is often applied to media access services, within which a user can choose a fee structure that would result in the lowest bill payment for his/her usage. Consumers typically prefer flat-rate to measured-rate pricing, because under such plans, a variety of communications services ranging from traditional telephony services to broadband internet access are bundled together into one flat-rate package. Train (1994) has provided empirical evidence to support this view, showing that 'consumers seem to value flat-rate service over measured service even when the bill that the consumer would receive under the two services would be the same'. Conversely, traditional economics has emphasized the dominance of measured rates, as they are effective in outlining economic efficiencies. It has been interpreted that the addiction to a flat rate is evidence of users' inclination to avoid the risks inherent in fluctuating monthly bills under measured-rate plans.

When considering flat-rate pricing, however, user demand is not sensitive to price, therefore creating the potential for unnecessary usage from full-time connections. At the same time, a higher flat-rate price may exclude small-scale users from subscribing to the service. From the perspective of media access providers, under such plans their supply would be increased but the revenue would not be proportional to the network usage. It is apparent then that flat-rate pricing does not attain resource allocation efficiency, which is considered 'unreasonable' within the context of traditional economic theory. As a result, few analyses of flat-rate pricing exist in the pricing literature. Mitomo (2001) has previously suggested that traditional economics could not be successfully applied to explain users' addiction to a flat rate, but instead that the integration of other academic perspectives would help to develop a more reasonable interpretation for consumer preferences for flat-rate pricing.

This chapter applies several important concepts from behavioural economics to provide more reasonable interpretations of consumer preferences for flat-rate pricing plans. Behavioural economics, although difficult to apply in an empirical investigation, provides deeper insights into consumer behaviour since it includes psychological factors which allow for the consideration of irrational choice behaviours. Mitomo et al. (2007) conducted empirical tests for the existence of biased preference for flat rates for mobile phones and examined how psychological factors can have an effect upon these preferences. They examined how fundamental concepts from Prospect Theory – including loss aversion, dependency upon reference points, and the shape of the probability weighting function – could explain consumer inclinations towards flat-rate plans. Other fundamental concepts – such as mental accounting, ambiguity aversion, cognitive dissonance, and so on – are also applied to further explain such preferences.

Towards this end, we extend the analysis. Initially, we test the existence of consumer preferences for flat-rate pricing plans. Then, we investigate the factors that can be used to further understand and explain such preferences. More concretely, the data used in this analysis were collected through web-based surveys, and include information on mobile phone and Internet access services. The statistical analyses employed both parametric and non-parametric methods.

The results show that loss aversion and dependency upon reference points have a significant influence on the existence of consumer preferences for flat rates, although the shape of the probability weight function could not be identified. Mental accounting, ambiguity aversion and cognitive dissonance were also recognized as influential factors for such preferences.

This chapter is organized as follows: Section 10.2 explains the behavioural economic concepts to be applied to explain the flat-rate preference. Sections 10.3 and 10.4 show the results of the empirical tests in which Internet access and post-paid mobile phone services are selected for the tests since they have been supplied under both flat and measured rates. Section 10.5 offers some concluding remarks.

10.2 Background and framework of the research

According to traditional economic theories, only a measured rate (a single price) can work as a parameter and achieve economic efficiency through market mechanisms. Flat rates are not believed to attain higher levels of economic efficiency. Consumers' preference for flat-rate pricing has been regarded as a consequence of consumers' *risk-averse behaviour*.

However, it has become clear from our everyday experience that human behaviour is not necessarily as rational as is assumed by the concepts of traditional economics. The hypothesis on consumers' behaviour that people maximize their utility represented with well-behaved utility functions would appear to be too simplistic. Our decisions or choices often violate the expected utility hypothesis. An interpretation based on risk avoidance is useful but not sufficient to explain the preference for flat rates. Therefore, the 'rationality' of consumer behaviour should be redefined by incorporating psychological factors to describe more realistic processes in decision making in order to reflect the diversity of human behaviour.

Behavioural economics, which was initiated by Kahneman and Tversky (1979) and others, has integrated insights from psychological research into economic science, especially in the areas of human judgement and decision making under uncertainty. Prospect theory, which is one of the important theories in behavioural economics, provides a framework for explaining how people prospect for and behave towards a risk, containing several important concepts such as *loss aversion, reference dependence* and *Overvaluation of a low probability* based on the shape of the value function and the probability weighting function.

Figure 10.1 illustrates the two functions which characterise the prospect theory: the *value function*, which replaces a utility function in the traditional economic theory; and the *probability weighting function*, which represents a modified expected value weighted by the subjective evaluation of the probability that a phenomenon is likely to happen.

Loss aversion explains tendencies that losses are weighted substantially more than objectively commensurate gains in the evaluation of prospects and trades (Kahneman and Tversky, 1979). This can be represented in Figure 10.1 by a steeper curve of a value function in the loss direction than in the gain direction in the neighbourhood of the reference point. Reference dependence represents a dependence of preference on one's reference point – for instance, the current endowment, which is shown as the origin in Figure 10.1. The shape of the probability weighting function shows tendencies that low probabilities

Value function

A loss is more serious than the gain of the same size.

Probability weighting function

Expected value: $p_1 v(x_1) + p_2 v(x_2)$
$\pi(p_1) v(x_1) + \pi(p_2) v(x_2)$
$\pi(p)$: Probability weighting function

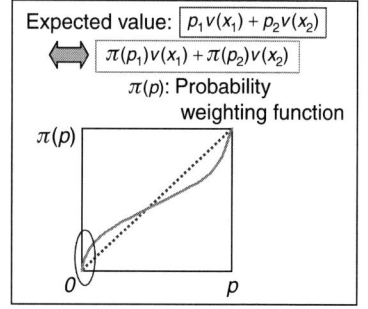

It tends to overestimate a lower probability.

Figure 10.1 The shape of a value function, and the shape of a probability weighting function
Source: Mitomo et al. (2007).

are overweighted while high probabilities are underweighted compared with the objective probabilities.

In addition to the concepts from prospect theory, we will employ other six behavioural economic concepts: *Overvaluation of a Low Probability, mental accounting, ambiguity aversion, Choice by Habit, Misunderstanding of Payment Reduction* and *Dependency on the Level of Usage*. Thaler (1985) brought out the concept of mental accounting which is an idea that people set up mental accounts for outcomes that are psychologically separate, describing the rules that govern the integration of gain and loss. Ambiguity aversion describes preference for known risks over unknown risks (Camerer, Loewenstein and Rabin, 2004, ch. 1). In other words, measures of certainty affect decisions and people tend to avoid decision making in uncertain situations. Other concepts have been discussed in articles of behavioural economics. These concepts can be applied to interpret the flat-rate preference or tendencies to avoid a measured rate in such a way as follows:

10.2.1 Loss aversion

If a monthly payment happens to be larger than the reference point (= the average monthly bill payment), users tend to overestimate the loss. To avoid the loss, they prefer flat rates.

10.2.2 Reference dependence

If the reference point represents a level of bill payment which a user is accustomed to paying, the level affects the subjective evaluation of the shift to a flat rate. Users' preference for flat rates is not affected by the absolute level of payment but by the diversion from the reference point.

10.2.3 Overvaluation of a low probability

With a typical probability weighting function, users with a low probability to overuse tend to overestimate the probability. They avoid an extraordinarily high amount of payment even if it does not seem to be likely to happen, and then choose a flat rate.

10.2.4 Mental accounting

This represents how expenditures are recognised by consumers in a psychological sense (Thaler, 1980). Under a measured rate, users are aware of their bill payment every month. Under flat rates, users are not aware of such a psychological burden.

10.2.5 Ambiguity aversion

This denotes behaviour to avoid uncertainty. Under measured rates, the amount of the bill is uncertain, while under flat rates the amount of payment is constant. In this instance, consumers prefer the latter to the former.

10.2.6 Choice by habit

This represents a kind of usage inertia. Users tend to use a billing plan with which they are familiar.

10.2.7 Misunderstanding of payment reduction

Users simply regard a new billing plan as one that brings about a reduction in payment.

10.2.8 Dependency on the level of usage

Prospective usage levels affect the choice of a billing plan. That is, large-scale users tend to choose flat rates while small-scale users prefer measured rates.

10.3 Questionnaire survey

In order to examine the existence of flat-rate preference and the reasons for its existence, the sample data were collected through the use of a questionnaire survey. As a result of the Japanese laws relating to the protection of personal information, random sampling using a postal mail questionnaire faces considerable difficulties. Instead, an online questionnaire survey was carried out over sample panels pre-registered by a survey research company. The data were collected in September 2006 and were taken from a pool of 400 mobile users ranged in age from teens to people in their forties. From each of these we collected 100 samples. These were selected randomly from the pre-registered consumer panels. The number of valid responses was 313, giving a response rate of 78.3 per cent. The questionnaire included 44 questions with regard to the choice of fee plans in addition to questions asking personnel information. Some demographic data of the respondents and their current level of payment for Internet and mobile access are shown in Table 10.1 and Figure 10.2.

Table 10.1 Basic attributes of the respondents

Sex	Male	48.6%
	Female	51.4%
Age	Teens	23.6%
	Twenties	25.2%
	Thirties	25.6%
	Forties and over	25.6%
Average monthly disposable money		¥35,424

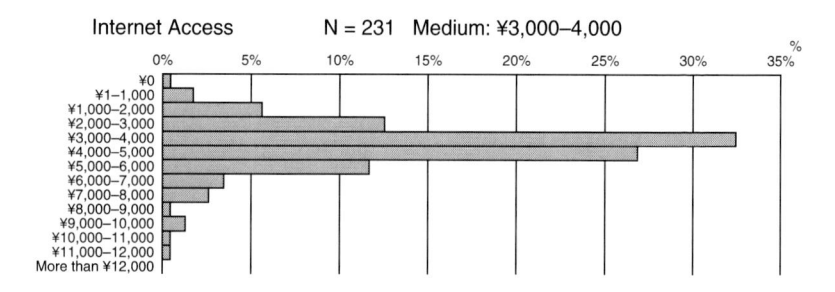

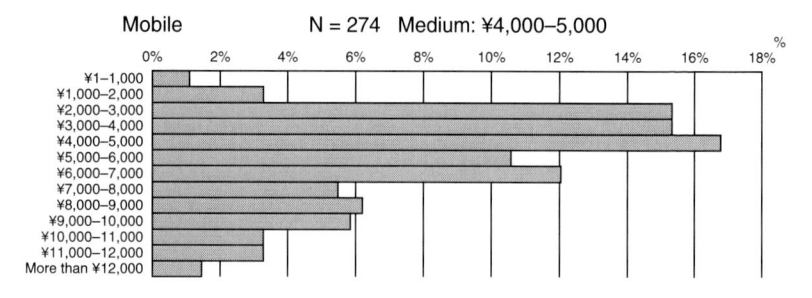

Figure 10.2 Current levels of payment for Internet access and mobile phones

Mobile and Internet access are selected because they are representative of current communication media. They offered an opportunity for comparison because Internet services have been supplied under a flat-rate pricing system while mobile phones generally operate under a system of measured rates.

The summary of the questionnaire survey is thus as follows:

Period: From 1 to 6 September 2006.
Method: Online questionnaire survey.
The number of valid response: 313 (The total number surveyed: 400).
Questions: 44 questions on the choice between flat and measured rates.

10.4 Flat-rate preference

10.4.1 Existence of flat-rate preference

A question was asked regarding the choice between a flat rate and a measured rate assuming that both rates are available and that bill payments in the both cases would eventually be the same amount. The result shows that the differences between those who selected flat rates and measured rates are 94 per cent points and 28 per cent points in the usage of the Internet and mobile phones, respectively (see Figure 10.3).

A chi-square test was applied to test the hypothesis that preferences on a flat rate and on a measured rate are the same (that is, users distribute evenly between the two rates). The hypothesis was rejected at $p < 0.01$. The result indicates that flat-rate preference exists in the both media.

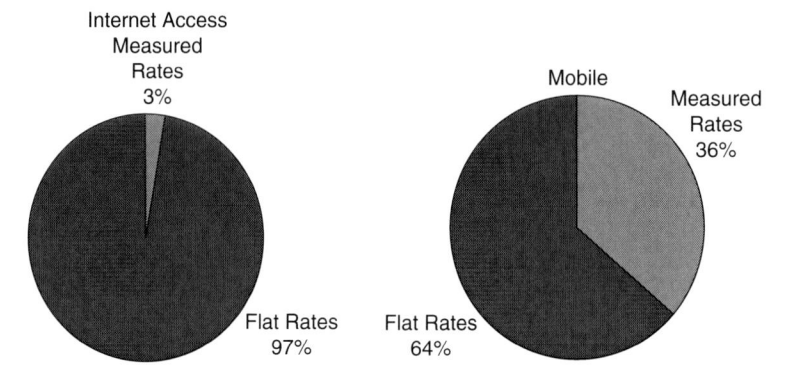

Figure 10.3 Choice between flat rates and measured rates

One may suspect that respondents who selected a fee system for one medium would select the same fee system for the other medium. Applying a MacNemar test which tests the difference between matched pairs of subjects with a dichotomous choice, the null hypothesis that no difference exists in the choice between the two media was rejected. This can also be shown by the cross-table (Table 10.2). Many users selected different fee systems for the both media.

Note that the respondents are Internet users and are used to flat rates because this has been the prevailing fee system. This can cause a biased preference for flat rates.

10.4.2 Differences between the fee system in use and the one each user is willing to use

By comparing the fee system currently chosen with one which they are willing to use, the extent of the users' biased preference on a specific fee system can be ascertained. The result of a chi-square test examines whether the ratio of users' current use between flat rates and measured rates is significantly different from the ratio of their willingness to choose ($p < 0.01$).

In the same way as above, it could be examined whether or not the respondents choose the same fee system as the one actually selected – that is, if the respondents' answers are influenced by the fee currently chosen. Without applying a McNemar test, a cross-tabulation (Table 10.3) can reveal that there is a difference between the current choice and the willingness to use in the ratios of the choice between flat and measured rates.

10.4.3 Differences of usage inertia

When a biased preference exists in respect of one fee system, users should have a stronger feeling of resistance to a shift to the other tariff than they have to a reverse shift. Usage inertia, that is, an inclination

Table 10.2 The choice between measured and flat rates for Internet access and mobile phones

		Mobile		Total
		Measured	Flat	
Internet Access	Measured	5	4	9
	Flat	109	195	304
Total		114	199	313

Table 10.3 Actual usage of tariff and the choices stated in the answers (the cross-tabulation)

Internet Access

		Choice		Total
		Measured	Flat	
Actual Usage	Measured	5	34	39
	Flat	4	270	274
Total		9	304	313

Mobile Access

		Choice		Total
		Measured	Flat	
Actual Usage	Measured	104	152	256
	Flat	10	45	55
Total		114	197	311

to stick to a choice, should be different between the two tariff systems. In order to analyse this, we examine what difference in price can trigger the adoption of the other tariff. The respondents are divided randomly into seven groups, each of which are asked if they shift to the other tariff when hypothetically faced by differences in bill payment from –30 per cent to +30 per cent (seven distinct levels).

The results are shown in Figure 10.4. The numbers of respondents in the respective levels varies from 30 to 58 due to the random allocation of valid responses.

In both media, the number of those who express willingness to shift from a measured rate to a flat rate is higher than the number of those who are willing to shift from a flat rate to a measured rate. Many of the differences are significant as a result of chi-square test ($p < 0.05$) as shown in the tables with asterisk.

Note that the curves in the graphs should be downward sloping. However, this does not hold at some parts of the figure. In that sense, the results do not display an overall consistency. This could be a result of the comparatively limited number of samples.

Then, let us consider the price difference which results in those willing to adopt the other tariff exceeding 50 per cent. This happens for measured-rate users when the bill payment with flat rates is equal to that with measured rates in terms of both Internet and mobile access (the top part of

Internet Access

Change in payment	Measured => Flat	# of samples	Flat => Measured	# of samples	Significance of the difference
−30%	88%	42	43%	46	*
−20%	87%	39	40%	43	*
−10%	87%	53	35%	46	*
0%	83%	41	11%	36	*
10%	45%	49	13%	47	*
20%	41%	44	12%	49	*
30%	60%	45	17%	46	*

Mobile

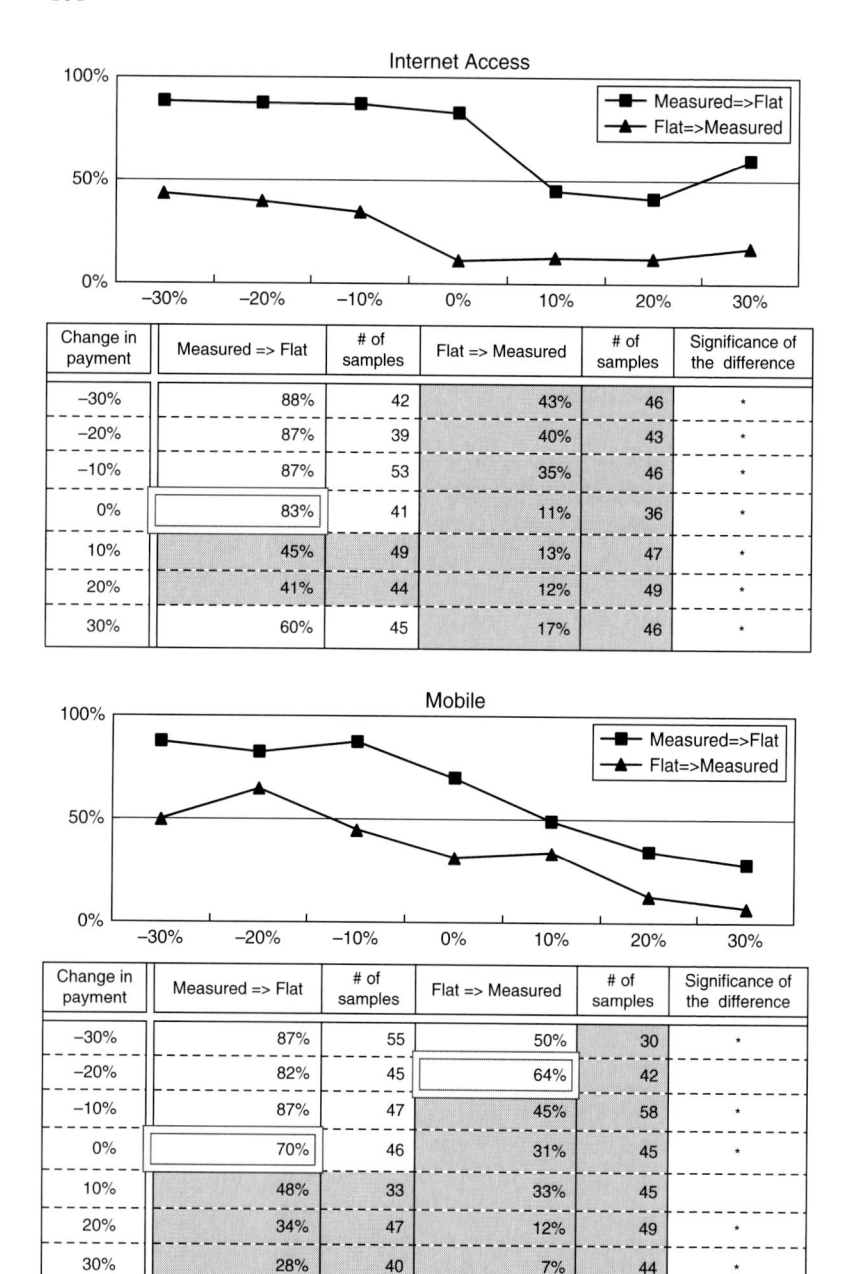

Change in payment	Measured => Flat	# of samples	Flat => Measured	# of samples	Significance of the difference
−30%	87%	55	50%	30	*
−20%	82%	45	64%	42	
−10%	87%	47	45%	58	*
0%	70%	46	31%	45	*
10%	48%	33	33%	45	
20%	34%	47	12%	49	*
30%	28%	40	7%	44	*

Figure 10.4 Comparison of trade-off points
Note: An asterisk in the table rejects the hypothesis that the difference in the two averages is equal to zero (a chi-square test, $p < 0.05$).

Table 10.4 Comparison of trade-off points between the media

Measured rates to flat rates

Change in Payment	Internet	Mobile	Significance of the difference
–30%	88%	87%	
–20%	87%	82%	
–10%	87%	87%	
0%	83%	70%	
10%	45%	48%	
20%	41%	34%	
30%	60%	28%	*

Flat rates to measured rates

Change in Payment	Internet	Mobile	Significance of the difference
–30%	43%	50%	*
–20%	40%	64%	*
–10%	35%	45%	*
0%	11%	31%	
10%	13%	33%	
20%	12%	12%	
30%	17%	7%	*

Note: An asterisk in the table rejects the hypothesis that the difference between the two averages is equal to zero (a chi-square test, $p < 0.05$).

Table 10.4). On the other hand, it happens for flat-rate users only when the payment with measured rates is 20 per cent lower in mobile access. It does not occur even when it is 30 per cent lower in the case of Internet access (the bottom part in Table 10.4). The result strongly suggests the existence of a preference for flat-rate schemes.

10.4.4 Preference factors contributing to the choice between flat rates and measured rates

To identify the reasons why users choose either a flat rate or a measured rate, we chose nine factors (shown in Table 10.5), which were collected from previous studies of behavioural economics. The statements to be examined are arranged based on these factors and modified according to the respective characteristics of measured rates and flat rates. We assume a hypothetical situation where each user should choose either a flat rate or a measured rate for Internet and mobile access under the condition that the bill payments in both cases are eventually the same. Each respondent was asked to indicate his or her degree of agreement with the statement, according to a five-point Likert scale.

Based on the result, we can identify the relative strength of each factor on the choice between measured rates and flat rates. The Wilcoxon

Table 10.5 The factors of preferences

		Factor	Statement
Measured Rates	1	Choice by Habit	I will select a measured rate because I have used it.
	2	Ambiguity Aversion	because total usage is not predictable.
	3	Misunderstanding of Payment Reduction	because the total payment is expected to be lower.
	4	Level of Usage	because I will not use mobile/Internet so often
	5	Loss Aversion	because a flat rate may result in a higher payment
	6	Reference Dependence	because a measured rate will bring about a lower payment.
	7	Overvaluation of a low probability	because I can't ignore the possibility of low usage
	8	Mental Accounting	because I can know how much I have used.
	9	Other External Factors	because I would not be responsible for the contract.
Flat Rates	1	Choice by Habit	I will select a flat rate because I have used it.
	2	Ambiguity Aversion	because total usage is not predictable.
	3	Misunderstanding of Payment Reduction	because the total payment is exected to be lower.
	4	Level of Usage	because I can use mobile/Internet without limit.
	5	Loss Aversion	because a measured rate may result in a higher payment
	6	Reference Dependence	because a flat rate will bring about a lower payment.
	7	Overvaluation of a low probability	because I can't ignore the possibility of excessive usage
	8	Mental Accounting	because I don't need to care how much I have used.
	9	Other External Factors	because I would not be responsible for the contract.

Note: Evaluation is based on a five-point Likert scale as follows: 5: Strongly agree, 4: Agree, 3: Neither agree or disagree, 2: Disagree, 1: Strongly disagree.

Table 10.6 Comparison of preference factors contributing to the choice between flat rates and measured rates

Internet Access

	Preference Factor	Measured Rates		Flat Rates	Significance Level
1	Choice by Habit	2.8	<	4.4	**
2	Ambiguity Aversion	3.4	<	4.4	**
3	Misunderstanding of Payment Reduction	3.3	<	4.4	**
4	Level of Usage	3.0	<	4.8	**
5	Loss Aversion	3.6	<	4.3	*
6	Reference Dependence	3.2	<	4.0	*
7	Overvaluation of a Low Probability	3.3	<	4.5	**
8	Mental Accounting	3.3	<	4.6	**
9	Other External Factors	2.1	>	2.0	

Mobile

	Preference Factor	Measured Rates		Flat Rates	Significance Level
1	Choice by Habit	3.6	>	3.5	
2	Ambiguity Aversion	4.1	<	4.2	
3	Misunderstanding of Payment Reduction	4.0	<	4.1	
4	Level of Usage	4.4	<	4.5	
5	Loss Aversion	4.3	>	4.1	*
6	Reference Dependence	3.8	>	3.7	
7	Overvaluation of a Low Probability	4.0	<	4.2	*
8	Mental Accounting	3.4	<	4.3	**
9	Other External Factors	1.6	<	2.0	**

Significance Level: *: 5%, **: 1%

signed-rank test is applied to test the equality of the means of two normal populations between the two related measurements. The results are given in Table 10.6.

In respect of Internet access, every factor apart from 'external factors' has a significantly greater influence on the choice of flat rates. On the other hand, 'loss aversion' is the only significant factor that has a greater impact on the choice of measured rates, and 'mental accounting', 'overvaluation of a low probability' and 'external factors' are significant factors affecting the choice of flat rates in respect of mobile access.

10.4.5 Relative contribution of the preference factors

Up to this point in the analysis we have applied non-parametric methods. A parametric approach, however, can be employed to estimate how each of the preference factors has a relative influence on the choice between measured and flat rates. A parametric approach has one advantage – it can deal with all of the factors influencing the choice within a single framework and can identify their relative importance. In this section, we will employ a binomial logit model. We will only show the results for access to mobile phones. With regard to Internet access, the estimation result was not statistically reliable because the number of those who chose flat rates were overwhelming in the majority (97 per cent) and the number of measured-rate users was too small.

In the model, the explained variable is the choice between a flat rate and a measured rate, and the explanatory variables are the six factors of preference listed in Table 10.5, excluding those related with prospect theory for keeping independence of the explanatory variables. A maximum likelihood method was applied for the model estimation. The results are shown in Table 10.7. If a coefficient is positive, the preference factor contributes to the choice of flat rates. If negative, it does to the choice of measured rates.

'Mental accounting' and 'Other external factors' are significant as positive contributors. In the Japanese post-paid mobile communication

Table 10.7 Relative contributions of the factors: the case of mobile access

	Mobile		
The Number of Samples	313		
Initial Likelihood	−205.27		
Maximum Likelihood	−175.59		
Likelihood Ratio Index	0.14		
Preference Factors	Estimated Coefficients	Standard Error	Significance Level
Ambiguity Aversion	0.126	0.157	
Misunderstanding of Payment Reduction	−0.203	0.188	
Dependency on the Level of Usage	−0.032	0.196	
Choice by Habit	−0.289	0.113	*
Mental Accounting	0.896	0.155	**
External Factors	0.356	0.123	**
Constant Term	−2.123	0.897	

**: $P \leq 0.01$, *: $P \leq 0.05$

market, in general measured rates have been applied; this means that users should be careful about their usage because it is hard for them to know how much they spend every time they use a mobile phone. 'Mental accounting' indicates the existence of such a psychological burden, which could promote the choice of flat rates. 'Other external factors' implies a situation in which parents give a mobile phone to their children or where business users are given mobile phones by their employer. We can imagine that these users would have an aversion to fluctuations in payments.

On the other hand, 'Choice by habit' is a significant factor in contributing to the choice of measured rates. 'Choice by habit' may suggest that a kind of inertia exists in the choice of a bill plan and that, once a plan has been chosen, people are reluctant to change to another – even if it appears to be more reasonable. Note that these interpretations are not exact; rather, they are based on possible scenarios.

10.5 Conclusion

It has been asserted that the application of flat-rate plans is likely to promote media access. In this chapter, the statistical tests based on the questionnaire survey strongly suggest the existence of flat-rate preferences in terms of both Internet access and mobile access services. Evaluations on flat rates are not the same and flat-rate preferences exist independently between the two media. Users' willingness to use flat rates does not show significant correlations with currently adopted fees.

Consumers' psychological factors employed from behavioural economics were used to explain the preference for flat rates and measured rates. The non-parametric statistical tests have identified that all of the factors with the exception of 'external factors' are contributing to the choice of flat rates in the case of Internet access. On the other hand, 'mental accounting', 'overvaluation of a low probability' and 'external factors' are influencing the choice in the case of mobile access.

The logit analysis could identify the relative strength of the factors contributing to the choice between measured rates and flat rates. The result suggests that choice by habit, meaning that current users have been accustomed to measured rates, has contributed to the choice of this method of payment. 'Mental accounting' is the significant factor in the choice of flat rates.

Therefore, behavioural economic factors can successfully explain flat-rate preferences. Despite the persuasive argument of behavioural economics, it is often faced with a number of difficulties in empirical tests.

The result may also be affected by the bias embedded in the data collected through the online survey, so we should be careful to the method of data collection. In order to describe the choice behaviour between flat rates and measured rates, we need to employ experimental methods and interviews as well as questionnaire surveys. Only then will we finally be able to reach an overall evaluation of users' choice behaviour and flat-rate preference.

Note

1. Hitoshi Mitomo is a Professor at Graduate School of Asia-Pacific Studies, Waseda University, Japan; Tokio Otsuda is an Assistant Professor, at Shumei University, Japan.

References

Camerer, C., Loewenstein, G. and Rabin, M. 2004. *Advances in Behavioral Economics*, Princeton University, NJ: Princeton University Press.

Kahneman, D. and Tversky, A. 1979. Prospect theory: an analysis of decision under risk, *Econometrica*, 43(2), 263–91.

Lambrecht, A., and Skiera, B. 2006. Paying too much and being happy about it: existence, causes and consequences of tariff-choice biases, *Journal of Marketing Research*, 43(2), 212–23.

Mitomo, H. 2001. An economic evaluation of flat-rate – a simulation of how a shift from a two-part tariff changes economic welfare, *Journal of The Japan Society of Information and Communication Research*, 39–54 (in Japanese).

Mitomo, H ., Otsuka, T. and Nakaba, K. 2007. A behavioral economic interpretation of the preference for flat rates: a case of post-paid mobile phone services, 18th European Regional ITS Conference, International Telecommunications Society, Istanbul.

Thaler, R. 1985. Mental accounting and consumer choice, *Marketing Science*, 4(3), 199–214.

Train, K.E. 1994. *Optimal Regulation*, Cambridge, MA: MIT Press.

Train, K.E., McFadden, D.L. and Ben-Akiva, M. 1987. The demand for local telephone service: a fully discrete model of residential calling patterns and service choices, *RAND Journal of Economics*, 18(1), 109–23.

11
Explaining Prices Paid for Television Ad Time: the Purchasing Profile Model

W. Wayne Fu, Hairong Li and Steven S. Wildman[1]

11.1 Introduction

Advertising plays a major role in the financing of the vast majority of television networks, the principal exceptions being premium pay services such as HBO and pay-per-view services, including video on demand. For many over-the-air broadcast networks, it is the sole source of revenue. According to the Television Bureau of Advertising (2009), advertisers spent $46.4 billion on television ads in the United States alone in 2008. Given the financial stakes involved, it is not surprising that the measurement of television audiences constitutes a substantial business in its own right and that reports on prices paid for ad time are often featured stories in the industry trade press.

Measured in per viewer terms, the prices advertisers pay for commercial time vary considerably among programmes, both within and across individual channels.[2] Efforts by academics and other researchers to empirically model the pricing of television ad time have focused primarily on variation among programmes in the size and the demographic composition of their audiences as measured by the commercial audience ratings services, principally A.C. Nielsen in the United States.[3] The argument for using demographic composition to explain price variation is both simple and intuitive. Because consumers' demographic traits are correlated with their product choices, advertisers use measures of audience demographics to estimate how many prospective customers are contained in the audiences for different programmes. The argument for including audience size in these models is that advertisers may be willing to pay more per viewer for ad time in programmes with larger audiences because per viewer transaction costs are reduced when eyeballs are purchased in larger lots.

When one examines the practices of the media buyers who plan and execute advertisers' media strategies, it is immediately apparent that they rely on a varied set of sources for information about programmes' audiences that extends considerably beyond the reports on audience size and demographic composition produced by audience measurement services. Clearly, advertisers believe that with the information on audiences from these alternative sources, they can do a better job of assessing the merits of ad buys in different programmes than would be possible if they relied on the commercial measures of audience size and demographics alone. Napoli's (2003) review of the substantial literature generated by audience researchers and media planners suggests that the demand for additional information about audiences arises because the demographic attributes reported for a typical television programme's audience are rather crude predictors of the types of products purchased by its viewers. Demographically similar viewers may, and apparently do, consume very different sets of products. Therefore information from other sources may enable an advertiser to improve considerably the accuracy with which it can predict the number of potential customer's in a programme's audience (Assael and Poltrack, 1996; D'Amico, 1999; Schroeder, 1998; Surowiecki, 2002).

One such source is Simmons Market Research Bureau (SMRB), which conducts an annual survey of over 20,000 US households, asking them about their patterns of purchasing and consumption. Simmons reports can be used to assess the correlation of consumer choices among products and television programmes for over 8,000 brands in 460 product categories. The SMRB surveys are widely employed within the advertising industry and, according to Assael and Poltrack (1991, 1993, 1996, 1999), the data generated by these surveys provide an advertiser with a much more accurate picture of the comparative benefits of purchasing time in different programmes than do the audience size and demographic data reported by Nielsen. This suggests that we might benefit from constructing empirical models of ad time pricing that incorporate more of the information used by buyers of ad time to compare programmes' audiences and other factors that might influence the amounts they are willing to pay for commercial time. Even if such models do not improve on the statistical fit of traditional demographics-based models, they might provide additional insight into the role of buyer-side considerations in the determination of prices for television ad time.

The heavy reliance on Nielsen audience measures to study the pricing of television ad time in the USA undoubtedly reflects in part the high visibility of the Nielsen ratings. The audiences for national television networks are measured by Nielsen on a nearly continuous basis, and the results are provided to clients electronically on a daily basis and are reported weekly in the trade press catering to both buyers and sellers of television ad time. By contrast, the SMRB survey is conducted annually[4] and its reports are used primarily by media planners who are working on behalf of advertisers. However, the most important factor limiting the use of findings from consumer surveys in ad time pricing models may be that it is not obvious how data on the correlation of purchases of specific products with the viewing of individual programmes might be aggregated in an empirical model.

Wildman (2003) published a 2-product model that constructs the demand for a programme's ad time from the demands of individual advertisers. The model, which we call the purchasing profile model (PPM), predicts that the price charged for ad time in a television programme will increase with: (1) the range of products consumed by viewers in the programme's audience; (2) the degree to which the programme's viewers resemble each other in their choices among advertised products; (3) advertisers' profit margins on the goods they intend to sell; and (4) the effectiveness of television ads in converting potential customers into actual customers for the types of products purchased by the members of the programme's audience. As long as advertisers' predictions of products purchased by programmes' viewers are not wholly inaccurate, the PPM suggests that variation in viewers' product choices will impact prices paid for television ad time in ways that cannot be captured by empirical models relying on demographic information as a proxy for the value of programmes' viewers to advertisers.

Using SMRB data advertisers might have used to evaluate the major US broadcast networks' primetime programmes in advance of the fall 1997 television season, we were able to construct measures, although at a high level of aggregation, of the range of products purchased by programmes' viewers and the extent to which different programmes' viewers resembled each other in their product choices. Data from other sources allowed us to construct estimates of the average profit per customer products earned on products purchased by programmes' viewers, and a proxy for the effectiveness of television advertising in inducing sales of these products. These variables are employed in a regression model used to explain prices reported for upfront market[5] sales of time in primetime network programmes for the fall 1997 television season. As is reported below, even though the constructed measures rely on highly aggregated data, the results show that empirical models that incorporate more relevant data can shed new light on how the demands of individual advertisers and factors influencing the way these demands are aggregated are reflected in prices paid for TV ad time, lending strong support for the PPM.

The next section of the chapter describes the PPM and presents four testable hypotheses derived from the model. Section 11.3 then describes the dataset and the empirical tests. The results are presented and discussed in section 11.4, and the findings are summarised and their implications discussed further in the final section.

11.2 The purchasing profile model (PPM)

The PPM constructs the demand for a programme's ad time from the demands of individual advertisers whose products might beneficially be promoted through commercials placed in television programmes. The focus is on the price paid for commercial time in a single television programme. We assume each advertiser distinguishes among viewers according to whether they are or are not potential buyers of its product. In addition, each advertiser possesses information about the programme's audience that it uses to predict the number of viewers in the audience that are potential customers for its product. We describe an advertiser's calculation of how much it would be willing to pay for a unit of commercial time in the programme as if it knew with certainty how many potential customers the audience contained. However, the basic logic of the model carries through if advertisers' estimates of numbers of potential customers in programmes' audiences embed some statistical error as long as the predictions do not suffer from excessive bias.

From an advertiser's perspective, a programme's viewers are either potential customers or they are not. The PPM assumes that the value of a programme's audience to an advertiser is proportional to the fraction of the audience comprised of people who might buy its product. For product i, let f_i designate this fraction. How much the advertiser selling i (advertiser i) is willing to pay for each potential customer in the programme's audience is a function of how much seeing its commercial in the programme contributes towards turning a potential customer into an actual customer and the profit it realises from sales to a representative customer. Let Δ_i be the increase in the likelihood that a potential i customer becomes an actual i customer after seeing a commercial for i in a television programme, given purchases of ad time or space advertiser i has made or expects to make from other media companies selling access to audiences, and define m_i and t_i, respectively, as the contribution the marginal unit of i sold makes to the advertiser's profits and the number of units of i purchased by a representative customer. $m_i t_i$ is the value of the marginal customer to advertiser i. Let w_i be the maximum amount advertiser i would be willing to pay for a unit of commercial time in the programme. Given f_i, m_i, t_i, and Δ_i, for n the number of viewers in the programme's audience we have:

$$w_i = nf_i\Delta_i m_i t_i. \qquad (11.1)$$

The amount i is willing to pay per viewer in the programme's audience is:

$$\frac{w_i}{n} = f_i\Delta_i m_i t_i. \qquad (11.2)$$

If we rank order advertisers according to willingness-to-pay such that $w_1 \geq w_2 \geq w_3$, and so on, and assume unit demands for commercial time by advertisers, this rank ordering describes the inverse demand function for the programme's commercial time.[6] Suppose advertisers are price takers and the programme sells a units of ad time. Then, the price paid for each unit of time sold by the programme will be at least w_a. If the programme sells all units of ad time at a common price, that price will be w_a. Increasing the homogeneity of the programme's viewers as measured by the sets of products they purchase will result in an audience whose purchases are concentrated in an increasingly small subset of the set of all products that might be advertised on television. As a consequence, the fractions of audience comprised of potential buyers for products advertised on the programme (the f_i) will increase. Therefore, as long as Δ_i, m_i, and t_i do not vary systematically with differences in the consumption heterogeneity of programmes' audiences, an ad for i has the same impact on a potential i consumer no matter what other types of consumers are in the audiences of the programmes in which the ad appears. We should expect to see the price of ad time increase with the consumption homogeneity of a programme's audience because, if more members of its audience purchase the same products, the network broadcasting the programme can sell the firms selling those products access to larger groups of potential customers.[7] This is an obvious consequence of increasing f_i in the expression for w_i in equation (11.2) for all $i \leq a$.[8]

Equally apparent from equation (11.2) is that increasing the profits the programme's advertisers earn from sales to their customers ($m_i t_i$) will also increase the per viewer price the programme can charge for its ad time, as will increasing Δ_i, the impact a television commercial has on the likelihood a viewer will purchase the product it promotes. We would also expect the price charged for a programme's ad time to increase if the number of products purchased by a representative audience member increased because more advertisers would have a positive demand for the programme's ad time.

Thus, the PPM generates four hypotheses about the price paid for a programme's ad time: that the per viewer price paid for a programme's television ad time will increase: (1) with the consumption homogeneity of the programme's audience; (2) with the per customer profits the sellers of products purchased by the programme's viewers would make on additional sales generated by advertising; (3) with the effectiveness of television ads for promoting the products purchased by members of the programme's audience; and (4) with the number of products purchased by a representative viewer in the programme's audience.

11.3 Data and variables

11.3.1 Variables specific to PPM-based models

We test the four hypotheses of this study and compare the ability of regression models based on the PPM to explain variation in per-rating-point prices for ad time to the performance of a traditional demographics-based model for 46 primetime series (out of 82 in total) that were renewed from the previous season and aired by the four major US broadcast networks (ABC, CBS, NBC, FOX) during the fall 1997 television season.[9] The trade publication, *Advertising Age*, published a list of 'average unit rates' paid for 30-second spots in prime time programmes during the 1997 upfront market (Mandese, 1997).[10] *Broadcasting and Cable* magazine publishes the weekly estimates of primetime network programmes' ratings (percentage of all viewers watching television who watch each programme) produced by Nielsen Media Research, the dominant audience measurement service in the USA.

For each programme, we computed the simple average of the weekly Nielsen ratings estimates reported by *Broadcasting and Cable* for the fall 1997 season. We then divided the 30-second rates published by *Advertising Age* by the corresponding season average Nielsen ratings to create *UnitRate*, an estimate of the average price per rating point (measured in thousands of dollars) paid by advertisers for each programme in the sample. *UnitRate* is the dependent variable in all the regression models described below. The range of variation in *UnitRate* is quite large, with the highest value more than five times the lowest, as shown in Figure 11.1.

Simons Market Research Bureau conducts annual surveys of over 20,000 consumers. It analyses their viewing habits and the products they purchase, recording survey responses for over 8,000 brands in 460 product categories. Survey participants are asked what television programmes they

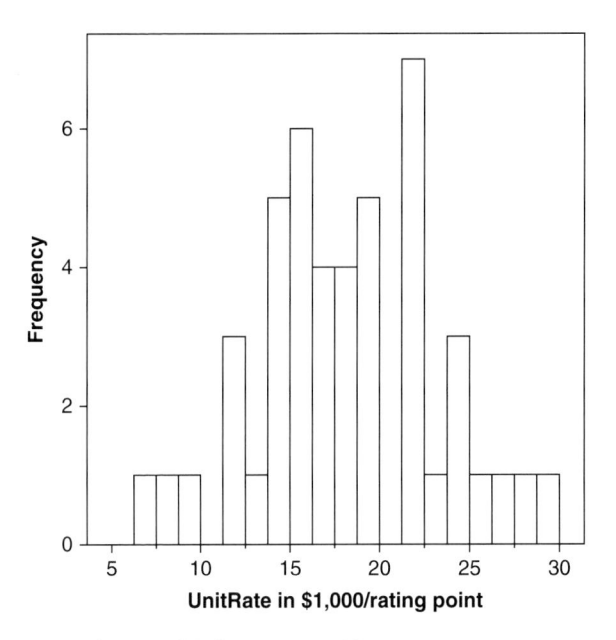

Figure 11.1 Distribution of *Unitrate* among 46 programmes

watch and the brands and types of products they purchase. To construct measures of the range and distribution of products purchased by viewers in the audiences for primetime programmes, we utilised data from the 1997 Simmons National Consumer Survey database (Simmons Market Research Bureau, 1997), which was based on consumer interviews from 1996 and 1997, all conducted prior to the fall 1997 television season. Because audience purchasing habits can be assessed only after a programme has been aired and has attracted an audience to be studied, we limited our sample of programmes to the 46 programmes in the networks' prime time schedules that were renewed from the previous television season. For survey participants indicating they watched a given programme, we calculated the percentages of those who also stated they purchased various brands and products from each of the Simmons product categories.

AdAge.com, the online affiliate of *Advertising Age*, reports annual US advertising expenditures broken down by media type for 33 aggregated product categories, where a product category is a set of closely related products. *AdAge.com* (AdAge.com(a)) reports that television advertising for products in its 33 product categories accounted for 98.38 per cent of network television advertising in 1997. We matched Simmons survey results on products purchased and programmes viewed to corresponding *AdAge.com* product categories in order to construct a measure of the fraction of a programme's audience purchasing products from each *AdAge.com* product category for all of the programmes in the sample. For each product category–programme pair, we used this measure as a proxy for the fraction of the programme's audience comprised of potential purchasers of the products in the category. By their respective descriptions, 20 of the *AdAge.com* categories appeared to have nearly direct matches in the Simmons product categories. For these *AdAge.com* categories we used the fraction of Simmons survey respondents who reported they watched a programme and purchased at least one product from the corresponding Simmons category as our measure of the fraction of the programme's audience purchasing products from the *AdAge.com* category, a variable we will refer to as the product category's penetration of the programme's audience. One *AdAge.com* category, 'government and organizations', had no corresponding product listing in the Simmons database and thus is not represented in any of the constructed variables described below. This category ranked number 20 among the 33 *AdAge.com* product categories in advertising expenditures.

For each of the remaining 12 *AdAge.com* categories, it was necessary to combine two or more Simmons categories to produce a close match for the *AdAge.com* category. The Simmons categories combined to produce a match for each of these *AdAge.com* categories are listed in Appendix 11.1 at the end of the chapter. For six of the 12, it was possible to combine a small number of Simmons categories to produce a close match with the *AdAge.com* category.[11] Each of the remaining *AdAge.com* product categories, which we will refer to as the MS (many Simmons) AdAge.com categories, included large numbers (from 21–119) of Simmons categories.[12] The *AdAge.com* product categories and the number of Simmons product categories combined to match each of them are listed in Table 11.1.

The larger number of Simmons categories for each of the MS AdAge.com categories increases the risk that an unweighted average over Simmons categories whose penetrations may differ considerably from each other may depart considerably from penetrations for Simmons products whose penetrations are more representative of the AdAge.com category. For example, included in the AdAge.com category 'food & food products' are Simmons categories for ethnic foods likely to be purchased by small fractions of the US population and staples consumed by the vast majority. To deal with the problem posed by averaging penetrations across so many potentially disparate Simmons categories, we employed principal

Table 11.1 *AdAge.com* and Simmons product categories

Top *AdAge.com* product categories	Number of Simmons categories matched to the *AdAge.com* category
Automotive, auto accessories, equipment & supplies	1
Retail, department and discount stores	1
Movies and media	1
Toiletries & cosmetics	10
Medicines & proprietary remedies	9
Food & food products	17
Financial	1
Restaurants & fast food	2
Airline & cruise travel, hotels & resorts	3
Telecommunications	1
Computers & software	1
Direct response companies	1
Insurance & real estate	3
Apparel	1
Beverages	8
Confectionery & snacks	7
Beer, wine, & liquor	13
Audio & video equipment & supplies	1
Games, toy, & hobby craft;	1
Household soaps, cleansers & polishes	1
Household paper, plastic & foil products	3
Building materials, equipment & fixtures	1
Sporting goods	1
Household appliances equipment	1
Schools, camps, seminars	1
Manufacturing, equipment, freight	1
Pets, pet foods & supplies	2
Gasoline & oil	1
Office machines, furniture & supplies	1
Household furnishings & accessories	1
Eye glasses, medical equipment & supplies	2
Fitness & diet programs and spas	1

component analysis and used the Kaiser rule for factor extraction to calculate the communalities for Simmons category penetrations for each of the six MS AdAge.com product categories. Those Simmons categories with communalities greater than 0.6 were used as representative subsets of the Simmons categories for the MS AdAge.com categories and the average penetrations for the subsets were assigned to the AdAge.com categories. The Simmons categories for each of the MS AdAge.com categories are listed in Appendix 11.2. Regressions using variables based on average penetrations for representative subsets of Simmons categories proved to have more explanatory power than regressions using simple averages over all Simmons categories in a MS AdAge.com category, with R^2 increased by around 0.05 to 0.07.

For each programme, the audience penetration figures for the 32 AdAge.com product categories were used to create two variables reflecting different aspects of the distribution of products purchased by members of its audience. The first, the Purchasing Profile Index, or PPI, is simply the sum of the percentages of a programme's viewers reporting purchases from each category (the sum of the programme's category penetrations). That is, for programme j, product categories indexed by $k = 1,\ldots,32$, and $\alpha_{j,k}$ the percentage of viewers in programme j's audience reporting purchases from product category k, $PPI_j = \sum_{k=1}^{32} \alpha_{j,k}$.

For example, consider a hypothetical programme for which Simmons records positive penetration rates for only three product categories and suppose they are 30 per cent, 40 per cent and 50 per cent. Then the PPI for this programme would be 0.3 + 0.4 + 0.5 = 1.20. We label the second variable describing the distribution of audience purchases the PPI-HHI because it is calculated with a formula identical to that the US antitrust agencies use to calculate a product market's HHI (Herfindahl–Hirschman Index). Antitrust authorities use the HHI to assess the degree of concentration in economic markets and the PPI-HHI plays an analogous role here. For antitrust analysis, a product market's HHI is calculated as the sum of the squared market shares of all firms serving the market. Because shares are squared, a market's HHI increases as the distribution of sales in the market becomes concentrated in the hands of fewer sellers. A product category's share of a programme's PPI plays the same role in calculating the programme's PPI-HHI as a seller's share of a product market in calculating the market's HHI. Thus for programme j and product category k, k's share of j's PPI is $\alpha_{j,k}$ divided by PPI_j.[13] The PPI-HHI for program j is calculated as: $PPI\text{-}HHI_j = \sum_{k=1}^{32} \left(\frac{\alpha_{jk}}{PPI_j} \right)^2$. A programme's PPI-HHI increases as consumption choices by the programme's viewers become concentrated in fewer product categories, which means that the programme's viewers are becoming more similar in their purchase choices.

Note that the value of the PPI-HHI is determined by the values of the product categories' shares of audience relative to each other, rather than by their absolute values, while the value of the PPI is determined by the absolute values of the category shares. The relationship between

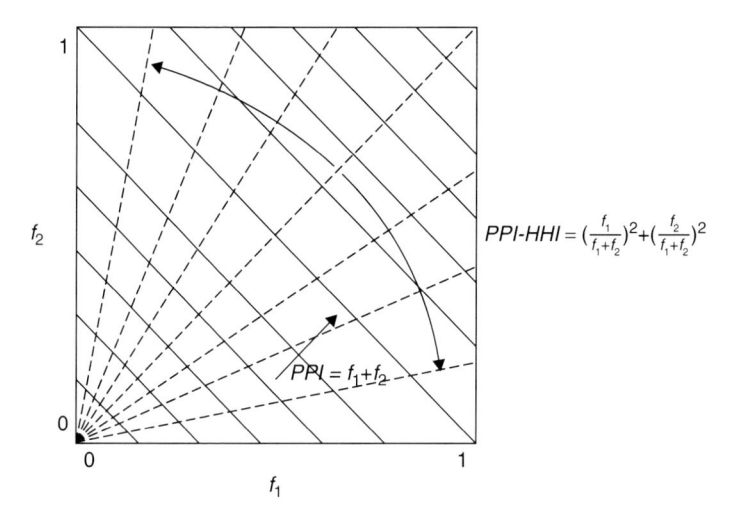

$$PPI\text{-}HHI = \left(\frac{f_1}{f_1+f_2}\right)^2 + \left(\frac{f_2}{f_1+f_2}\right)^2$$

$$PPI = f_1 + f_2$$

Figure 11.2 Relationship between PPI and PPI-HHI for the case of two products

a programme's PPI and its PPI-HHI is illustrated in Figure 11.2 for a programme with two advertised products, 1 and 2, with f_1 and f_2 the fractions of the programme's audience purchasing products 1 and 2 respectively. The dashed rays through the origin are PPI-HHI isoquants because along a ray the relative shares of viewers purchasing the two products are always the same. The straight solid lines with 45-degree negative slopes are PPI isoquants because the sum of f_1 and f_2 is not changed by movement along one of these lines. It is always possible to shift to a higher or lower PPI isoquant along any PPI-HHI isoquant and vice versa. We may thus treat the PPI and PPI-HHI as orthogonal for our regressions.

In a regression with price per rating point as the dependent variable, we can interpret the sign of the coefficient for PPI as a test of the PPM hypothesis that the price per viewer paid by advertisers purchasing time in a programme will increase as members of the programme's audience increase the number of products they purchase, and we can interpret the sign of the coefficient for PPI-HHI as a test of the hypothesis that the per viewer price for ad time will increase with the consumption homogeneity of a programme's viewers. According to the PPM, the signs of both coefficients should be positive.

AdAge.com reports national advertising expenditures by year for each of its 33 product categories (AdAge.com(a)) and advertising to sales and margin to sales ratios for 4-digit Standard Industrial Classification (SIC) industries (AdAge.com(b)), where margin is calculated as an industry's net sales minus the cost of goods sold. For all but nine of the 33 *AdAge.com* product categories, products within the category match up directly with those included in a corresponding 4-digit SIC industry (which often has the identical name). For the categories with direct matches, the 4-digit SIC industry margin to sales ratio was applied directly to the category. The 'government and organizations' category had no match in the SIC list, as was the case with the Simmons product categories. The eight remaining *AdAge.com* product categories[14] include products produced by two or more 4-digit SIC industries. For each of these product categories, we calculated the margin to sales ratio for the category as a weighted average of the margin to sales ratios of the corresponding 4-digit SIC industries using their relative industry sales as weights.[15]

To produce estimates of category profits, we divided a category's margin to sales ratio by its advertising to sales ratio and multiplied by category ad expenditures. Taking the Simmons sample as representative of the US population, we used category penetrations for the Simmons sample as estimates of category penetrations for the US population as a whole. Multiplying these estimates of category penetration by the US population in 1997[16] produces an estimate of the number of people in the USA who purchased products from each of the 32 categories used in this study.

For each category, we divided estimated category profits by the estimated number of people in the USA purchasing from the category to produce an estimate of the level of profit per customer. For representative product i, this is $m_i t_i$ in equations (11.1) and (11.2). For any given programme and product category i, the percentage of the Simmons survey participants who watch the programme and reported purchasing at least one product from category i is used as a proxy for f_i, so the product of category profits per customer and the percentage of the programme's viewers purchasing from the category is a proxy for the potential per viewer profits from the sale of products in the category, which corresponds to $f_i m_i t_i$ in equations (11.1) and (11.2).

We created the variable *AveSalePrft* for each programme by summing the potential per viewer profits proxies ($f_i m_i t_i$s) for all 32 categories and dividing this sum by the programme's PPI. *AveSalePrft* is a measure of the value to a representative advertiser of sales induced by advertising on the programme. Paralleling the construction of *AveSalePrft*, we created *AveTVAdtoSales* by first creating for each product category a weighted average of the television advertising to sales ratios for the component 4-digit SIC industries (again using relative industry sales as weights).

Television advertising to sales figures were calculated by multiplying 4-digit SIC industry advertising to sales ratios by the fraction of all category advertising expenditures for television reported by *AdAge.com* for each category (AdAge.com(b)). For each programme, *AveTVAdtoSales*, a weighted average of the 32 categories' TV advertising to sales ratios was created using category audience penetrations as weights. Assuming television advertising to sales ratios are higher for products for which television makes a larger contribution to generating new sales, we use *AveTVAdtoSales* as a measure for the effectiveness of television advertising in promoting sales of the products in a product category. This is the final variable employed in the empirical model corresponding to the PPM.

11.3.2 Variables specific to demographics-based models

Nielsen Media Research (1996, 1997) reports estimates for various measures of demographic composition for programme audiences. For the demographics-based pricing model, we included the natural logs of Nielsen's estimated percentages of audience that are females 18–49, males 18–49, women with four or more years of college education, and African American females. (*lnPctFemale18-49, lnPctMale18-49, lnPctWomen-college, lnPctWomen-black*). The male counterparts for the last two variables were dropped from the regressions because they were highly collinear with the measures for women. It is generally accepted that advertisers value viewers in the 18–49 age group more highly than others, and, depending upon the product being advertised, women may be valued more or less than men. In addition, education and minority status are also believed to influence buying behaviour and thereby advertisers' valuations of the audiences. We also included two measures of viewer income – the percentage of the audience earning more than $60,000 annually and less than $30,000 annually (*Pct > $60K* and *Pct < $30K*). If advertisers pay more for access to wealthier audiences, the regression coefficients for *Pct > $60K* and *Pct < $30K* should be positive and negative, respectively.

Variables common to both sets of models

Viewership, measured as the season's average primetime rating for each programme, is included as an independent variable in both sets of models because it is sometimes argued that the size of a programme's audience influences the per viewer price charged for its advertising time. Dummy variables for ABC, CBS and NBC are included in both sets of models to allow for the possibility of network-specific pricing effects. Summary statistics for the variables are reported in Table 11.2.

184   The Media Industries and their Markets

Table 11.2   Descriptive statistics of variables

Variable	M	SD
UnitRate	18.233	5.117
Viewership	9.624	3.299
Pct$30Kless	0.394	0.086
Pct$60Kmore	0.288	0.072
PctWomen18to49	0.436	0.105
PctMen18to49	0.304	0.089
PctWomen-college	0.123	0.042
PctWomen-black	0.048	0.045
PPI	24.718	2.103
AveSalePrft	229.230	12.547
AveTVAdtoSales	0.038	0.007
PPI-HHI	0.054	0.013
ABC	0.188	0.394
CBS	0.333	0.476
NBC	0.333	0.476

11.4   Results

Regression results for the demographics-based model, four equations that sequentially introduce the four variables specific to the PPM, and an equation that includes the explanatory variables for both models are presented in Table 11.3. The natural log of price per rating point (*lnUnitRate*) is the dependent variable in all regressions. All models were estimated with ordinary least squares. The White test procedure was conducted for each regression specification and no test statistics (χ^2) rejected the null hypothesis of homoscedasticity. The regression models used the natural logs of all non-binary variables. Results for models with the untransformed variables were qualitatively stable with the same signs as reported below for their log form counterparts, although their significance levels were slightly lower. However, use of variables in the log form yielded some increase in the adjusted r-squares as is often the case with price regressions.

The results for the demographics-based model are presented in the second and third columns of Table 11.3. Although only the coefficients for women 18–49 and CBS achieve high levels of statistical significance, the model still accounts for well over half the variation in *lnUnitRate*. The relatively high explanatory power of demographics-based models such as this one explains why they have for decades played such a prominent in studies of media pricing. Regression results for four versions of the purchasing profile model are presented in the columns of Tables 11.3 and 11.4.

Table 11.3 Demographic and PPM regressions (variables PPM1 and PPM2) for ln*UnitRate*

Variables	Demographic model β	t	PPM 1 β	t	PPM 2 β	t
Constant	−1.749	−1.230	−15.274**	−2.807	−27.615*	−2.304
ln*Viewership*	−0.041	−0.257	0.147	0.850	0.293	1.289
ln*Pct$30Kless*	−0.369	−0.450				
ln*Pct$60Kmore*	0.319	0.638				
ln*PctWomen18to49*	1.415**	3.380				
ln*PctMen18to49*	0.015	0.068				
ln*PctWomen-college*	−0.358	−1.511				
ln*PctWomen-black*	0.020	0.195				
ABC	0.189	1.463	−0.084	−0.757	−0.116	−0.983
CBS	0.492**	3.460	−0.015	−0.082	0.081	0.627
NBC	0.144	1.096	−0.095	−0.664	−0.133	−1.060
ln*PPI*			6.580***	4.629	2.396**	3.822
ln*PPI-HHI*					0.770**	3.119
ln*AveSalePrft*						
ln*AveTVAdtoSales*						
R^2	0.683		0.511		0.544	
Adjusted R^2	0.592		0.450		0.474	

Note: $N = 46$. *$p < .05$. **$p < .01$. ***$p < .001$.

Table 11.4 PPM regressions for ln*UnitRate* (Variable PPM3 and PPM4)

Variables	PPM 3 β	PPM 3 t	PPM 4 β	PPM 4 t	Combined β	Combined t
Constant	−32.215**	−2.877	−25.077	−1.308	−4.846	−0.277
ln*Viewership*	0.310	1.656	0.394*	2.255	0.033	0.180
ln*Pct$30Kless*					−0.427	−0.702
ln*Pct$60Kmore*					−0.059	−0.105
ln*PctWomen18to49*					0.839	1.583
ln*PctMen18to49*					0.024	0.071
ln*PctWomen-college*					−0.155	−0.347
ln*PctWomen-black*					0.032	0.276
ABC	−0.104	−0.692	−0.074	−0.367	0.240	1.456
CBS	0.152	0.968	0.221	1.590	0.586**	3.472
NBC	−0.066	−0.373	0.019	0.144	0.150	1.633
ln*PPI*	1.483**	2.916	1.899***	2.875	1.139	1.082
ln*PPI-HHI*	0.747**	2.798	0.701*	2.262	2.512	0.972
ln*AveSalePrft*			1.517**	3.891	1.381	1.259
ln*AveTVAdtoSales*	1.475*	2.500	4.686*	2.205	4.218	1.247
R^2	0.603		0.635		0.714	
Adjusted R^2	0.530		0.556		0.585	

Note: $N = 46$. *$p < .05$. **$p < .01$. ***$p < .001$.

PPM1 is the simplest version of the model and includes, in addition to the network dummies and audience size, only *PPI* as a variable specific to the PPM. As is shown, this measure of the distribution of products purchased by programmes' audiences by itself explains a fair amount of the variation in *lnUnitRate*. *lnPPI-HHI*, *lnAveSalePrft*, and *lnAveTVAdtoSales* are in turn added to the model in the equations labeled PPM2, PPM3, and PPM4. Each variable is statistically significant, has the predicted sign, and increases the equation's adjusted r-square.

While the adjusted R^2 for the PPM never quite reaches that of the demographics model, it still explains a substantial amount of the variation in the dependent variable. As shown in the last two columns of Table 11.4, the highest R^2 and adjusted R^2 are produced by a regression that combines the demographic and PPM variables, although the increase in adjusted R^2 over that for the basic demographics model is slight. Neither demographic data nor PPM variables by themselves carry much weight in the combined model. This cancelling out of variable significance is consistent with the argument advanced in this study that advertisers use audience demographic measures to estimate the numbers of potential customers in programmes' audiences, more direct estimates of which are used to construct programmes' *PPI*s and *PPI-HHI*s.

11.5 Discussion

The PPM regressions reported in Table 11.3 support our contention that, while they are very useful for predicting the prices paid for television ad time, demographics-based models obscure critical factors individual advertisers consider in assessing the value of advertisements placed in specific programmes, as well as the nature of the process through which individual advertisers' valuations of audiences are aggregated to generate the market demands and influence the prices paid for ad time in these programmes. The PPM model starts from the individual advertiser's perspective and identifies four factors critical to the determination of prices paid for television ad time. Even though we were forced to work with highly aggregated data (460 product categories collapsed to 32), the findings reported in Table 11.3 strongly support the PPM model. As predicted by the model, the higher are the per viewer prices paid for ad time, the more extensive is the set of products purchased by a programme's audience, the more similar are a programme's viewers' product choices, the more profitable (at the margin) are the products purchased by a programme's viewers, and (if our proxy is accepted) the more effective are television ads for promoting the products consumed by a programme's viewers. While the empirical application of the PPM presented here does not improve on the statistical fit of the demographics model, it does not fall far short. More important, it provides an enlightening below the surface view of economic forces at work in markets for television ad time.

Appendix 11.1

List of Simmons Product Subcategories Under the 12 *AdAge.com* Categories

List of Simmons Product Subcategories for each category Between brackets: Number of Simmons subcategories Under an *AdAge.com* category

Toiletries & cosmetics (24): facial cleansing creams, lotions, gels; bath & shower additives; facial moisturizers; loose powder & pressed powder; foundation makeup; blusher; nail care products; nail polish; Mascara; eye shadow/liner/brow pencil; lipstick & lip gloss; tampons; sanitary pads & napkins; feminine hygiene products; menstrual & period pain; pre-menstrual tension & pain; home pregnancy tests; ovulation predictors; vaginal dryness products; yeast infection products; perfume, cologne, & toilet water; gift purchases of fragrances/cosmetic; cosmetic products; fragrance products

Medicines & proprietary remedies (24): cold/allergy/sinus remedies; sleep aids; lactose intolerance products; headache & pain relievers; indigestion aids/stomach remedies; nasal sprays; laxatives; incontinence products; groin irritation remedies; corn removers; cough syrup; sore throat products; wart removers; pain relief rubs/liquid; oral pain relievers; athlete's foot remedies; hemorrhoid remedies; first air prod/topical antibiotic remedy; adhesive bandages; in-home diagnostic tests-devices; vitamin/mineral tables/caps/liquid; diet control; health care services; hospital care

Food & food products (119): cold breakfast cereals; hot breakfast cereals; toaster pastries; breakfast pastries; donuts; bagels; croissants; English muffins; packaged muffins; bread; peanut butter; jams, jellies, & preservatives; butter; butter sprinkles/mixes; blends (butter/ margarine); margarine spread; sour cream; cream cheese; cottage cheese; spread cheese; American pasteurized processed cheese; national cheese; low fat/cal/cholesterol cheese; grated cheese; ice cream/milk/sherbet; frozen novelty treats; packaged instant potatoes; frozen potato products; frozen vegetables; frozen corn-on-the-cob; fresh vegetables; canned or jarred vegetables; sloppy Joe preparations; pork & beans or baked beans; frozen hot snacks; frozen soup; canned soup & broth; dry soup/lunch mix & dry bouillon; shelf-to-microwave dinners/entrees/soup; microwave food products; frozen complete dinners (TV dinners); frozen main courses (casseroles/entrees); single serving size purchases; pizza crust; frozen pizza; pizza; rice/rice dishes; fresh refrigerated packaged pasta; can/jar spaghetti/macaroni; dry packaged pasta; complete packaged dishes and dinner mix; frozen fried chicken; pre-cooked packaged poultry; jarred recipe/simmer sauces; meat, fish & poultry; canned chicken/meat products; meat snacks & beef jerky; cold cuts; prepared lunch kits; ham (unsliced); bacon; sausages; frankfurters & wieners; meat & fish extenders; canned tuna; frozen prepared seafood; non-stick cooking spray; shortening; salad or cooking oil; salad toppings; prepared salad dressing; dry mix salad dressing; mayonnaise or mayo type salad dressing; spaghetti sauce; canned tomatoes and tomato sauce; catsup/ketchup; mustard; salsa; barbecue & seasoning sauces; gravy and sauce mixes; Mexican food & ingredients; bread crumb, coating & stuffing mixes; pancake & table syrup; canned or jarred pineapple; other canned/jarred fruit; fresh fruits; frozen fruits; dried fruits & raisins; white granulated sugar; sugar substitutes/artificial sweeteners; frozen waffles, pancakes, fresh toast; frozen breakfast entrees and sandwiches; dry pancake/waffle mix; frozen muffins; frozen dessert pies, cakes and pastries; packaged pie crusts; refrigerated/frozen dough products; dry cake mixes (non four); dry brownie mixes; other baking mixes; flour; corn starch; baking from scratch; baking chips & pieces; frosting; pudding; pie fillings; flavored gelatin deserts; ice cream toppings; whipped topping; non-dairy cream substitutes; eggs; egg substitutes; salt substitutes/alternatives; seasoning/spices; vinegar; olives; pickles; low fat/fat free products

Restaurants & fast food (2): fast food & drive-in restaurant; family rest & steak houses

Airline & cruise travel, hotels & resorts (3): cruise ship vacation-taken last 3 years; domestic travel-stay at hotel/motel last year; foreign travel last three years

Insurance & real estate (3): life insurance; home owners, tenant's insurance; medical/hospital/health insurance

Beverages (27): thirst/quenchers/activity drinks; Iced tea (ready to drink); diet or sugar free colas; other carbonated (non-cola) diet drinks; regular cola (non diet); other regular carbonated (non-cola) drinks; sparkling waters/seltzers/natural sodas; non-carbonated bottled spring water; milk flavorings; canned milk; milk flavorings; instant hot cocoa mix; powder soft drinks; herbal tea; regular tea; Instant tea; instant iced tea mix; decaf instant coffee; caffeinated instant coffee; international flavored instant coffee; Espresso/Cappuccino; Ground or whole bean coffee; frozen orange juice; orange juice; other fruit juices/drinks; tomato & vegetable juices; liquid breakfast/nutritional supplements

Confectionery & snacks (21): chewing gum/bubble gum; snack mixes; boxed chocolates; hard roll candy/candy breath mints; individual full size candy bars & packs; miniature snack-size candy bars; yogurt; frozen yogurt; nutritional snacks; rice/grain cakes; nuts for cooking & snacks; pretzels; potato chips; popcorns products; corn & tortilla chip & snacks; other chips and snacks; variety packs of snacks; snack, saltines, graham crackers; cookies; snack cakes; dips for snacks and vegetables

Beer, wine, & liquor (35): Non-alcohol/low alcohol beer; ale; malt liquor; draft beer; imported beer; light low cal domestic beer; regular domestic beer; ice beer; micro brewed beer; coolers; sangria/pop/party wines; port, sherry & dessert wines; aperitif & specialty wines; cases purchases; domestic dinner/table wines; imported dinner/table wines; champagne/cold duck/spark wine; vermouth; cocktails & mixed drinks; rum; tequila; brandy & Armagnac; cognac; prep cocktail mixes with liquor; prep cocktail mixes-no liquor; cordials & liqueurs; Canadian whiskey; Bourbon whiskey; Scotch whiskey; Irish whiskey; Aquavit; blended whiskey or rye; gin; vodka; gift purchase liquor/wine

Household paper, plastic & foil products (3): plastic-type kitchen wrap; aluminum foil; paper napkin

Pets, pet foods & supplies (2): dogs owned; cats owned

Eye glasses, medical equipment & supplies prescription (2): eyeglasses & contact lenses; contact lens, cleaning solutions

Appendix 11.2

Simmons Subcategories Selected Using Factor Analysis for the Six MS *AdAge.com* Product Categories

> ### List of Simmons Product Subcategories for each category
>
> **Toiletries & cosmetics:** facial cleansing creams, lotions; facial moisturizers; loose & pressed face powder; foundation makeup; blusher; eye shadow/liner/eye brow pencil; lipstick & lip gloss; feminine hygiene products; cosmetic products; fragrance products
>
> **Medicines & proprietary remedies:** cold/allergy/sinus remedies; sleep aids; headache/pain relievers; indigestion aids/stomach remedies; nasal sprays (non-prescription); incontinence products; cough syrup (non-presc); pain relief rubs/liquids(non-presc); hemorrhoid remedies (non-presc)
>
> **Food & food products:** cold breakfast cereals; donuts; croissants; bread; peanut butter; jams, jellies & preserves; cream cheese; fresh vegetables; microwave food products; frozen pizzas (bought frozen); can/jar spaghetti/macaroni; frozen fried chicken; bacon; frozen prepared seafood; pudding; pie fillings; pickles
>
> **Beverages:** thirst quencher/activity drinks; diet or sugar free colas; regular cola (not diet); spark waters/seltzers/nat sodas; milk (liq in bottles/cartons); internat flavored inst coffee; espresso/cappuccino; tomato & vegetable juices
>
> **Confectionery & snacks:** chewing gum/bubble gum; boxed chocolates; indiv full size candy bars/packs; nuts for cooking & snacks; pretzels; corn/tortilla chips & snacks; cookies (ready-to-eat) (ready-to-eat)
>
> **Beer, wine, & liquor:** malt liquor; draft beer; reg dom beer; micro brewed beer; domestic dinner/table wines; champ/cold duck/sparkling wine; rum; tequila; brandy & Armagnac; cognac; scotch whisky; gin; vodka

Notes

1. Wayne Fu is an Associate Professor at the Wee Kim Wee School of Communication and Information, Nanyang Technological University; Hairong Li is

a Professor in the Department of Advertising, Public Relations, and Retailing at Michigan State University; Steven S. Wildman is a Professor in the Department of Telecommunication, Information Studies and Media of Michigan State University, East Lansing, Michigan, and co-director of the university's Quello Center for Telecommunication Management and Law.
2. Webster and Phalen (1997) and Napoli (2003) review and extend the substantial literature that explores this relationship.
3. When the prices examined are for local spot time, demographic variables are typically combined with variables reflecting variations in the structure and condition of local markets, such as the number of over-the-air broadcast stations, retail sales per capita, and rates of home ownership. See, for example, Fournier and Martin (1983).
4. The instrument for the annual survey is presented twice during a year with a six month interval to two separate subsamples of consumers. Semi-annual reports based on the subsamples are also available for purchase.
5. The upfront market is a period in early to mid-summer during which networks and advertisers negotiate prices for packages of ad time in programmes that will be broadcast starting in the forthcoming fall television season.
6. Allowing for individual advertisers to have positive valuations for more than one unit of the programme's ad time does not materially alter this description of the inverse demand function for the programme's ad time because the amount a given advertiser would be willing to pay for a second or subsequent unit of ad time can be treated as the demand of an entirely separate advertiser.
7. Chandra (2007) found that advertisers are willing to pay higher prices for ad space in newspapers with more consumption-homogeneous audiences.
8. This conclusion also depends on *a* being smaller than the number of products purchased by a representative viewer. This seems to be a reasonable assumption. At most an hour-long programme will have 17–18 minutes of commercial time, which permits a maximum of 36 standard 30 second commercial units – a number far smaller than the number of products purchased by most consumers.
9. The 46 prime time programmes are 20/20, 3rd Rock, 48 Hours, Beverly Hill 90210, Boy Meets World, Caroline in the City, Chicago Hope, Cops, Cosby Bill, Cybill, Dateline NBC-Friday, Dateline NBC-Tuesday, Diagnosis Murder, Dr. Quinn Medicine Woman, Drew Carey, Early Edition, ER, Ellen, Family Matters, Fox Tuesday Night Movie, Frasier, Friends, Home Improvement, Homicide: Life on the Street, JAG, Law & Order, Living Single, Mad About You, Melrose Place, Millennium, Murphy Brown, Naked Truth, The Nanny, Nash Bridges, News Radio, NYPD Blue, Party of Five, The Pretender, Prime Time Live, Profiler, Promised Land, Sabrina, Seinfeld, Spin City, Suddenly Susan, and Walker, Texas Ranger.
10. Prior to each fall television season, advertisers negotiate with networks for packages of commercial availabilities. These negotiations, which take place during June and July, are referred to as the 'up front market'.
11. The six *AdAge.com* categories that could be matched to a small number of Simmons categories are: restaurants & fast food; airline & cruise travel, hotels & resorts; insurance & real estate; household paper, plastic & foil products; pets, pet foods & supplies; and eye glasses, medical equipment & supplies.

12. The MS AdAge.com categories are: toiletries & cosmetics; medicines & proprietary remedies; food & food products; beverages; confectionery & snacks; and beer, wine, & liquor.
13. Given the shares, the only difference between the HHI and the PPI-HHI is that the U.S. antitrust authorities measure sellers' shares as percentages with values varying from 0 to 100, while PPI-HHI shares are entered as decimal values varying from 0 to 1. This difference in scaling does not affect the critical mathematical properties of the measure.
14. These categories are (1) automotive, auto accessories, equipment & supplies; (2) retail, department and discount stores; (3) movies and media; (4) financial; (5) airline & cruise travel, hotels & resorts; (6) telecommunications; (7) computers & software; (8) insurance & real estate.
15. The receipts or revenues of product industries for 1997 by SIC codes are posted on the US Census Department's website: http://www.census.gov/epcd/ec97sic/E97SUS.HTM.
16. The 1997 Population Profile of the United States (US Census Bureau, 1997) reports the US population to be 266,490,000.

References

AdAge.com(a). Total measured US ad spending by category and media in 1997. (http://AdAge.com, accessed on 16 August 2004).
AdAge.com(b). 1997 advertising-to-sales ratios for the 200 largest ad spending industries. (http://AdAge.com, accessed on 16 August 2004).
Assael, H. and Poltrack, D.F. 1991. Using single-source data to select TV programs based on purchasing behavior, *Journal of Advertising Research*, 31(4), 9–17.
Assael, H. and Poltrack, D.F. 1993. Using single-source data to select TV programs: Part 2, *Journal of Advertising Research*, 33(1), 48–56.
Assael, H. and Poltrack, D.F. 1996. Single-versus double-source data or TV program selection, *Journal of Advertising Research*, 36(6), 73–81.
Assael, H. and Poltrack, D.F. 1999. Relating products to TV program clusters, *Jour nal of Advertising Research*, 39(2), 42–52.
Chandra, A. 2007. Targeted advertising: the role of subscriber characteristics in media markets. Mimeo. University of British Columbia.
D'Amico, T.F. 1999. Magazines' secret weapon: Media selection on the basis of behavior, as opposed to demography, *Journal of Advertising Research*, 35(6), 53–60.
Fournier, G.M. and Martin, D.L. 1983. Does government-restricted entry produce market power? New evidence from the market for television advertising, *Bell Journal of Economics*, 14(1), 44–56.
Mandese, J. 1997. 'Seinfeld' nears price ceiling as sophomore shows soar, *Advertising Age*, 15 September, 1, 18.
Napoli, P.M. 2003. *Audience Economics: Media Institutions and the Audience Marketplace*, New York: Columbia University Press.
Nielsen Media Research. 1996 and 1997. *Nielsen Television Index: National Audience Demographics, Volume 2*, November 1996, February 1997, May 1997, and July 1997. New York.

Schroeder, G. 1998. Marketing research: Behavioral optimization, *American Demographics*, August, p. 34.

Simmons Market Research Bureau. 1997. *Choices II*, CD-ROM. Simmons National Consumer Survey.

Surowiecki, J. 2002. Ageism in advertising, *New Yorker*, 1 April, p. 40.

Television Bureau of Advertising. 2009. 1 April. Broadcast TV revenues were down 0.4% in 2008 (http://www.tvb.org/rcentral/adrevenuetrack/revenue/2008/ad_figures_1.asp, accessed on 1 August 2009).

Webster, J.G. and Phalen, P.F. 1997. *The Mass Audience: Rediscovering the Dominant Model*, Mahwah, NJ: Lawrence Erlbaum Associates.

Wildman, S.S. 2003. Modeling the ad revenue potential of media audiences: an underdeveloped side of media economics, *Journal of Media Economics and Culture*, 1(2), 7–37.

12
Advertising Media Strategies in the Film Industry

Caroline Elliott and Rob Simmons[1]

12.1 Introduction

The film industry remains both important and high profile. Cinema attendance appears buoyant in many countries, for example with cinema admissions rising in the UK over the previous decade, and 170 million visits recorded for 2004 alone (UK Film Council Statistical Yearbook 2004–5). An increasing number of academic papers have investigated the factors contributing to the success of films at the box office. Influential recent studies of the factors contributing to US box office success include those of De Vany and Walls (1999), Ravid (1999), Reinstein and Snyder (2005) and Chang and Ki (2005). Analyses of UK film box office success include Collins et al. (2002) and Elliott and Simmons (2008), with a limited number of cross-country analyses also being available, such as Elberse and Eliashberg (2003). A subset of papers examines the impact of total advertising on film revenues (Prag and Casavant 1994; Elberse and Eliashberg 2003; Hennig-Thurau *et al.* 2006; and Elliott and Simmons 2008). Each of these papers concludes that aggregate advertising can have a positive, significant impact on box office revenues.

If we accept that total film advertising is correlated with film revenues, as is indicated by the literature cited above, it is also important to consider the determinants of film advertising expenditure. This chapter makes a substantial contribution to the literature on the film industry. The dataset is believed to be unique as it contains not only a large number of films compared to many studies, but advertising expenditures are also disaggregated to the advertising media level. Thus, we are able to investigate the determinants of total advertising expenditure when a film is released, and also the factors determining film advertising expenditures in each of four different advertising media, a question not yet addressed in the literature.

The structure of the remainder of this contribution is as follows. Variables under consideration and data sources are first outlined, as well as the empirical methodology adopted. Results relating to the factors determining film total advertising expenditures and the amounts spent advertising films in different traditional media are then described before conclusions are presented.

12.2 Data and research methodology

12.2.1 Data collection

Between 1999 and 2003 Nielsen ADC provided total amounts spent in the UK on each of four categories of advertising by film and year. These categories are television, press, outdoor (poster campaigns) and radio. Care was taken to remove films for which advertising expenditure occurred in 1998 and 2004, to avoid any censoring of the data. As is common in the analyses of the impact of advertising on box office revenues, values were expressed in log values at constant prices; zero values were inserted where no advertising spending occurred. The resulting variables are denoted by *log TV*, *log outdoor*, *log press*, and *log radio* and this sequence is also the ranking of conditional mean values of advertising. As in the USA, television advertising is both the most expensive medium and the category attracting the highest level of expenditure (Elberse and Anand 2005).

The process by which films are released in the UK is clearly important for the determination of advertising expenditure. Advertising expenditure is financed by distributors, rather than directly by producers or exhibitors. The distribution sector is dominated by a number of studios, with a competitive fringe of independents. Exhibition is dominated by a small number of nationwide cinema chains, such as Odeon and Vue, which will usually book the same films for exhibition across their screens. These screens are placed in multiplex cinemas and bigger films will occupy several screens. Distributors will approach exhibitors with a slate of films, which will vary in terms of budget and potential consumer appeal. By United Kingdom law, an initial contract between the distributor and the exhibitor for the screening of a film can only last two weeks. During these first two weeks, the distributor will seek to persuade the exhibitors that their films deserve an extended release. Prior to release, much advertising expenditure will already have been incurred, as billboards have to be prepared and television advertising slots have to be booked. But during the initial release, distributors can raise their advertising expenditures on particularly promising films in order to encourage audience demand and hopefully secure an extended release. The first two weeks of release are therefore vital for the success of a film, as exhibitors assess whether a film 'has legs' in industry parlance. The purpose of film advertising is then twofold: to raise consumer awareness of films directly, but also to secure an extended release in the exhibition network. Therefore, cinema advertising has both supply-side and demand-side effects.

Our model examines advertising expenditure over the life of a film as we lack week-by-week data. A number of explanatory variables were considered as potentially determining both total UK film advertising expenditures, and the advertising in different media. Data on the number of screens on which films are shown in their opening week of release were obtained from the Internet Movie Database (www.imdb.com). This database also provided details of film budget (which comprises all production and public relations expenses incurred by production companies but not advertising expenditures), genre, certificate (namely U, PG, 12, 15 and 18), and distribution company; all potentially important explanatory variables. The distribution sector is dominated by a small number of major studios, namely Buena Vista, Columbia Tristar, Paramount, 20th Century Fox, Universal International Pictures and Warner. Hence, we can test whether these different distribution companies are associated with different strategies for advertising films in the various media commonly used.

Information provided on the Internet Movie Database also allowed us to create a number of additional explanatory variables. The dummy variable *ukproduction* indicates films produced in the UK (rather than the USA), with *ukindep* indicating UK films distributed by an independent distribution company. It is still the case that the majority of films are still released in the USA prior to their UK release. Distribution companies then have the opportunity to discover just how successful a film is at the US box office, selecting UK advertising strategies and expenditures and in some cases the length of time before the UK release date, in the light of this information. Consequently, we allow advertising expenditures to depend on log US opening weekend revenue, *lusopen*. If no US opening revenue is reported or the US opening follows or is simultaneous to the UK opening, a zero value is inserted. This essentially creates a slope dummy for films that open in the USA before the UK. Films that have a long release gap between the USA and the UK may be deliberately held back by distributors and exhibitors as these are unlikely to be successful. Presumably, any favourable momentum from strong US box office performance is dissipated as the UK release is delayed. Rational audiences can spot long release gaps and may view these films as being of inferior quality. Conversely, a film that opens strongly in the US can benefit from enhanced publicity when it opens quickly in the UK. It appears that, on average, gaps in release date are shortening and more use is now being made of simultaneous release (with 36 such films in our sample). Industry sources claim that a quicker release strategy is designed to combat piracy but we suspect that the management of publicity is also a relevant factor. Consequently, we include an explanatory variable that is a simple count of the number of weeks between the US and UK releases (*wks diff*), and can identify if films delayed for UK release are advertised in a different manner. We also create a variable, *sameopeningcount*, of the number of other films in the dataset, released in the same week. Film release dates are announced in advance, allowing a test of whether advertising expenditures are partly determined by the number of other films released simultaneously.

A dummy variable for the appearance of major stars (*star power*) was derived from the *Hollywood Reporter*'s 2002 ranking of 'A list' actors. Actors were identified from the Maximum Star Power category, based on a survey of Hollywood studio executives of those stars who are deemed to be 'bankable' in terms of securing finance for production, major studio distribution and additional opening box office revenues. The 14 actors included in the top category are Tom Cruise, Tom Hanks, Julia Roberts, Mel Gibson, Jim Carrey, George Clooney, Russell Crowe, Harrison Ford, Bruce Willis, Brad Pitt, Nicolas Cage, Leonardo DiCaprio, Will Smith and Denzel Washington. In this study we wanted to test whether the appearance of such stars impacted upon the advertising media strategies adopted.

Some US literature has examined the impact of the status of film directors on opening US revenues, with positive and significant effects, controlling inter alia for presence of stars (Litman and Kohl 1989; Sochay 1994). As with *star power*, we create a dummy variable (*director*) for directors who attract considerable media publicity for their films. Lacking a generally approved list, we impose our own categorization and this comprises Robert Altman, Stanley Kubrick, George Lucas, Michael Moore, Guy Ritchie, Martin Scorsese, Steven Soderbergh and Steven Spielberg, testing whether the use of such high-profile directors has an impact upon the advertising strategies adopted.

Dummy variables were also created to highlight if a film's release coincided with the summer school holidays or 1–24 December inclusive. It may be that film distributors release films that are expected to appeal to family audiences, or audiences with greater leisure time at holiday periods. The existing literature produces conflicting expectations about the expected signs and sizes of the impact of summer and Christmas release dates on box office returns, for example, Litman (1983) concludes that a Christmas release has a significant impact on the financial success of a film, although Sochay (1994) concludes that summer is the optimum time to release a film. However, the alternative aim in this paper is to test the effect of releasing films in these periods on the advertising media used to promote the releases.

We have a dummy variable for films that represent a *sequel*. Significantly, films nominated for Best Actor, Best Actress or Best Film awards at the BAFTA and/or Oscar ceremonies each spring are represented by a dummy variable, *prize*; 48 such films being identified. It is possible that producers and distributors raise their advertising efforts for films that they perceive will win awards. Indeed, the mean level of (real) television advertising for films nominated for award is £426,627 compared with £299,291 for non-nominated films. A one-sided *t*-test rejects the null of equality of means (p value = 0.01). A similar *t*-test rejects equality of means of press advertising between nominated and non-nominated films (p value = 0.00). All *t*-tests of differences in sample means permit unequal variance between the two sub-samples.

Note that all monetary values were converted to real sterling at 1996 prices. Ultimately, we found consistent data for 534 films released between 1999 and 2003.

12.2.2 Empirical methodology

Initially, interest focused on the factors determining total advertising expenditures when films are released in the UK. Given the heterogeneity of films released and in the dataset we were unsurprised to find that the residuals from Ordinary Least Squares (OLS) regression results suffered from heteroscedasticity. Hence, Huber's Robust regression method was adopted in our final total advertising expenditure regressions. Robust regression is an estimator designed to eliminate gross outliers. The procedure is to perform an initial screening of the data based on Cook's distance > 1. Once any gross outliers are removed, iterations are performed, using Huber weights and biweights sequentially, until convergence is achieved. The resulting standard errors are then robust to heteroscedasticity. This procedure can be applied whenever a distribution exhibits excess kurtosis due to the presence of outliers.

It seemed likely that decisions regarding film advertising expenditures in different media are not taken independently. Hence, it seems reasonable to allow for correlation of the disturbances across advertising media equations. The seemingly unrelated regression estimation (SURE) method was therefore used to account for both heteroscedasticity and contemporaneous correlation in the errors across equations. The confirmation of the validity of this approach came from the rejection of the null hypothesis of the Breusch–Pagan test for the independence of residuals in all of the SURE systems of advertising media equations estimated, always at least at a 1% significance level.

12.3 Results

12.3.1 Determinants of total film advertising expenditure

Initially, attention focused on modelling the factors determining total logged advertising expenditure for the films in the dataset. A general to specific methodology was adopted, with each successive regression eliminating explanatory variables where the associated coefficient had been found to be significant, only at more than a 10 per cent significance level. Table 12.1 contains a full list of the explanatory variables that were included initially.

As noted above, Huber's Robust regression method was used to correct for the persistent heteroscedasticity in initial OLS regression residuals. Preferred regressions are reported here for the sake of brevity. Full details of all regressions are available on request. The two final iterations of regressions run are reported in Table 12.2. The robustness of the results should be noted and all coefficients in the regressions have the expected associated signs.

Films for which distribution companies are able to negotiate a larger number of screens in the opening week of film release attract greater advertising expenditures, as do films with larger budgets. Similarly, films that are at least nominated for major BAFTA or Oscar awards are advertised more heavily.

If a film's UK release follows (or continues after) the announcement of the nominations then additional advertising can be used to highlight any nominations and prizes to potential audiences. Alternatively, if a film is released prior to the announcement of the BAFTA and Oscar nominations, a higher advertising expenditure may signal a distribution company's confidence in a film's quality, the theory that advertising can indirectly signal quality being first put forward by Nelson (1974). The presence of a high-profile director also results in greater total advertising expenditures associated with a film's release, but interestingly the coefficient on the *star power* variable was never significantly different from zero. It was hypothesized above that longer lags between the US and UK

Table 12.1 Complete list of explanatory variables

Explanatory variable	Description
lukscreens	Logged number of opening week screens
lbudget	Logged total production budget
lusopen	Logged US opening week revenue
wks diff	Lag in weeks between US and UK release
Sameopeningcount	Number of dataset films released simultaneously
Certificate Dummies: *certu; certpg; cert12; cert18*	Films classified *Certificate 15* were considered the base category and so omitted in regressions.
Genre Dummies: *action; animation; comedy; romantic comedy; horror; scifi; thriller*	Dramas were considered the base category and so omitted from regressions.
Major Distribution Company Dummies: *buenavista; columbia; fox; paramount; universal; warner;*	
Further Dummies: *Starpower*	Unity if a film's actors contain at least one of 14 high profile actors.
Director	Unity when a high profile director is used
Ukproduction	Unity if a film was produced in the UK
Ukindep	Unity if a film is distributed by an independent company
Ukfirst	Unity if a film is released in the UK before the USA
Sequel	Unity if a film is a sequel
Prize	Unity if a film is nominated for a major BAFTA/Oscar
Christmas	Unity if a film is released in the UK 1–24/12
Summer	Unity if a film is released in the UK1/7–24/8

release dates for films indicate 'lower-quality' films that may have suffered poor US reviews and may not have done relatively well in terms of US box office success. This is reflected in the significantly lower advertising expenditures associated with these films when they are released in the UK market.

12.3.2 Determinants of film advertising in four advertising media

The primary aim of this chapter is to gain a deeper appreciation of the factors determining film advertising strategies, by focusing on the determinants of advertising expenditure in the predominant four media.

Table 12.2 Determinants of total logged advertising expenditure

Explanatory Variables	Regression 1	Regression 2
lukscreens	1.0975	1.0989
	(0.00)	(0.00)
lbudget	0.0619	0.0650
	(0.05)	(0.04)
Wks diff	−0.0211	−0.0211
	(0.00)	(0.00)
prize	0.5603	0.5579
	(0.00)	(0.00)
director	0.3359	0.3008
	(0.04)	(0.06)
Cert18	−0.1285	
	(0.11)	
buena vista	−0.2823	−0.2835
	(0.00)	(0.00)
Constant	1.5835	1.5094
	(0.00)	(0.00)
$\bar{R}^2$	0.7441	0.7449
F	215.72	252.64
	(0.00)	(0.00)
N	518	518

Note: *p* values in parentheses.

Once again a general to specific methodology was adopted, but the use of the SURE regression method which, while allowing for correlation in the residuals, does not restrict each related equation to identical sets of explanatory variables. Nevertheless, the initial regressions for logged advertising expenditure in each advertising media included identical sets of explanatory variables, those being the same as were used in the total advertising expenditure regressions above and detailed in Table 12.1. Table 12.3 summarizes the preferred SURE regression results with Table 12.4 giving correlation matrix of residuals. Again previous iterations of regressions are not reported to ensure conciseness, but are available on request. Note that while the coefficients of determination in the final regressions are relatively low, this was expected, partly a consequence of the number of zero advertising expenditures in the less commonly used advertising media.

As in the analysis of total film advertising expenditures, distribution companies invest more heavily in promoting films in all four advertising media when they negotiate a larger number of screens on which films are shown in their opening week of release, and when films are nominated for major awards. However, although all categories of advertising

Table 12.3 Determinants of advertising media usage

Explanatory variables	log TV	log outdoor	log press	log radio
lukscreens	2.0498	2.2791	0.8073	1.3573
	(0.00)	(0.00)	(0.00)	(0.00)
lusopen	0.1600		−0.0767	0.1945
	(0.00)		(0.07)	(0.01)
lbudget			0.1861	−0.5953
			(0.09)	(0.02)
Wks diff	−0.0009			
	(0.04)			
Prize	1.8998	2.6508	1.6158	1.8190
	(0.00)	(0.00)	(0.00)	(0.01)
Star power		1.2735		
		(0.04)		
Ukfirst	1.5890	3.2902	1.0054	
	(0.00)	(0.00)	(0.01)	
Sequel		1.4509		
		(0.06)		
summer			−0.6497	
			(0.01)	
sameopeningcount		−0.5504		−0.3984
		(0.01)		(0.03)
animation	0.9417	3.1862		
	(0.01)	(0.00)		
Scifi				−2.4548
				(0.00)
Certpg		−1.3098		
		(0.05)		
buena vista		−1.4357		2.5982
		(0.05)		(0.00)
columbia		−2.5101		1.5365
		(0.00)		(0.01)
Fox		−1.8822	0.9676	
		(0.02)	(0.00)	
paramount		−5.2779	−0.9913	−2.1048
		(0.00)	(0.09)	(0.09)
universal		−4.7083		
		(0.00)		
Warner		−1.5211	−0.5938	
		(0.04)	(0.02)	
Constant	−7.1211	−3.9682	4.3327	7.7040
	(0.00)	(0.03)	(0.01)	(0.04)
R^2	0.37	0.18	0.15	0.13
p	0.00	0.00	0.00	0.00
N	534	534	534	534

Notes: p values in parentheses. Breusch-Pagan test of independence $\chi(6) = 289.95$; p = 0.00.

Table 12.4 Correlation matrix of residuals

	log TV	log outdoor	log press	log radio
log TV	1.00			
log outdoor	0.28	1.00		
log press	0.44	0.29	1.00	
log radio	0.23	0.12	0.35	1.00

are affected positively by numbers of opening screens and prize nominations, impacts vary across types. Television and radio advertising each also respond positively to US opening revenues, while press advertising is negatively related to these revenues.

Television advertising shows no response at all to production inputs, here taken to comprise production budget and star quality and director indicators. Hence, the decision on whether and how much to advertise in these categories depends instead upon signals of film performance that appear when the film is ready for release. Peer review and initial consumer appeal determine these forms of advertising and not production and cost factors. Note that radio advertising, which is the smallest and cheapest medium and in the UK relates primarily to small local commercial stations, is negatively correlated with the production budget. Of course, the production budget is a sunk cost and, given the inherent uncertainty involved in predicting consumer preferences for particular films, it is rational for distributors to have a flexible response to interim signals of film quality, such as US opening revenues and award nominations. Successful film advertising is largely about 'backing winners'. Expectations of the numbers of opening screens and prestige awards, especially Oscars, determine the initial level of advertising which then responds flexibly as the opening run unfolds. The role of advertising is then largely to facilitate and promote 'word of mouth' dissemination of the film's quality early in its release.

The longer the lag between the US and UK release dates, a potential signal of film quality, the less money that is invested in television advertising, the most expensive advertising media. In addition, as noted above, films with greater opening week US revenues are associated with greater television and radio advertising.

Billboards are a preferred medium for the promotion of animated films and those films containing arguably the highest-profile actors – that is, films for which large posters may have a particularly strong visual impact. Similarly, animated films are associated with greater levels of television advertising. These films are likely often to appeal to younger and family audiences, for which mass audience advertising is likely to be effective. Meanwhile, science fiction movies are advertised significantly less through the medium of radio. Perhaps reassuringly, these results seem quite intuitive. Finally, we notice significant differences in the major distribution companies' preferences for using the alternative media available, holding all other variables constant.

12.4 Conclusions

The primary contribution of this contribution to the advertising literature is to look more closely at the advertising strategies used to promote films released in the UK, by using the SURE regression method to identify factors influencing the use of four advertising media – namely, television, outdoor, press and radio advertising. While there are differences in the strategies of the major distribution companies, some general principles seem to emerge. We show that the expenditure on different types of advertising media for films is not arbitrary. Distributors use advertising to back 'winners'. In particular, they use information on film award nominations and the number of opening screens to plough more expenditure into the four main media – namely, television, press, outdoor and radio advertising. Their advertising response is proportionally greater for the most expensive, but most productive, medium, which is television advertising. In contrast, television and press advertising are not responsive to what may be termed 'inputs' to the film production process, such as the production expenditure (budget) and use of top stars in the cast list. This suggests an element of rationality in the advertising decision. Information offered by award nominations, US opening box office revenue for films released at a later date in the UK, and the number of opening screens are used as signals for extra advertising expenditures to promote likely 'winners'. As Internet advertising in general, and for films in particular, becomes increasingly important, of course future research should be extended to examine the factors determining expenditure on the online advertising of films.

Acknowledgements

Many thanks to participants of the Media and Communication Conference, Applied Econometric Association, Paris 2007, for comments. Any errors of course remain the responsibility of the authors.

Note

1. Caroline Elliott is a Senior Lecturer at the Department of Economics of the University of Lancaster; Rob Simmons is a Senior Lecturer at the Department of Economics of the University of Lancaster.

References

Chang, B.-H. and Ki, E.-J. 2005. Devising a practical model for predicting theatrical movie success: focusing on the experience good property, *Journal of Media Economics*, 18, 247–69.

Collins, A., Hand, C. and Snell, M. 2002. What makes a blockbuster? Economic analysis of film success in the UK, *Managerial and Decision Economics*, 23, 343–54.

De Vany, A. and Walls W.D. 1999. Uncertainty in the movies: can star power reduce the terror of the box office?, *Journal of Cultural Economics*, 23, 285–318.

Elberse, A. and Anand, B. 2005. The effectiveness of pre-release advertising for motion pictures, Harvard Business School Working Paper 06-002.

Elberse, A. and Eliashberg, J. 2003. Demand and supply dynamics for sequentially released products in international markets: the case of motion pictures, *Marketing Science*, 22, 329–54.

Elliott, C. and Simmons R., 2008. Determinants of UK box office success: the impact of quality signals, *Review of Industrial Organization*, 33(2), 93–111.

Hennig-Thurau, T., Houston, M.B. and Sridhar, S. 2006. Can good marketing carry a bad product? Evidence from the motion picture industry, *Marketing Letters*, 17, 205–19.

Litman, B. 1983. Predicting success of theatrical movies: an empirical study, *Journal of Popular Culture*, 16, 159–75.

Litman, B. and Kohl, L. 1989. Predicting financial success of motion pictures: the 80s experience, *Journal of Media Economics*, 2, 35–50.

Nelson, P. 1974. Advertising as information, *Journal of Political Economy*, 82, 729–54.

Prag, J. and Casavant, J. 1994. An empirical study of the determinants of revenues and marketing expenditures in the motion picture industry, *Journal of Cultural Economics*, 18, 217–35.

Ravid, S.A. 1999. Information, blockbusters and stars: a study of the film industry, *Journal of Business*, 72, 463–92.

Reinstein, D. and Snyder, C. 2005. The influence of expert reviews on consumer demand for experience goods: a case study of movie critics, *Journal of Industrial Economics*, 53, 27–52.

Sochay, S. 1994. Predicting the performance of motion pictures, *Journal of Media Economics*, 7(4), 1–20.

13
Demand for Movies in Europe and the Effects of Multiplex Diffusion

Orietta Dessy and Marco Gambaro[1]

13.1 Introduction

After three decades of falling admissions, cinema attendance in Europe showed a significant rise during the 1990s despite competition from several audiovisual media. This growth in ticket sales must be compared with the declining share of exhibition in total film revenues. During this period exhibition in cinemas became for movies just the first stage of a complex multi-release strategy that includes home video, various form of pay television and finally free-to-air TV.

Exhibition is still very important in order to signal the quality of a movie, revealing through the number of tickets sold the preferences of consumers, but its proportion of the overall revenues of the film industry has declined from a share of 50 per cent in 1980 to less than 15 per cent in 2008, at least for Hollywood productions. However, a declining share of a growing market can still mean an increase in the number of tickets sold.

There are different explanations in literature for this growth, ranging from a different approach in film production to a spillover effect resulting from the rising production costs, to the improved condition in movie theatres following this extensive process of renovation.

In this chapter we attempt to test the role of the multiplex. While multiplex is usually analysed in terms of the supply side so that it can look to reduce the cost of exhibition through economies of scale in several of its functions, we will focus on the demand side. The positive role of the multiplex is related to risk reduction on the part of the audience and the improved conditions in the new cinemas. The possible negative role is related to the competition of large multiplex chains towards traditional theatres that can be moved out of the market, thereby eventually reducing the density of movie theatres and the overall level of supply.

This chapter explores the evolution of movie demand in Europe using a dataset of 15 countries from 1989 to 2003. We use a panel approach to estimate a simple demand function of film exhibition with yearly tickets per inhabitant as the dependent variable where as expected price coefficient is negative and income coefficient is positive. Multiplex diffusion, indicated as the percentage of multiplex seats in the total number of seats, appears to be moderately positive and is significant at the 1% level. The results are robust to different model specifications.

13.2 Evolution of the exhibition market

In several countries cinema attendance reached a maximum in the postwar years and declined sharply with the advent of television in the 1950s and 1960s.

The global pattern is quite similar. In the United States tickets peaked at 4 billion (24 per capita) in 1946 before declining to 1 billion 15 years later; in the UK cinema attendance reached 1.4 billion in 1950 before dropping to under 100 million in the 1980s; in Germany the peak was 800 million tickets in 1956 (15 tickets per capita) before a decline set in to 1990; finally, in Italy the peak occurred in 1955 with 819 million tickets sold and the lowest point was the sale of 81 million tickets in 1992.

In the postwar years television offered a free alternative to the casual entertainment consumption supplied by the cinema. Together with a drop in attendance there were structural changes across the whole industry. On the supply side producers tried to differentiate movies through the rise of production budgets and the search for blockbusters (Storper 1989). On the demand side, the casual consumption of films gradually became an event with people having to choose the single movie they would watch, considering such quality signals as newspaper reviews, stars or directors.

By the 1990s the average attendance per capita was around once or twice per year while television consumption had soared to around three hours per day – 300 more times than cinema.

The introduction of the multiplex accompanied the slight growth in audience figures that has occurred in several countries since 1990. However, to some extent this recovery may be a result of the satisfaction of previously unsatisfied demand, as more sites were opened and more screens became available, particularly in the suburbs (Collins, Hands and Ryder 2005).

Before 1990 there were only a small number of multiplexes. However, by 2003 in several European countries they accounted for around 20–30 per cent of the total number of screens (with the UK and Belgium both exceeding 50 per cent). Over the same period the total number of seats have grown between 10 per cent and 30 per cent.

A cinema is considered to be multiplex if they have more than seven screens. In addition, there are now megaplex cinemas (with more than 20 screens) and also miniplexes in the city centres (with on average around three or four screens). They offer a wider choice of films, easy parking, more modern and more spacious auditoria and several related services – from food and drink to book and video sellers.

Multiplex diffusion represent both a process and product innovation in exhibition industry that can be viewed as having a number of similarities to the development of supermarket and shopping malls in the retail sector. On the supply side they can achieve scale economies in management and general services while on the demand side the bundle of services offered can attract a larger number of consumers and the wider choice of movies reduces the risks that the consumer faces when she plans a trip to the movies.

In some countries growth in the number of theatre screens during the 1990s far exceeded the growth in industry revenues. In the US the number of screens grew by 50 per cent and in 2000 and 2001 four of the six largest movie theatre circuits filed for bankruptcy. Davis (2002) finds a large business-stealing effect that can create a situation of overcapacity.

Furthermore in Australia and the UK overinvestment in multiplexes led to a consolidation in the industry with a rise in concentration and bargaining power vs studio distributors.

13.3 Previous literature

The exploration of cinema demand has followed different paths. A number of studies analysed demand evolution in a single country over a long period.

In the case of Great Britain Macmillan and Smith (2001) use a dataset from 1950 to 1997 to estimate a near VAR model in which television ownership impacts negatively on cinema screen stock and, consequently, on the level of admissions. The large price elasticity that emerges explains why the price increase decided by theatres in the 1960s accelerated the decline in attendances, while the capacity increase that accompanied multiplex diffusion was a better policy for sustaining the growth in demand.

In Spain Fernandez-Blanco and Banos Pino (1977) investigate cinema attendance between 1968 and 1992 applying co-integration analysis to the annual data and find an unusually high long-run price elasticity

(−3.8) and an income elasticity greater than one, indicating that cinema can be classified as a luxury good. The negative impact of television is measured with the increase of commercial programming and seems to be responsible for a maximum of 9 per cent of the drop in cinema attendance during the 1980s.

Dewenter and Westermann (2005) analyse the demand for cinema attendance in Germany between 1950 and 2002 using time series data. They estimate both a demand equation and a simultaneous equation specification, in which they take account of the relationship of the number of seats to the level of cinema admissions. They find a strong long-run impact of price and income on attendance that decreases when adding other variables and using simultaneous equations. While TV and other cultural activities have been identified as substitutes for cinema, the effect of VCRs is ambiguous.

A series of papers use micro-level data to investigate the revenues of the movies as a function of different attributes. Smith and Smith (1986) and Prag and Casavant (1994) consider critical reviews and the cost of production and MPAA rating as signal of quality. Collins, Hands and Snell (2002) repeat the exercise using data from the UK instead of the USA and find that both good reviews and the presence of stars have a positive influence on movie revenues. In similar studies De Vany and Walls (2004) and Walls (2004) examine the role of movie stars and Bagella and Becchetti (1999) the popularity of directors using Italian data.

Some studies focus on the issues of differentiation and collusion in the exhibition market. Theatres differentiate themselves in the long run through location, seat capacity, peripheral services and in the short run mostly through programming choice. Chisholm, McMillan and Norman (2005) analyse film selection of pairs of first-run US movie theatres, extending the Hotelling framework in a multi-characteristic space. Theatre pairs located more closely in geographical space make less similar programming choices. Although the contractual constraints of movie distributors may force a similarity in programming around major holidays or on major movie releases, strategic considerations lead to a reduction in similarity during other periods. Moreover they find that theatres under common ownership make more similar programming choices than theatres with different owners.

Filson, Fabre, Nava and Rodriguez (2000) conduct a similar investigation, but focusing instead on the vertical relationship between multiplex owners and movie distributors. They simulate a dynamic model that explains the practice of staggering the release dates of hit movies and consider how vertical integration affects release patterns and the allocation of movies to screens. In this case the suppliers are the ones that want to avoid head-to-head competition. When two big movies are released simultaneously, they erode each other's productivity and demand is shared between the two movies. In a multiplex the exhibitor chooses multiple movies, so cross-effects on demand can be examined. Their model confirms that distributors avoid the release of two new hits at the same time and allow their old hits to play out before releasing new ones. They also avoid the release of new hits when their competitors are releasing new hits and they let their competitors' old hits to play out.

As with our analysis, Collins, Hand and Ryder (2005) address specifically the influence of multiplex on cinema attendance, but they use survey data at an individual level and estimate a model that can take account of travel cost and travel time. They use the Travel Cost Approach (Smith 1989) which has been employed frequently in the United States in order to evaluate consumer surplus from outdoor sites such as country parks, the distance decay function for football (Forrest et al. 2003) and in the area of cultural goods to investigate the demand for the Royal Exchange Theatre in Manchester (Forrest et al. 2000). Transport costs can be a very substantial proportion of the total cost of attending cinema and other cultural services, but they find it to be significant for non-multiplex cinemas and insignificant in the case of multiplexes. Multiplex visitors seem willing to travel long distances to these venues, so long as it is easy to park and one can book tickets ahead of the visit. For those customers in the age range 30 to 50 years the multiplex model predicts a higher frequency of visit than the non-multiplex model, but it is not possible to explain within that framework if it emerges as a simple correlation or if multiplex diffusion can cause a higher visit rate.

Finally, Sisto and Zanola (2004) – who, like us, use the Mediasalles data – produce an estimate of cinema demand, following the rational addiction model proposed by Becker and Murphy (1988) and often employed in the consumption analysis of cultural goods. They find strong evidence that an increase in past consumption leads to an increase in present consumption. In the area of cultural goods this can be attributed to a sort of learning by consuming.

13.4 Empirical specification

We are interested in exploring the determinants of cinema demand and in particular in assessing the impact of multiplex diffusion. We attempt a panel approach using national annual data for 15 European countries over a 15-year period.

This allows us to try to estimate the general relationships that encompass specific national dynamics. Moreover the spread of multiplexes during the 1990s and with annual data the single-country approach offer an insufficient number of observations.

The dataset used is the *European Cinema Yearbook* (2004), collected and published by Mediasalles, an organisation linked to the exhibition industry and funded in part by the European Union. It covers the period 1989–2003 and includes data from 18 European countries: Austria, Belgium, Switzerland, Germany, Denmark, Spain, France, Finland, Greece, Italy, Ireland, Luxembourg, Norway, Netherlands, Portugal, Sweden, the UK and Iceland. We have excluded Denmark, Greece, Luxembourg, Portugal, and Iceland restricting the analysis to 15 countries over 15 years.

These data have been integrated with general country macro-indicators taken from Eurostat, such as *Gross Domestic Product*, price indexes, population (disaggregated in 16 brackets), and various indicators of the level of education in the country.

13.5 Econometric analysis

We estimate the demand equation for cinema using the following specification:

$$y_{it} = \alpha + \beta x_{it} + u_{it} \qquad (13.1)$$

where, $u_{it} + \lambda_i + \varepsilon_{it}$ and ε_{it} are assumed to be not auto-correlated, and not correlated with the explanatory variables x_{it}. The component λ_i of the composite error takes into account the possibility of time-invariant unobserved individual heterogeneity across countries, as for any standard model of panel data.

In order to interpret the parameters of the model in terms of elasticity, we consider a log-linear form, using the following variables:

$$\log freqpc_{it} = \alpha + \beta_{0_{it}} \log gpdppc + \beta_{1_{it}} \log pmer + \beta_{2_{it}} \log multiplex \\ + \beta_{3_{it}} \log inhab\_screen + \beta_{4_{it}} \log seatpop + u_{it} \qquad (13.2)$$

The dependent variable ($freqpc_{it}$) is the annual frequency per capita. Among the explanatory variables we have selected, as the ones resulting significant, in order: the GDP per capita (*gdppc*), as a measure of income of individuals; the average price of tickets in real terms (*pmer*), with 1989 as the reference period; the density of screens in multiplexes (*multiplex*);[2] the number of inhabitants per screen (*inhab_screen*); and the number of seats per capita (*seatpop*).

We compare three different estimators: pooled OLS, random effects and fixed effects. In the pooled OLS regression unobserved heterogeneity is not considered. In the fixed or random effect model instead it is taken into account, but whereas in the random effects model λ_is are assumed to be not correlated to x_{it}s, in the fixed effect model the correlation between λ_is and x_{it}s is left unrestricted.

Results for the three regressions are presented in Table 13.1. Although the coefficients are not reported in the table, we have also included time dummies in each regression. As we can see, the results are qualitatively similar across the three estimation techniques. However, in order to choose the correct coefficients, we need to carry out some tests that allow us to compare the different regressions and select the best. But, first of all, we need to test for the absence of intra-group serial correlation and groupwise heteroscedasticity in the idiosyncratic errors ε_{it}. It is important to check this because in the presence of either form of departure from the conventional assumptions on the variance–covariance matrix of ε_{it}'s, the standard error estimates for all models would be biased and a White-correction would be required. The absence of intra-group serial correlation is tested following the procedure suggested in Wooldrige (2002) and implemented in Stata by the xtserial command written and described in Drukker (2003). For a null hypothesis of no first-order autocorrelation, we obtain an $F_{(1,8)}=0.057$ (p-value=0.81), and therefore we cannot reject the absence of serial correlation in the ε_{it}'s at any conventional significance level. The absence of heteroscedasticity is tested using the xttest3 command in Stata, written by Kit Baum, that implements the procedure in Greene (2008). Obtaining a $\chi^2_{(9)}=9.63$ we cannot reject homoscedasticity in the ε_{it}'s at any conventional significance level. We conclude that the ε_{it}'s are white noise, therefore we do not need to correct the standard errors of the coefficients estimated and move on in the procedure of selecting the appropriate regression.

First of all, we want to test if the classical regression model without individual effects offers a valid specification for our demand function. As is well known, the classical regression model is a particular case of our baseline model when $\lambda_i = 0$ (if λ_is are treated as fixed parameters as in the fixed effects model) or $\sigma^2_\lambda = 0$ (if λ_is are treated as random disturbances as in the random effects model). The first case is tested through an F-test on the fixed effects model, whose null hypothesis is that all

Table 13.1 Results of regressions

Dependent variable: Lfreqpc	Pooled Regression	Random Effects Model[1]	Fixed Effects Model
Lgdppc	−.0304	.3794**	.4275**
	(.853)	(.002)	(.003)
Lpmer	.1046	−.2687**	−.3249**
	(.585)	(.034)	(.028)
lmultiplex	.1567**	.0696**	.0619**
	(.000)	(.000)	(.007)
Linh_screen	−.1151	.0722	−.0459
	(.611)	(.637)	(.797)
lseatpop	.5263**	.5224**	.4941**
	(.033)	(.001)	(.007)
constant	4.2774**	.1700	−.2583
	(.004)	(.913)	(.888)
	$R^2 = 0.7731$		$R^2_{within} = 0.892$
		Log likelihood=131.95	$R^2_{between} = 0.358$
			$R^2_{overall} = 0.459$

[1] This model has been estimated through Maximum Likelihood method, because the default in Stata collapses to the OLS. Therefore, R^2's are not given.
P-values in parenthesis
**significant at 5%
*significant at 10%

individual effects are equal. We obtain that $F_{(8,62)} = 80.05$, therefore individual heterogeneity emerges as important and the OLS estimates of the Pooled regression are clearly biased. The same conclusion is drawn using the OLS residuals in a Breusch Pagan Lagrange multiplier test, which rejects the null of $\sigma^2_\lambda = 0$ at any conventional significance level, giving a $\chi^2_{(1)} = 108.62$. We conclude that both the fixed effects and the random effects model perform better than the pooled model. For selecting between the fixed effects and the random effects model, we carry out the usual Hausman test, whose null hypothesis is the absence of correlation between λ_i and x_{it}, obtaining a $\chi^2_{(18)} = 1.54$. We cannot reject this assumption at any conventional significance level, and therefore select the *random effect* as the regression that fits out data at best and we focus on this specification for our comments on coefficients.

As we can see from Table 13.1, GDP per capita is significant with the expected positive sign showing an elasticity of 0.37. Price is significant, with an elasticity of −0.26. Multiplex has a positive impact on the demand for cinema, with an elasticity of 0.07. The number of seats per capita is also highly significant with a positive elasticity of about 0.5.

As for all cultural goods, habit formation may also play a crucial part in the demand for cinema. Its more relevant implication is the slow short-run response of the demand for cinema to exogenous shocks, including relative-price variation. This dynamic effect, neglected by the panel data specifications implemented to date, may be captured by the inclusion of the first and, possibly, further lags of y_{it} (lfreqpc) as explanatory variables. As a result of the small time dimension in our data we restrict the dynamic specification to the first lag, $y_{i,t-1}$:

$$y_{it} = \alpha + \gamma y_{i,t-1} + \beta x_{it} + u_{it} \qquad (13.3)$$

It is well known that both fixed and random effect methods fail to provide consistent estimators for the foregoing dynamic panel data (DPD) model. To the opposite IV and GMM first-differenced estimators, like the well-used Arellano and Bond (1991), have appealing properties for N large, being consistent and also asymptotically efficient.

Unfortunately, the finite-sample performance of GMM-DPD estimators turns out to be very poor when the cross-sectional dimension is small (say N = 10, 20 or 40), as demonstrated in a number of Monte Carlo experiments (Kiviet 1995; Judson and Owen 1999; and Bruno 2005b, among others), which makes the Arellano and Bond estimator as well as other GMM estimators unfeasible in our case. The same Monte Carlo experiments, however, show that the biased-corrected fixed effect estimator (LSDVC), as derived by Kiviet (1995) and extended to unbalanced panel data by Bruno (2005a, 2005b), has good small-sample performances, always outperforming GMM-DPD estimators both in terms of bias and root mean squared error. Therefore, as a robustness check for the results of our static regressions, we estimate the DPD model using the LSDVC estimator.[3] The results are reported in Table 13.2.

The dynamic effect does not seem strong, and indeed the coefficients on the other regressors are quite robust to the dynamic specification, in terms of both sign and size. Moreover, bootstrapped standard errors for LSDVC reveal that the coefficient on the one-time lagged dependent variable is not even significant at any conventional level. We therefore conclude that dynamic underspecification does not seem to be an issue for our static panel regressions.

Table 13.2 DPD regression (bootstrapped standard errors, 1,000 iterations)

Dependent variable:	LSDVC
Lfreqpc (−1)	.1457
	(.261)
Lgdppc	.3639**
	(.05)
Lpmer	−.2659
	(.119)
lmultiplex	.0560*
	(.053)
Linh_screen	.0579
	(.799)
lseatpop	.4383*
	(.059)

P-values in parenthesis
**significant at 5%
*significant at 10%

13.5 Concluding remarks

As we can see from Table 13.1, GDP per capita is significant with the expected positive sign showing an elasticity of 0.37, thus movies cannot be identified as a luxury good.

Price is significant, with an elasticity of −0.26. The demand seems to be quite inelastic respect to price and the value is lower than what is found in some other studies conducted at a national level.

Multiplex has a positive impact on the demand for cinema, with an elasticity of 0.07. The coefficient is rather small, but the effect is net once considered the rise in total supply captured by the variable *seatpop* that has a strong positive value confirming that competition in exhibition works in geographical limited markets and that the availability of theatres influences positively the demand. The elasticity value of 0.5 suggests anyway that marginal capacity expansion displays diminishing returns.

Contrary to the view of many theatre owners, multiplexes do not simply get their market share from traditional theatres; rather, they contribute to an overall demand growth probably as a result of the service innovations they introduce.

We measured the effect of other demographic factors such as the share of young people or the levels of literacy level, but we found them not to be significant and therefore we exclude them from the final equations.

In future works we plan to include some measures of substitute consumption like television or DVD, even though data gathering and definitions are fairly different across countries.

Notes

1. Orietta Dessy is a Lecturer at the Institute for Industrial and Labour Economics, Catholic University, Milan, Italy; Marco Gambaro is a Professor of Media Economics at Department of Economics and Business (DEAS), Università degli Studi di Milano, Italy.
2. Defined as the number of screens situated in multiplexes, i.e. theatres with at least 8 screens, as a percentage of the total number of screens in each country, in each of the years under consideration. This is the degree of penetration of multiplexes.
3. LSDVC is implemented through the Stata code xtlsdvc written by Bruno (2005b).

References

Alderson, D., Karish J., and Price, R. 2002. Revenge of multiplex, *The McKinsey Quarterly*.
Allison, D. 2006, Multiplex programming in the UK: the economics of homogeneity, *Screen* 47(1), 81–90.
Arellano, M. and Bond, S. 1991. Some Tests of Specification for Panel Data: Monte Carlo Evidence and an Application to Employment Equations, *Review of Economic Studies*, 58, 277–97.
Bagella, M. and Becchetti, L. 1999. The determinants of motion picture box office performance: evidence from movies produced in Italy, *Journal of Cultural Economics*, 23(4), 237–56.
Becker, G.S. and Murphy, K.M. 1988. A theory of rational addiction, *Journal of Political Economy*, 96(4), 675–700.
Bensi, P. 2004. Decrease in the power of multiplex to draw spectators away from other cinema, *European Cinema Journal*, 3, 3–4.
Bruno, G.S.F. 2005a. Approximating the bias of the LSDV estimator for dynamic unbalanced panel data models, *Economics Letters*, 87, 361–6.
Bruno, G.S.F. 2005b. Estimation and inference in dynamic unbalanced panel data models with a small number of individuals, *The Stata Journal*, 5, 473–500.
Cameron, S. 1986. The supply and demand for cinema tickets: some UK evidence, *Journal of Cultural Economics*, 10, 38–62.
Chisholm, D., McMillan, M. and Norman, G. 2005. Product differentiation and film programming choice: do first-run movie theatres show the same film, Working Paper.
Collins, A., Hands, C. and Ryder, A. 2005. The lure of the multiplex? The interplay of time, distance, and cinema attendance, *Environment and Planning*, 37, 483–501.

Collins, A., Hands, C. and Snell, M. 2002. What makes a blockbuster? Economic analysis of film success in the United Kingdom, *Managerial and Decision Economics*, 23, 343–54.

Corts, K. 2001. The strategic effects of vertical market structure: Comkmon Agency and divisionalization in the US motion picture industry, *Journal of Economics and Management Strategy*, 10(4), 509–28.

Davis, P. 2002. Entry cannibalization and bankruptcy in the US motion picture exhibition market, LSE Working Paper.

De Vany, A. 2004. *Hollywood Economics*, New York: Routledge.

De Vany, A.S. and Walls, V.D. 2004. Motion picture profit, the stable Paretian hypothesis, and the curse of the superstar, *Journal of Economic Dynamics and Control*, 28(6), 1035–57.

Dewenter, R. and Westermann, M. 2005. Cinema demand in Germany, *Journal of Cultural Economics*, 29(3), 213–31.

Drukker, D. 2003. Testing for serial correlation in linear panel-data models, *The Stata Journal*, 3(2), 168–77.

Fernandez-Blanco, V., and Banos Pino, J. 1997. Cinema Demand in Spain: A Cointegration Analysis, *Journal of Cultural Economics*, 21(1), 57–75.

Filson, D., Fabre, F., Nava, A. and Rodriguez, P. 2001. *At the Movies: Risk Sharing and the Economics of Exhibition Contracts*, Claremont, CA, USA: Claremont-McKenna College Economics Working Paper 2001-1. Available at http://www.claremontmckenna.edu/econ/papers/.

Filson, D., Switzer, D. and Besoke, P. 2005. At the movies: the economics of exhibition contracts, *Economic Inquiry*, 43(2), 354–69.

Forrest, D., Grime, K. and Woods, R. 2000. Is it worth subsidising regional repertory theatre?, *Oxford Economic Papers*, 52(2), 381–97.

Forrest, D., Simmons, R. and Feeham, P. 2003. A spatial cross-sectional elasticity of demand for soccer, *Scottish Journal of Political Economy*, 49(3), 336–55.

Greene, W. 2008. *Econometric Analysis*, Upple Saddle River, NJ: Prentice Hall.

Judson, R.A. and Owen, A.L. 1999. Estimating dynamic panel data models: a guide for macroeconomists, *Economics Letters*, 65, 9–15.

Kiviet, J.F. 1995. On bias, inconsistency and efficiency of various estimators in dynamic panel data models, *Journal of Econometrics*, 68, 53–78.

Macmillan, P. and Smith, I. 2001. Explaining post-war attendance in Great Britain, *Journal of Cultural Economics*, 25, 91–108.

McCosker, P.M. 2004. A brief history of cinema exhibition in the UK, www.mediasalles.it/research.

Mediasalles. 2004. *European Cinema Yearbook*, Milan, Italy: Mediasalles.

Moul, C.C. (ed.). 2005. *A Concise Handbook of Movie Industry Economics*, New York: Cambridge University Press.

Prag, J. and Casavant, J. 1994. An empirical study of the determinants of revenues and marketing expenditures in the motion picture industry, *Journal of Cultural Economics*, 18(3), 217–35.

Ravid, A. 1999. Information blockbusters and stars: a study of the film industry, *Journal of Business*, 72(4), 463–92.

Sisto A., and Zanola, R. 2004. *Rationally Addicted to Cinema and TV? An Empirical Investigation of Italian Consumers*, POLIS Working Paper 52. Vercelli, Italy: Università del Piemonte Orientale.

Smith, S.P., and Smith, V.K. 1986. Successful movies: an empirical analysis, *Applied Economics*, 18(5), 501–7.

Smith, V.K. 1989. Travel cost recreation demand methods: theory and implication, Discussion Paper QE89-03. Washington, DC: Resources for the Future.

Storper, M. 1989. The transition to flexible specialisation in the US film industry: external economies, the division of labour, and the crossing of industrial divides, *Cambridge Journal of Economics*, 13, 273–305.

Waterman, D., and Sung Choon, L. 2003. Time consistency and the distribution of theatrical films: an empirical study of the video window, Allied Social Science Association Annual Meeting Working Paper.

Wooldridge, J. 2002. *Econometric Analysis of Cross Section and Panel Data*, Cambridge, MA: The MIT Press.

14
Quantitative Analyses of the Media Industries and of Their Markets: Concluding Comments

Orhan Güvenen[1]

14.1 Introduction

The quantitative statistical and econometric studies elaborated by the authors of this volume entitled *The Media Industries and Their Markets: Quantitative Analyses* have made a substantial contribution to applied and theoretical research.

The complexities of various aspects of the media industries' economic structures and the management of media enterprises are clarified by the use of quantitative and econometric analysis. This leads to a more efficient decision-making process in respect of socioeconomic, behavioural, technological and managerial phenomena.

14.2 Impacts of technologies on the media industries and their markets

As can be seen from Figure 14.1, the development of information and communication technologies (ICTs) leads to a rupture which can be interpreted in terms of mathematical chaos. One could even describe this break as a second industrial revolution, more important than the first industrial revolution, which resulted from the development of steam power.

It generates a multi-factorial, multi-sectorial productivity growth in the economy, which of course also concerns the media industries and their markets. Taking as a base-point the nonlinear socioeconomic phenomena trends, the technological impacts move to upper strata the dynamics of societies. This evolution continues and is in interaction with other technologies; the most influential impacts coming from nanotechnology and genome projects. Nanoscience and nanotechnologies,

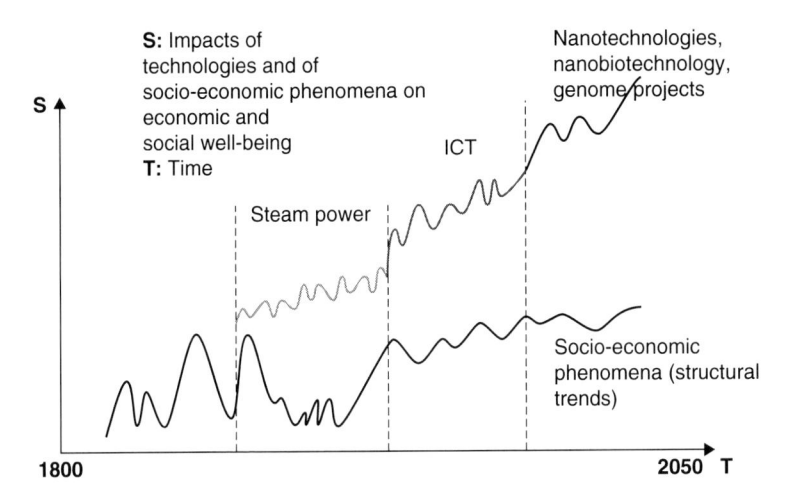

Figure 14.1 The impact of technologies on socioeconomic phenomena in time dynamics
Source: Güvenen (2008).

nanobiotechnology, and genome projects create a new major revolution with 'mathematical chaos', which will continue throughout the oncoming decades. The probability that this change will be more intensive and more substantial in its dynamics than the first industrial revolution can be considered to be relatively high.

The media and their markets cannot remain exogenous to these evolutions. It is likely that the impacts of both ICT and nanotechnologies will increase; all of these developments can bring about an exponential path to changes in the media industries and their markets.

14.3 Some comments on measurement and quantification in the context of media industries and their markets

In the dynamics of these trends the important and original value added of this volume is to bring about measurements, quantifications and to improve our knowledge of our subject. In terms of research dynamics, as shown in our previous work (Güvenen, 2000), and in Figure 14.2, this will provide new signals for future research, applications, decision systems and decision making at international, national, industrial and corporation level, that can be endogenised in their dynamics.

Quantitative analyses of the media industries and their markets require dealing with structures which are mathematically complex, chaotic and

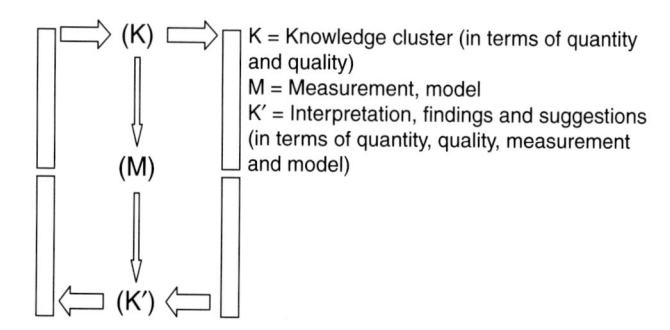

```
         ┌──> (K) ──>┐  K = Knowledge cluster (in terms of quantity
         │           │      and quality)
         │           │  M = Measurement, model
         ▼           │  K' = Interpretation, findings and suggestions
        (M)          │      (in terms of quantity, quality, measurement
         │           │      and model)
         │           │
         ▼           │
        (K') <──────┘
```

Figure 14.2 Dynamics of knowledge, measurements, models and interpretations
Source: Güvenen (2000).

of low predictability. It also requires endogenisation of the underlying dynamics of interactions, and a cross-disciplinary scientific methodology (Güvenen and Oztürk, 2008).

The methodological capacity to create interactions with various disciplines in science, art, culture and life requires understanding, solving, interpreting and acting on complex problems. Iterative and continuous learning processes between theory and applications appear to be a necessary condition.

Science methodologies in the twentieth and twenty-first centuries, especially in the social sciences, have predominantly made use of approaches that use subset and partial analysis. Apart from providing short-term solutions in the analysis of social and economic phenomena, subset and partial analysis approach creates, especially in the medium to long term; mechanistic, short-termist structures and non-negligible socioeconomic costs in the dynamics of society. These costs have fundamental consequences for the global media industries and their markets.

The twenty-first century requires interdisciplinary and polymath convergence approaches, as well as ethics and value systems that should be considered endogenous to decision sciences and decision-making.

Future quantitative analyses on the media industries and their markets may give more importance to the endogenisation of ethics, social responsibility, environmental and educational issues. It is well known that media do play a very important role in shaping political decision making, and on influencing societal and human behaviour. As is shown by Figure 14.3, all of these factors can contribute substantially to the transformation of the society from its present dynamics involving

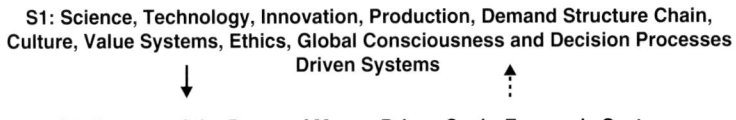

> **S1: Science, Technology, Innovation, Production, Demand Structure Chain, Culture, Value Systems, Ethics, Global Consciousness and Decision Processes Driven Systems**
>
> ↓ ⁝
>
> **S2: Power and the Power of Money Driven Socio-Economic Systems**
>
> S1: The Structure of world dynamics targeting "human optimality", a normative approach.
> S2: The structure of world dynamics in 2009

Figure 14.3 Present world system and normative system
Source: Güvenen (2008).

the power of money-driven socio-economic systems (S2) to science, technology, innovation, production, the demand structure chain, culture, value systems, ethics, global consciousness, and decision processes-driven systems (S1).

14.4 The media industries, media markets, quantitative analyses, information distortion, ethics and decision making

The main actors in decision-making processes are nation-states, international institutions, transnational corporations, non-governmental organisations and individuals. For all of these actors, knowledge generates opportunity and power. It requires responsibility, accountability, transparency, and value systems. Discrepancies created by access to knowledge and to technology create inequities. This requires a redefinition of the objective function of the decision sciences, and making ethics and value systems endogenous to the decision system analysis.

In research and decision systems, most of the time, data, information level, statistics are used without a systematic evaluation of error margins. The alternative costs and misunderstanding that is caused is an important fact that has to be considered carefully in the national and global research and applications.

All of these considerations have strong implications for the various parts of this volume.

Picard's comments about the obstacles to the creation of a global information society in chapter 2, are of great significance as the 'digital divide' which is under discussion reflects the inequities of our complex present world system, especially in terms of the access to information. In chapter 3, Garonne and Weygand offer an explanatory institution that compares the business models of some of the largest Internet companies. They illustrate what has been discussed above about the 'digital revolution' in respect of its implications for global corporate strategies. Zilic Fiser (chapter 4) comments on profit-maximising objectives as well as public service social responsibility objectives in the public service media, illustrating clearly the necessity of moving from the power-driven system to a normative world optimal system. They show that the media industries and markets represent subsystems which exert a substantial influence on the overall dynamics. Chapter 5, by Badillo and Bourgeois, reflects the importance of technologies and their impacts on the long-term dynamics and strategic issues in the management of the media industries.

In chapter 6, Noam's analyses of media concentration and private power over the media, insisting that advances in the information and communication technologies, and in particular digital convergence, are a fundamental driving force in the dynamics of the media industries. These analyses are very pertinent to explaining complexities in policy implications. In chapter 7 Iosifidis develops monitoring tools for assessing media pluralism, offering new dimensions that go beyond the usual analyses of markets. The investigations of chapter 8, by Badillo and Lesourd, emphasise the economic and technological environments, which is an original dimension, especially in the context of analysing the complexities of the dynamics of the media industries and their markets. The study by Artero et al. (chapter 9) concentrates on the critical factors that influence the profitability of television networks, in particular attracting substantial audiences, the final targets being to sell products to both media buyers and advertisers. This finding can be considered to be a constraint towards achieving the value system approach discussed above.

A remarkable empirical analysis employing techniques from behavioural economics and psychological factors is presented in chapter 10 by Mitomo and Otsuda. This experimental methodology is especially valuable and lends itself to further qualitative and quantitative research in the field of the media industries and markets. In the next contribution, Fu, Li and Wildman analyse the purchasing profile model in order to explain the prices paid for television ad time. These authors emphasise the complexities of advertising price determination in this context. Elliott and Simmons (chapter 12) highlight, in their analysis of the multiple determinants of film advertising expenditures, the importance of potential film quality signals and the rather complex interactions between various media industries. Finally, in chapter 13, the panel studies of Dessy and Gambaro investigate the long-term decline in the level of movie theatre audiences. They conclude that this decline may be at least partially overcome through technical and organisational innovations.

Taken as a whole, the contributions to this volume create a very strong analytical base, and they can generate further research concerned with world dynamics, sustainability, transparency, and peace.

Acknowledgements

We owe our thanks to the editors, P.-Y. Badillo and J.-B. Lesourd, and to all of the contributors to this volume which represents a great step forward in the quantitative analyses of the media industries and their markets.

Note

1. Orhan Güvenen is a Professor at Bilkent University, Ankara, Turkey, as well as Founder and Director of the University's Institute of World Systems, Economic and Srategic Research.

References

Güvenen, O. 2000. The interaction between econometrics, information systems and statistical infrastructure: anticipation and comparative analysis in a decisional structure, *Journal of the Turkish Statistical Association*, 3(1–2), 22–43.

Güvenen, O. and Öztürk, M.H. 2008. *Transdisciplinarity in Decision Sciences: a Discourse on Poly-math Renaissance Man Methodology*, presented at the Institute of Operations Research and the Management Sciences – INFORMS, Washington, DC.

Güvenen, O. 2008. Economic prosperity, interaction with science, knowledge and value systems, in A.M. Herzberg (ed.), *Statistics, Science and Public Policy*, vol. XII, Ontario: Queen's University.

Index

addiction model (for cinema demand) 211
advertiser 10–11, 18, 40–1, 51, 58, 121, 149–50, 171–6, 181–183, 187, 192, 224
advertising 5–6, 10–11, 36–7, 39–42, 44–5, 52–3, 56–8, 61, 64–7, 72–9, 81, 108, 117, 122, 140, 143, 149–50, 152–3, 171–3, 176–8, 181–3, 193–206, 224
  expenditures 11, 149–50, 178, 181, 195–202, 205, 224
  industry 61, 172
  for films 11, 195–206
  market 53, 57
  revenue 45, 57, 61, 65–6, 76, 79, 108
  share 56–8
  time 10, 52, 171–94
aggregate information sector 8
Amaury (press group) 132, 135
Amazon 5, 39–42, 45
ambiguity 10, 45, 156, 158–9, 166–8
  aversion 156, 158–9, 166–8
American 16, 66–7, 87–8, 101, 103, 105–106, 128, 130, 134, 183, 188, 193
  media concentration 87–107
Ask Network 5, 32, 38–42, 46
audience 4, 9–10, 41, 108–9, 111–12, 115–17, 119–22, 128, 135, 139, 141–2, 146–51, 171–8, 180–1, 183, 187, 192–4, 197–8, 200, 205, 207–8, 224
  movie theatre 224
audiovisual 144, 207
Australia 7, 12, 23, 44, 137, 209
Austria 12, 23, 212
aversion for ambiguity 10

barriers to entry 7, 29, 71, 118–19
BBC 5, 50–2, 56–7, 63, 85, 144, 154
BBC1 56–7

behavioural economics 10, 155–8, 165, 169, 224
Belgium 12, 23, 132, 212
biotechnology 31, 40–8
  nano- 221
blended media 64, 75, 80, 82, 84
Bertelsmann (Prima-Bertelsmann media group) 130, 132, 137
blockbuster 206, 208, 218
Brazil 7, 19
broadband internet 155
broadcast 2, 7, 10, 94, 125, 141, 152, 171, 173, 176, 192, 194
  TV 7, 94, 194
broadcaster 50–4, 56, 58–63, 116, 146, 153
broadcasting 55–6, 58, 60–3, 99–100, 109–11, 113, 116–17, 123, 126, 147, 152–3, 175–6
business 3–6, 211, 13, 26–48, 64–86, 143–4, 169, 223
  model 3–6, 11, 13, 26–48, 64–86, 144, 223

cable 7, 94, 100–2, 152, 154
  TV 94, 152, 154
Canada 17–18, 21, 23, 137
Channel (TV) 54–9, 61, 88, 100–1, 111–12, 141, 143–4, 146, 151
Channel 4 5, 50, 52, 56, 59
Channel 5 5, 49–63
China 4, 19, 137
choice by habit 158–9, 166–9
cinema 7, 11, 117, 195–7, 207–12, 215–18
  attendance 207–11
  demand 209, 211, 218
commercial 6, 55, 144, 150, 152–3, 171–2, 174–5, 192, 204, 210
  broadcaster 50–2, 59, 61–2
  broadcasting 50, 62
  channel 55

television 144, 152–3
time 172, 174–5, 192
commercialise 30
competition 9, 17–18, 37, 66, 70, 74, 79–80, 82, 127, 128, 138, 141, 143, 146, 148–54, 207, 211, 216
competitor 7, 66, 80–1, 85–6, 136, 150, 211
competitive 42, 85, 137, 142, 150, 196
 fringe 196
competitiveness 86
concentration (in the media industries) 4, 6–8, 87–107, 108–40, 142–4, 148, 152–4, 180, 209, 224
 indicators 7, 94–5, 108–24, 127–9, 134–5
 in the French press industry 125–40
 ratio 114–15, 128
content(s) 2–3, 8, 45, 69, 75, 84, 86, 88–9, 105–6, 111–12, 122, 142, 144
cycle 7, 92–3
Czech Republic 22–3

Dassault (media Group) 126, 129–30, 132
data 1, 17, 27, 30, 32, 70–1, 84, 134, 136, 145–7, 156, 159–60, 170, 172–3, 176–7, 187, 193, 195–201, 208–12, 214–15, 217–19, 223
 set 32, 36, 41, 43, 174, 195, 198–201, 208–9, 212
 transmission 17
 Panel 146–7
daily press 5, 73–5, 119, 129–30, 134–6, 138
 French 136
 national (French) 129, 134–5, 138
demand 4, 10, 21, 67, 120, 153, 155, 170–6, 187, 192, 197, 206, 208–13, 215–19, 223
demographic (in the context of models for TV time pricing) 10–11, 171–3, 183, 185, 187, 192
demographics (-based model for TV time pricing) 172, 176, 183–4, 187–8, 193

dependency on the level of usage 158–9, 168
dependent variables 145, 147–8, 151
Denmark 12, 23, 212
developed 15–16, 18, 20–2, 24, 125
 areas 18
 countries 15–16, 22
 economies 3–4
 nations 15, 18, 20–1
developing economies 3–4, 125
developing nations 3–4
disintermediation 36–7, 39, 42
digit (4-digit standard industrial classification) 181–183
digital 7, 15–17, 29–30, 32, 34–5, 40–4, 46, 48, 55, 82, 86, 88–9, 93–4, 99, 106, 109, 126, 140, 150, 152, 223–4
 channel 55, 150, 152
 convergence 7, 89, 93, 106, 224
 divide 4, 14–15, 24, 223
 economy 29–30, 32, 34–5, 40–4, 46, 48
 enterprise 48
 media 86
 revolution 7, 89, 109, 224
 technology 89
digitalisation 126, 144
digitally 117
digitise (digitalise) 1, 126
diversity 7–8, 106, 108–15, 117–23, 127–8, 134–6, 138–9, 142, 144, 152–4, 157
 index (DI) 7, 115, 127–8, 134–6, 138–9
dot.com burst 5, 26–48
DVD 217

E-Bay 5
ebusiness 28, 30–1, 46–8
 model 28, 30–1, 46–8
econometric 11–12, 212, 218–20
 study 11–12
econometrics 225
economies 3–4, 7, 76, 81–2, 84, 89–93, 100, 142, 207, 209
 of scale (scale economies) 7, 76, 81, 84, 89–93, 100, 207, 209
 of scope 7, 81–2, 84

economy 220
Egypt 22
emerging economies 3–4, 137
Europe 125, 143, 153–4, 207–8
European 130, 137–8, 141, 144–5, 208, 212, 217–18
experimental 10, 224
  economics 10
explanatory variables 9, 147, 149, 168, 184, 212, 215

feature film 53, 55
film 1, 11, 52–3, 55, 89–90, 93–4, 99–100, 195–202, 204–6, 207–10, 217–19, 224
  advertising 195, 197, 199–202, 204, 224
  distribution 7, 11, 94
  industry 195, 206–7, 218–19
  production 7, 11, 205, 207
  revenues 195, 207
Finland 17, 22–3, 212
flat rate 10, 155–70
  preference 10, 155–6, 158–9, 161, 169–70
France 9, 12, 17, 23, 126–7, 129–30, 135, 139, 145, 153–4, 212

Germany 9, 12, 17, 22–3, 145, 212
global 3, 16, 18–20, 24, 57, 67, 72, 109–10, 125, 128, 131, 139, 153–4, 208, 222–4
  advertising market 57, 72
  consciousness 223
  corporate strategies 224
  information 19–20
  information society 3–4, 14, 16, 18, 20, 24, 223
  media market 110
  media industries 222
globalisation 125
Google 5
Greece 12, 22–3, 212
group 31, 34–6, 104–5, 110–12, 116, 123, 127–35, 137–8, 151, 163, 175, 183
group diversity 8, 111

Haiti 17
HHI (Herfindahl–Hirschman Index) 8–9, 95–101, 114–15, 127–9, 134–8
Hungary 22–3
hybrid 5, 30–2, 44, 50–2, 60–2
  business model 5, 30–2, 44
  model 50–1, 60, 62
hybrid broadcasting model 49–63

India 4, 17, 19, 22
Industrial revolution 220–1
  Second 220
industry meltdown 126, 136
infomediation 36–7, 39
information 1–2, 4, 7–8, 10, 14–16, 20–4, 27–9, 35–40, 42–3, 45–7, 64–9, 72–3, 76–7, 80–2, 84–6, 88–9, 91–4, 96–9, 101–6, 108–9, 111–12, 116, 121–3, 125–6, 131, 135–6, 138–40, 141, 145–7, 151, 156, 159–60, 172–4, 197, 205–6, 218, 220, 223–4
  and communication products 20–2
  and communication technologies 12, 14, 69, 77, 125–6, 138, 220, 224
  asymmetry 36–40, 42–3
  definition 1
  economy 45
  industries 7
  press 65, 72–4, 81
  products and services 15, 20
  sector 7–8, 88–9, 91–4, 96–9, 101–6
  society 3, 14–24, 77, 125, 138–40, 223
  systems 16, 47, 225
  technology, IT 8, 46, 96–8, 101–2, 104–5
  technologies 14, 15, 18, 20, 23–4
innovation 125–6, 209, 216, 223, 225
innovative 5, 52, 58–9
Ireland 12, 23, 212
ITV 5, 50–2, 56–7, 59
informational activities 20
Italy 22–3, 132, 208, 212, 217–18
Internet 6, 15, 17, 19–21, 24–5, 26–31, 34–8, 41–8, 65–76, 78–86,

87–9, 94, 96–102, 117–19, 144, 155–6, 160–9, 197, 205, 223
-based companies   27, 223
bubble   26, 30, 34
burst   44
newspapers   71, 86
services   21

Japan   4, 17–18, 21–3

knowledge   3, 30–1, 35, 42, 47, 125, 138, 221–3, 225
  cluster   222
knowledge-information society   3, 125, 138
Korea (South)   4, 23, 137

Lagardère (media group)   83, 126, 130, 132, 137
Le Monde (press group)   129–30, 132, 135
less developed   3, 18, 21
  countries   3
  nations   18, 21
  regions   18
libertarian   7, 87
life cycle   68–71, 75, 79–80
loss aversion   156–8, 166–7

meaningful information   2
medium, media   1–3, 34, 45, 50–3, 58–9, 61–3, 85–6, 105–7, 117–23, 129–32, 134, 138–9, 141–6, 148, 150, 152–5, 161–3, 165, 169, 172–4, 177, 184, 193–4, 199–205, 207, 220, 222–5
  concentration   87–9, 91, 100–1, 117, 139, 143, 224
  definition   1
  economy   62
  enterprise   2, 134
  group   5
  industry (industries)   3–4, 6–7, 12, 34, 45, 68–9, 98, 108, 123, 125–8, 130–1, 137–8, 223–4
  market   117, 119–20, 141
  ownership   119
  pluralism   121, 123
  sector   105, 120

media-optimistic (-optimist)   7, 106
media-pessimistic (-pessimist)   7, 106
media-realistic   106
mental accounting   156, 158–9, 167–70
metamediation   36–7, 39
Mexico   21–3
misunderstanding of payment reduction   158–9, 166–7
mobile phone   10, 144, 156, 160–2, 168–70
model   3–6, 10–11, 26–48, 49–52, 60–2, 89, 93, 115–16, 139, 143–4, 147–9, 168, 170, 171–4, 176, 183–5, 187–8, 208–15, 217–18, 222–4
  Discrete   170
    estimation   168
  Logit   168
    specification   208
Mondadori (media group)   83, 132, 137
motion picture   206, 217–18
movie   2, 53, 197, 206–11, 216–19, 224
  demand   208
  film   11
  industry (industries)   7, 11–12
  theatre   11–12, 207, 209–10, 217, 224
multichannel   50–1, 56–8, 99
  TV   99
multimedia   32, 118, 122, 130
  industry   32
multiplex (movie theatre, facilities)   11–12, 207–13, 216–17
  diffusion   207–9, 211
  model   211
music   89, 100–1

Netherlands (the)   12, 23, 212
newspapers   6, 64–8, 70–4, 78, 80, 82, 85–6, 87, 89, 94, 116–18, 124, 129–31, 136–7, 139–40, 192
nonlinear   220
not-for-profit   41, 131
Norway   12, 23, 212

OLS regression   200
online   66–7, 69–70, 75–6, 78, 85–6, 159, 161, 170, 177, 205
  advertising   205
  content   69
  newspaper   66–7, 70, 86
  questionnaire   159, 161
  survey   170
overvaluation of a low probability   157–9, 166–7, 169

Pakistan   19
panel   146–7, 160, 208, 212, 215, 217–19
Poland   22–3
Portugal   9, 12, 22–3, 145, 212
press   2, 5, 11, 64–82, 84–6, 109, 117, 119, 125–7, 129–32, 134–40, 171, 173, 199, 203–5
  free   78–82, 54, 86
  French   9, 66, 70–3, 85, 125–40
  paid-for   72, 75–6, 78–9
  periodical   5
  trade   171, 173
production (film, TV)   52, 59–61, 153, 197, 201, 204–5, 207–8, 210, 223
  independent   52, 59–91
print   87, 93, 99–100, 104
PRISA (media group)   132, 137
profit   5, 41, 47, 51, 57–8, 61, 80, 92, 105, 145, 149–51, 173–6, 182, 218, 224
  maximising   5, 224
profitable   30, 80, 120, 143, 187
profitability   27, 45, 64, 67, 69, 81, 141, 145–51, 224
  of European television channels (effect of competition on)   141–54
public   1, 5–6, 11, 18, 26, 31, 49–53, 56, 58–63, 108–11, 114, 117–19, 123, 129, 131, 134, 141, 144–5, 150, 152, 197, 224
  channel   144
  good   1, 49
  information   1
  television   144

public service   5–6, 50, 52–3, 56, 58–63, 144, 224
  broadcaster   50, 56, 58, 62–3
  broadcasting   50, 53, 58, 63
  company   5
  remit   50, 52, 61
  television   5, 49–63
publicity   198
purchasing profile model (for ad time)   171–94

quantitative   3, 7–9, 12, 125, 127, 144, 151, 222–3, 225
  analysis (analyses)   3, 7, 151, 222–3, 225
questionnaire   159–61, 169–70

radio   2, 11, 24, 66, 68, 72–3, 82–4, 116–17, 125, 128, 196, 204–5
readership   64, 66–7, 74–9, 109, 119
reference dependence   157–8, 166–7
regression   200–2, 205, 213–16
return   47, 145, 149, 151, 216
Return on Assets (ROA)   9, 145, 151
Return on Equity (ROE)   9, 145, 151
Return on Sales (ROS)   149
Roularta (media group)   130, 132, 137

Second industrial revolution   12, 220
Simmons product subcategories under the 12 *AdAge.com* categories (list of) (individual products in the list have not been indexed)   188–90
Simmons subcategories selected using factor analysis for the six MS *AdAge.com* product categories (list) (individual products in the list have not been indexed)   191
Singapore   137
Socpresse (media group)   129–30, 135
Spain   9, 145, 209, 212, 218
start-up   5, 41–4, 46, 48
supply   3–4, 6, 25, 36, 50, 69, 112, 197, 206–9, 216–17
SURE regression   202, 205
Sweden   12, 17, 21–2, 212
Switzerland   23, 212

tariff 10, 155, 162–3, 170
technological 12, 26, 32, 46, 55, 69, 86, 114, 125–6, 138, 141, 144, 220, 224
  advances 12, 55
technology 26–7, 30–2, 47, 62, 68–9, 85–6, 88–90, 93–4, 104, 109, 125–6, 138–9, 144, 150, 153–4
Telecom, Telecommunication(s) 10, 17, 88, 93, 96–8, 101–5, 117, 126, 139, 142, 154
telephone 21, 126, 170
telephony 17–18
  fixed 17
  mobile 17
television 1–2, 5, 9, 24, 49–64, 66, 68, 70–3, 77, 82, 84, 116–17, 124, 125–6, 139, 141–54, 171–7, 182–3, 187–8, 192–4, 196, 199, 204–5, 207–10, 217, 224
  ad time 171–3, 176, 187–8, 224
  channels 2
terrestrial 50, 52, 56–7, 61, 152
  advertising 57
  broadcasting 50
  channel 52, 56, 61
  movie 53
transmission 1, 17
  and processing of information 1
  technology 2
Turkey 23
TV 7, 9–10, 66–7, 84, 93–4, 99, 102, 110, 116–19, 128, 174, 183, 193–4, 207, 210, 218
  ad time 174
  channel 9

film 11
viewing time 9
watching time 9

UK 5, 8–9, 11–12, 17–18, 22–3, 50–3, 56, 58, 60–1, 63, 108, 114, 116–17, 124, 152, 197–201, 204–6, 212
United Kingdom 18, 22–3, 62, 122, 145, 208–9, 217–18
United States 17, 87–8, 107, 123, 126–7, 137, 139, 208, 211
US/USA 7, 18–19, 21–2, 24, 26, 64, 87, 94–5, 97–9, 109–10, 114, 128, 136, 138, 139, 153–4, 172–3, 176–8, 180, 182, 193, 195, 196, 197–8, 200, 201, 204–5, 210, 218
  newspapers 64
usage 155, 158–9, 161–3, 166–9

VAR model 209
versioning 64, 80–2, 84

web 26–7, 31–2, 34–5, 41, 43, 45–6, 48, 125, 156
  -based media 125
  2.0 26–7, 31–2, 34–5, 45
website 35–6, 40, 42–3, 45–6
Wikipedia 5, 32, 36, 38–41
written press 4, 71, 73–5, 125–7, 131, 137
  French 125–7, 131, 137
World Trade Organisation (WTO) 125

Yahoo! 5, 38–42, 45, 48